Happiness, Ethics and Economics

Despite decades of empirical happiness research, there is still little evidence for the positive effect of economic growth on life satisfaction. This poses a major challenge to welfare economic theory and to normative conceptions of socio-economic development. This book endeavors to explain these findings and to make sense of their ethical implications.

While most of the existing literature on empirical happiness research is ultimately interested in understanding how to improve human lives and societal development, the ethical backdrop against which these findings are evaluated is rarely made explicit. In contrast to this, Professor Hirata focuses on the role happiness should play in an ethically founded conception of good development. Taking a development ethics perspective, this book proposes a nuanced conception of happiness that includes both its affective and its normative dimensions and embeds this in a comprehensive conception of good development.

The argument is that happiness should not be regarded as the only thing that determines a good life and that good development cannot sensibly be thought of as a matter of maximizing happiness. Happiness should rather be seen as an important indicator for the presence or absence of those concerns that really matter to people: the reasons that give rise to happiness. This book should be of interest to students and researchers of economics, psychology, and development studies.

Johannes Hirata is Professor of Economics at the University of Applied Sciences of Osnabrück, Germany.

Routledge frontiers of political economy

Happiness, Ethics and Economics

Johannes Hirata

Routledge
Taylor & Francis Group
LONDON AND NEW YORK

First published 2011
by Routledge
2 Park Square, Milton Park, Abingdon, Oxon OX14 4RN

Simultaneously published in the USA and Canada
by Routledge
711 Third Avenue, New York, NY 10017

Routledge is an imprint of the Taylor & Francis Group, an informa business

British Library Cataloguing in Publication Data
A catalogue record for this book is available from the British Library

Library of Congress Cataloging in Publication Data
Hirata, Johannes.
Happiness, ethics and economics / by Johannes Hirata.
p. cm.
Includes bibliographical references and index.
1. Happiness–Economic aspects. 2. Economics–Psychological aspects.
I. Title.
BF575.H27.H57 2010
338.9001–dc22
2010039674

ISBN: 978-0-415-58404-3 (hbk)
ISBN: 978-0-203-82847-2 (ebk)

Typeset in Times
by Wearset Ltd, Boldon, Tyne and Wear
Printed and bound by TJI Digital, Padstow, Cornwall

Contents

Figures and tables

Figures

Tables

Preface

I had the privilege to research and write this study, originally as a doctoral thesis, in quite different geographical, economic, and cultural settings. Of three and a half years, I spent two years in St. Gallen (Switzerland), 12 months in São Paulo (Brazil), and three months in Thimphu (Bhutan). Each of these places gave me unique experiences and widely different cultural perspectives on happiness, economics, and ethics. Owing to the universalistic and conceptual approach of this book, these experiences could of course not find much explicit expression in the text. However, they contributed immensely to a more differentiated and better-reflected understanding of the major issues dealt with in this book.

Other major sources of inspiration were regular meetings with other researchers on the intersection of ethics and economics. There were the semi-annual meetings of the "Berliner Forum", which provided a great opportunity to present one's research in a scholarly and, at the same time, amicable atmosphere. There were also occasional retreats with a small group of doctoral students from St. Gallen's Institute for Business Ethics in the picturesque setting of a Black Forest cottage. These weekend meetings, which we labeled the "Wittenschwand Talks" after the village where they took place, were as inspiring intellectually as they were rewarding personally. I am grateful to Matthias Glasmeyer for making these meetings possible.

There are many more persons and institutions toward whom and which I feel indebted. Prof. Peter Ulrich was not only the major intellectual source of inspiration for this whole undertaking, but also an exceptionally dedicated thesis supervisor. Prof. Dieter Thomä, my second thesis supervisor, gave valuable guidance in the vast terrain of philosophical thought. Ulrich Thielemann of the Institute for Business Ethics sacrificed lots of his time in extensive conversations about fundamental questions of ethics and economics. Prof. Eduardo Giannetti of Insper (São Paulo) gave valuable advice and spent many hours answering my questions and discussing the growing manuscript. I also want to thank the directorate of Insper for the overwhelming hospitality and the excellent research conditions I enjoyed during the 12 months of my stay. On my second research stay abroad, at the Center for Bhutan Studies, it is Dasho Karma Ura, the center's director, and Karma Galay who deserve particular mention for their support of my research and for organizing a memorable field trip. Finally, I want to thank the Swiss National Science Foundation (SNF) for one year's generous funding of my research abroad and the Hochschule Osnabrück, University of Applied Sciences, for a reduction of my teaching load, which allowed me to update and improve the text.

There are many more people who contributed to this study – by proofreading, suggesting literature, participating in discussions, granting interviews, sending me their writings, etc. Among these were Dorothea Baur, Luigino Bruni, Francisco S. Cavalcante Junior, Jesús Conill, Ed Diener, Richard Easterlin, Robert H. Frank, Lopen Lungten Gyatsho, Rinzin Jamtsho, Sanjeev Mehta, Roberto Shinyashiki, Heiko Spitzeck, Alois Stutzer, Robert Sugden, Sherab Tenzin, Karma Tshiteem, Akiko Ueda, Robert Urquhart, Maarten Vendrik, and Pema Wangda. I am also grateful for the very helpful comments and suggestions of two anonymous referees.

A different kind of support came from my family. I thank my parents for their wholehearted and unconditional support of my studies and Karen and our children for their patience and understanding, even during the more taxing phases of my research.

Johannes Hirata

1 Introduction

A good society will be inhabited by happy people. They need not be euphoric all of the time and may even experience occasional episodes of unhappiness. A good society will also be characterized by many other distinct features apart from happiness. But if most of a society's members are not generally happy most of the time, we would hardly speak of a good society.

Even a good society will not be perfect, however. Believing in the possibility of the reality of a perfect society would not only be naïvely utopian but also sketch an implausibly deterministic image of the ethical idea of goodness. Societies do not construe a model of the perfect world after which they strive; they rather seek to improve their condition in a continuous struggle toward a less deficient world. Even with an incomplete and vague notion of the ultimate ideal destiny, it is of course still possible to meaningfully reason about what ought to be the next step in the right direction. This is the challenge of good development – the dynamic corollary of the static idea of the good society – and all societies are confronted with it as long as they are not perfect; in other words, for eternity.

If happiness is a characteristic of a good society and development a gradual movement toward a good, or better, society, then happiness appears to be a natural candidate as an objective for development policies. Yet, if happiness is not the only characteristic of a good society, good development cannot simply be the maximization of happiness regardless of all other possible considerations. The role of happiness will, therefore, have to be more subtle than this. This is what the following reflections are about.

The problem

Earlier generations could not have imagined the speed and extent of the technological and economic progress that has taken place in the wealthier countries over the last couple of decades. Over a period of only about 100 years, revolutionary luxuries like telecommunication, automobiles, washing machines, running hot water, etc. have become standard goods, accessible to almost every household. In less than ten years, mobile phones, personal computers, e-mail, and internet access have become widely available and affordable, radically changing people's daily lives.

Yet, at the same time, these same societies continue to struggle with social ills. Persistently high unemployment is a problem in many high-income countries. Violence, crime, and vandalism show no sign of abatement, with some societies having close to 1 percent of their population imprisoned at any given point in time. Loneliness, depression, alcoholism, and suicide continue to afflict wealthy societies and even appear to have risen in some countries. Obesity and other pathological symptoms of affluence are rising rapidly around the world, and work-related stress and sleep deprivation are becoming serious concerns in an increasing number of societies.

The disparity between economic progress and continuing social ills is striking. We are probably, on the whole, living better lives than any generation before us, but that is not a satisfactory accomplishment once we recognize that we could, and should, be living better lives than we are currently doing. There is an apparent paradox: We clearly have more options to choose from, more resources to transform into what we like, better living conditions to satisfy even our fanciest needs, but yet our lives appear to be riddled with many of the same problems as those of our forefathers, minus some that we have managed to reduce (such as mortality and morbidity), plus a couple of new ones (such as obesity and stress).

For a long time, the question of whether we are happier today than were earlier generations was a rather speculative debate, based on purely intuitive inferences from some arbitrary selection of indicators and, therefore, easily refutable. Recent empirical research on happiness, however, now allows us to come to much more precise conclusions. More importantly, it allows us to analyze the relationship between a person's degree of happiness and that person's living conditions and life concerns. Whereas the answer to the question of whether we have become happier or not will merely satisfy a curiosity, detailed evidence on the relationship between happiness and other factors may help us to better understand the effects of economic progress on our well-being and enable us to improve on the way our societies develop.

Getting a better understanding of what makes us happy would be a formidable achievement, but, if it is agreed that happiness does not exhaust the relevant concerns of a society, it would not by itself provide any normative conclusions. Knowledge and understanding of happiness can help us take better decisions only when they are embedded in a comprehensive conception of good development.

The question that organizes this text is therefore as follows: *What is the appropriate role of happiness within a comprehensive conception of good development?* The underlying ambition is thus to understand if and to what extent good development is a matter of happiness.

Perspective and methodology

The focus of this book is clearly normative, as indicated by the terms "appropriate" and "good" (as an attribute of "development"). The answer to a normative question must of course also be normative; any attempt to give a positive or "objective" answer would be bound to miss the point. Yet, the kind of normative answer that the above question demands is not of a prescriptive nature but rather of an orientating one. In other words, instead of moral judgments of what ought to be done, or technical knowledge of what can or will be done, we will be looking for ethical *orientation* as a basis for sound and well-reasoned judgments.

The systematic basis for this kind of normative reflection and affirmation is not a given set of values that is intuitively affirmed or not, but rather the universal grammar of reason that we implicitly adhere to – and expect others to adhere to – each time we sincerely engage in an argumentative conversation, i.e. in a discourse (cf. ch. 4).

The natural way to proceed on this course is a critique of the normative content of incumbent theories of happiness and of development. Contrary to what their proponents might believe, such theories are never value-free or value-neutral – and neither should they try to be. The challenge is therefore not to separate the "pure" theory from its normative "contaminations", but to come up with a well-reflected normative conception and to bring it to the light of day (Ulrich 2008: 3, 79ff.). Only such a normatively well-founded conception can provide normative orientation that can meaningfully guide judgment. It cannot, however, deliver a toolbox of prescriptions or precise evaluative criteria for "optimal" development.

The deeper reason for this has to do with the nature of ethics itself. Dealing essentially with the question of the proper use of human freedom (of will and of choice), ethics must be inherently indeterminate. This is a major, perhaps the fundamental, characteristic that distinguishes the ethical perspective from other scientific disciplines. Respecting indeterminacy means that one must not expect to find a grand unifying principle and that one must be prepared to live with theoretical incompleteness and irreducible ambiguities. This methodological problem reflects the normative-practical problem of the normative irreducibility of conflicting interests (which in turn is a corollary of freedom itself). Since it is apparently not possible to ethically defend a grand "objective" principle by which conflicts of interests could be "solved", the "correct" intermediation between conflicting interests becomes a matter of an (indeterminate) discursive appraisal of the specific reasons the concerned individuals may have. The implications of the indeterminacy of ethics will be a recurrent theme throughout each of the following chapters.

While the perspective of this study is ethical, it will make extensive use of empirical evidence to inform and test the normative conclusions. To be sure, empirical evidence itself cannot deliver any normative conclusions out of itself (that would mean committing the "naturalistic fallacy"). Yet, ethical theory would remain purely formal, and therefore of little significance to real-world problems if its general principles were not explicated with respect to concrete situations, however contestable any such exercise must ultimately remain. After all, ethical problems of relevance are those posed by real life, and practical ethical orientation therefore always requires the concretization of formal ethical principles.

An evaluative approach to questions of societal development can take one of two basic forms. It can be *comparative*, comparing the state of a given society at different points in time or of different societies at the same point in time. Such an approach would answer questions of the type "Are we living better today than 50 years ago or than society *X*?" Alternatively, the approach can be *systematic*, investigating to which degree a society is realizing its potential, answering questions of the type "Are we living as well as we could?" The approach adopted here will be the systematic one, even though some comparisons will also be made to enrich the analysis.

Ambition and scope

The theme of this study revolves around the two concepts that dominate the research question: happiness and good development. These two concepts will therefore form the gravitational center around which the reflections will be organized and which will delimit the boundaries for the discussion.

Happiness is a concept that can be looked at from a number of angles. In the present context, happiness will be of interest in so far as it relates to the question of societal development. To clarify the concept as such and to prepare the ground for a meaningful discussion of happiness with respect to development, a number of different approaches to happiness will need to be touched upon. These include a psychological and social psychological, a linguistic, and a philosophical approach. Notably, and in contrast to most recent contributions to the happiness literature, the approach taken here will specifically address the problem of conflicts between one person's happiness and that of others. This also means that a society's aggregate (or average) happiness will only be referred to as a potentially informative figure but not as an indicator with immediate ethical significance. In other words, the harmonious idea of "social welfare" as the consolidated balance of a society's well-being (cf. p. 103) is dropped in favor of a more differentiated, albeit technically less accessible, appraisal.

The discussion of the concept of good development will be restricted to two disciplinary approaches. Primarily it will be analyzed as an ethical concept. In order to keep the argument comprehensible, even for those unacquainted with ethical theory, and to avoid misunderstandings due to particular presumptions, the conception of ethics adopted here, including its key concepts, will be explained and defended. As will become clear, a conception of good development will depend fundamentally on a conception of the good life, which therefore will need to be included.

The discussion of good development from an ethical point of view will then fade into the (closely related) perspective of political philosophy. The latter will allow us to develop some policy implications. However, instead of formulating "policy recommendations" as known from, for example, normative economics, the practical conclusions will be embedded into a refined concept of democracy, specifying *in which way* the results of this study ought to affect policy decisions, rather than which precise policy decisions ought to be taken.

Economics will come into play in two different roles. First, its normative theory of good development and its model of human decision-making will be the object of a critical analysis. Second, the argument will make use of economic theory to understand the nature of economic growth and of competition.

The concept of development will be looked at in a wider sense. In particular, it will not be understood merely as a matter of policies or "rules of the game", but also as a matter of individuals actually being able to do particular things and to be who they want to be ("capabilities", cf. p. 78). What is more, the question of the good life will be considered not only as a matter of living conditions (what people could do), but also as a matter of what people actually do within these conditions, including how they feel and how they evaluate their lives and the state of the world they live in.

Outline and reading guide

In an attempt to make the argument comprehensible for the non-specialist reader, the main concepts will be carefully introduced with a minimum of formal language. Just a minimum of statistical literacy is expected (such as the meaning of correlation coefficients and statistical significance), but no deeper familiarity with the economic, psychological, or philosophical literature is expected.

The text will begin, in Chapter 2, with a presentation of evidence on the problem described above, i.e. the "happiness paradox" of the coexistence of tremendous economic growth and stagnating subjective well-being (SWB). In preparation of this evidence, the concept and methodology of subjective well-being research will be discussed.

Chapter 3 will deliver an interpretation of that evidence from within the (welfare) economic perspective, suggesting a set of concepts that may (partly) explain the observations. As will become clear, however, the internal perspective is too limited to adequately understand the phenomenon of happiness, making it necessary to step beyond the methodological confines of the welfare economic perspective.

This is the starting point for Chapter 4, in which happiness is discussed from an ethical perspective. The first part of the chapter will clarify the ethical point of view, making a distinction between a teleological and a deontological perspective (a recurrent theme). Subsequently, the concept of happiness itself will be discussed, culminating in a normative conception of happiness as a self-transcendent phenomenon.

The connection of the concepts of happiness and good development is the subject of Chapter 5. It begins with a discussion of the normative notion of good development along the lines of the two-dimensional conception of ethics introduced in the preceding chapter. The subsequent section addresses the question of how the ideal notion of good development relates to the practice of development in the face of concrete challenges, arguing that practice must always be oriented by ideal ethical principles ("regulative ideas", cf. p. 16). Finally, the role of happiness within a conception of good development will be discussed.

Chapter 6 is concerned with the practical implications of the findings on the practice of development under the premise of democracy. It will not formulate any prescriptions ("policy recommendations"), though. Instead, it will explain how the way of thinking and decision-making – of individuals or societies – might change when happiness is taken seriously. The chapter concludes with an outline of the limitations of the happiness perspective.

The conclusion (Chapter 7) will close the text with some general reflections on the results obtained. It will close the circle that has been opened in the problem statement through a reassessment of the role of economic growth in good development.

2 The evidence on happiness

Empirical happiness research of roughly four decades has established a peculiar pattern of rather robust correlations between income and happiness.[1] This configuration seems to defy a neat generalization of the kind "When income rises, happiness rises/stagnates/declines" and has therefore come to be known as the "happiness paradox", at least among those happiness researchers interested in the role of material living conditions.[2] More specifically, the happiness paradox actually consists of two distinct paradoxes: the first one is the observation that, over an individual's life cycle, people do not report increasing happiness as their incomes increase, and average happiness for nations as a whole shows at best a modest upward trend over time in some countries. This can be considered a paradox, as will be argued below, because one would expect a clear positive effect of income on happiness on the basis of behavioral observations. The second paradox refers to the observation that this result (i.e. the virtual independence of happiness from income) does not hold when comparing the happiness of individuals or of countries-as-a-whole *at a given point in time*. In this perspective, individuals and nations with higher incomes do in fact have a higher likelihood of being particularly happy.

To start with the first paradox, it might be objected that expecting rising incomes to raise happiness would reflect a questionable attitude or, more explicitly, a materialistic ideology and that it would therefore be presumptuous to talk of a paradox here. Indeed, the idea that "money will *not* make you happy" seems to be as old as money itself. Various Greek and Roman philosophical schools, most famously the Stoics, already recommended moderating one's material ambitions for the sake of a better life, and even older religious texts give the same advice (cf. Giannetti 2002: 116ff.). In our days, social critics and self-help books try to convince us that we can, and should, lead perfectly happy lives without a further increase in consumption.

In fact, however, when saying that the evidence of stagnant happiness in time series contradicts expectations, these expectations are not merely based on a particular ideology but rather on the quite unideological observation that most people in market economies go to great lengths to increase, or at least maintain, their income. They usually sacrifice real resources – most noteworthy, time – in order to earn more money and to consume more, even if that comes at the expense of things they know (or so one might assume) would make them happy, such as spending time with family and friends.

When we try to generalize this point, we see that the deeper reason why it is appropriate to talk of a paradox here has to do with the nature of economic growth. Applying the standard macroeconomic distinction between technological progress on the one hand and inputs of labor and (physical and human) capital on the other, we know that, historically, sustained economic growth is ultimately driven by technological progress (Solow 1956). While "technological progress" is a somewhat problematic catch-all term, it should be unproblematic in this context when it is understood as an increase in labor productivity that is not based on an increase in the capital stock. In other words, it is the increase in the intangible asset that makes it possible to increase the output per one hour of labor without increasing the rate of investment over and above the rate of depreciation of (physical and human) capital. This intangible asset is basically skill and knowledge, and its growth can often take very inconspicuous shapes. The mailman who discovers a shorter route to deliver the mail; the railway company that redesigns its timetable so as to reduce the idle time of its trains; or the engineer who makes an existing process more energy efficient; all these innovations are instances of technological progress. In essence, then, technological progress enhances our possibilities of reaching specific goals with fewer resources, or of reaching more goals with the same resources, and all this without the sacrifice of extra savings (as in the case of productivity gains based on an expansion of the capital base). In this perspective, technological progress should be a pure gain for society: while knowledge and options are gained, nothing is lost. In other words, technological progress is essentially an expansion of our options, and we are basically free to do with them whatever we want, including the option to transform them into more leisure time while changing nothing else (in particular, keeping consumption constant). Notably, technological progress can usually not be negative since the cost of conserving knowledge is comparably small. Only a dramatic failure to educate a generation or a catastrophic event that would irrecoverably wipe out a significant part of knowledge could be thought of as leading to technological regress on a global scale.

When we now assume that people are eager to use their increased options in a way that, whether intentionally or incidentally, also contributes to their happiness, we should, *ceteris paribus*, expect that technological progress gives rise to an increase in happiness. Whether people transform their increased options into more leisure time or into more consumption (or a little of both) cannot be predicted on the basis of this kind of reasoning, but we happen to observe that there is hardly any evidence for a concomitant increase in happiness.

Coming back to the second paradox – the fact that cross-section evidence shows a positive correlation between happiness and income whereas time-series data produce a zero correlation – I would like to take the opportunity to highlight two caveats. The first one, rather familiar but nevertheless worth stating, is that statistical evidence of correlation does not imply causality. A correlation, or its absence, can always be due to overlooked factors, and the strongest support we can expect from statistical evidence is the failure to contradict a hypothesis. No evidence whatsoever will ever prove a hypothesis (Popper 1959/1934) and, even less, establish a causal effect. Causality can only be made plausible by means of inductive reasoning, and statistical evidence can at most support, or weaken, such reasoning.

The second caveat concerns the practice of cross-country comparison of happiness data. While routinely done in the literature, such comparisons should be treated with a good deal of caution, since happiness surveys are inherently dependent on the precise meaning a language community or cultural community assigns to the survey questions asked. In the following section, I shall say more on this in the context of a discussion of the concepts that have been established for the purpose of empirical happiness research.

From happiness to subjective well-being

Happiness is, of course, not a physical state that is somewhere out there and only awaits the invention of the appropriate instrument to be precisely and objectively measured. The reason is that happiness is not, like "temperature", a concept that is defined with respect to objective, physical, or physiological criteria, and it therefore does not make sense to expect that one day happiness can be measured by means of a "hedonimeter", as Edgeworth (1881: 101) once hoped. Rather, it is an inherently subjective, value-laden, and indeterminate, but nonetheless real, mental concept that cannot be separated from an underlying judgment. Unless one believes the human mind to be determinate, which would have implications few people would be ready to accept (cf. Hirata 2004), one must face up to the fact that happiness as such cannot be measured. What can be measured, though, is a closely related psychological construct that has been christened "subjective well-being" (SWB). This section will argue that this construct delivers valid clues to the more elusive phenomenon of happiness and that it has the psychometrical properties required to run meaningful statistical analyses on this measure. An in-depth discussion of the concept of happiness itself, which will require the prior clarification of additional philosophical concepts, will follow in Chapter 4. For the time being, the discussion can proceed on the basis of the common understanding of "happiness" that every speaker of the English language has, prior to any scholarly analysis of the concept.

Interpersonal comparability and the question of cardinality

For measurement of SWB to make sense at all, SWB data must be at least either interpersonally comparable or cardinal. If only interpersonal comparison is accepted, one can at least do comparative studies using an ordinal SWB scale. If, on the other hand, only cardinality is accepted, one can still make time-series studies of individuals, as long as it is accepted that a given individual will use the SWB scale consistently over time (i.e. if one accepts *intra*personal comparability). Rejecting both interpersonal comparability and cardinality, as the so-called "new welfare economics" did on theoretical grounds, dramatically reduces the significance of SWB data. Incidentally, skepticism with respect to interpersonal comparability and cardinality is largely limited to the economic profession, whereas most psychologists find it natural to assume both to be given. If the non-economist reader finds it a waste of time to even consider the implausibility of interpersonal comparability and cardinality of SWB data, she is invited to skip the following paragraphs.

Accepting interpersonal comparability effectively means that we can be sure that a person who declares to be "very happy" is in fact happier than another person declaring to be "fairly happy". Clearly, interpersonal comparison is not a question of yes or no but a matter of degree. Of course there must a basis for the comparison of self-reports about subjective states – claiming otherwise would mean denying the possibility of meaningful verbal communication about subjective states in general. Thanks to our ability to empathize and to the common understanding of a shared language, we can in fact understand what a person intends to tell us about his or her degree of happiness, and we know which words we must choose in order to let others understand how we feel.

It is a slightly different question whether different respondents use the answer scales in precisely the same way. It may be objected that respondents do not all set the threshold between, say, "happy" and "very happy" at exactly the same level. At closer inspection, however, this objection merely says that the accuracy of SWB measures is less than perfect, which is certainly true. As will be shown below, the psychometrical evidence confirms that SWB measures suffer from imprecision and limited validity, but it also indicates that SWB data are of reasonable quality. Again, we can trust in empathy and language that two individuals who say the same thing will also feel roughly the same. Moreover, even seemingly "hard" data – in particular income – are far from accurate. It would therefore be inappropriate to expect absolute precision from SWB data.

Saying that SWB data are cardinal means that increments in SWB are quantitatively comparable with each other so that one can meaningfully say, for example, that a glass of wine will raise one's SWB by twice as much as a glass of beer. When applied to answer scales, this is usually interpreted as requiring that distances between any two adjacent answer categories be of the same magnitude, i.e. that answer categories be equidistant. (Even though, strictly speaking, cardinality would also hold if the distances were heterogeneous as long as they are quantitatively comparable, equidistance is for all practical matters the most reasonable requirement.) Accepting cardinality then means that all kinds of algebraic and statistical operations can be made on the data, such as taking averages, determining correlation coefficients, and so on.

By contrast, saying that SWB data are ordinal means that the answer categories can merely be ranked in terms of intensity while the distances between the categories cannot be compared and that, as a consequence, it is meaningless to calculate averages or correlation coefficients.

The appropriate question to ask is not whether SWB or happiness as such *is a cardinal concept* but rather whether it is meaningful to *interpret SWB data cardinally* and to what extent a cardinal interpretation delivers valid insights. After all, cardinality is not a manifest property of a concept that can be determined in isolation but rather a description of the relation between that concept and a particular evaluational space. For example, luminosity (say, of a light bulb) may be cardinal with respect to the space of energy but perhaps not with respect to the space of human perception (is it meaningful to say that I find one light bulb twice as light as another?). Or even if it is, it may be cardinal along a different scale (I may judge that to double the perceived luminosity, I need three identical light bulbs rather than two). By analogy, cardinality of SWB requires that there be some space with respect to which SWB can meaningfully be interpreted cardinally, and this will be the case if we find a robust statistical relationship with a relevant space (such as living conditions) that establishes a particular quantitative pattern along the entire scale of SWB. These relationships need of course not be linear but can also be exponential, polynomial, or logarithmic (for example, when SWB rises by a constant increment for each doubling of income).

Moreover, as in the case of interpersonal comparison, the nature of language goes a long way in making a cardinal interpretation plausible because people naturally use category labels as a way to maximize the informativeness of their judgments (Parducci 1995: 81; Kahneman 1999: 11). Experimental research by Bernard van Praag (1991) suggests that, provided that cardinality is accepted at all, respondents do actually interpret normative answer scales (i.e. answers involving normative judgments) in a way that the distances between any two adjacent labels represent roughly equal intervals.

Insisting on ordinality does not mean, however, that quantitative analysis becomes impossible because there are statistical methods to deal with ordinal data. For example, instead of using ordinary least squares (OLS) regression, it is possible to use ordered logit or ordered probit regression (even though these methods impose other requirements that are arguably not much less rigorous than cardinality). Such models do not give estimates of the magnitude of an effect but on the probabilistic influence of an independent variable, which is not much of a loss of information.

From an empirical perspective, the question of cardinality or ordinality appears to be less critical, however, because studies that compare OLS and ordered logit/probit regressions side-by-side regularly find that the results are largely consistent (e.g. Ferrer-i-Carbonell and Frijters 2004: 653; Frey and Stutzer 2000: 924, 2002: 188–9). In other words, while skeptics will still find it inadmissible to interpret the results cardinally, the evidence suggests that the cardinal interpretation will not lead to contradictory conclusions.

Terminological distinctions

A person's degree of subjective well-being is elicited through survey questions that ask respondents to indicate "How satisfied are you with your life as a whole these days?" (answer on a seven-point scale "completely satisfied … completely dissatisfied"; Andrews and Withey 1976: 67), "Taking all things together, would you say you are – very happy, quite happy, not very happy, not at all happy?" (World Values Survey; Inglehart 1997: 351), or "On the whole, are you very satisfied, fairly satisfied, not very satisfied, or not at all satisfied with the life you lead?" (Eurobarometer, cf. Di Tella *et al.* 2003: 810–11). The values obtained do of course not reflect happiness as such, but rather the respondent's self-assessment as elicited by the particular survey question, his or her *self-reported life satisfaction*. I will use the terms SWB, "self-reported happiness", "self-reported life satisfaction", etc. interchangeably, depending on the particular context. I will continue to use the term "happiness" in collocations where this terminology is firmly established and where confusions between *happiness* and *subjective well-being* can be ruled out, such as in "empirical happiness research" and "happiness surveys".

A basic distinction in empirical happiness research is that between a hedonic and a cognitive dimension. As an emotion, happiness includes "a reference to 'feeling', a reference to 'thinking', and a reference to a person's body".[3] It is therefore a "thought-related feeling" (Wierzbicka 1999: 2, 15). To grasp this distinction terminologically, psychologists have coined a number of terms that will reappear throughout this chapter. Generally speaking, terms that can be classified as belonging to the "hedonic" category refer to pre-reflective feelings that are experienced as either good or bad (or, in the limiting case, as neutral), associated physiologically with a tendency toward approach or avoidance, respectively (Kahneman 1999: 7). These feelings will typically occur as a response to bodily stimuli (such as an injury), but they can also be a response to non-bodily stimuli (such as an irritating noise). These purely hedonic feelings are termed (positive or negative) "hedonic affect", the balance between positive and negative hedonic affect is called "hedonic balance" or "hedonic level". Semantically, "pleasure" also falls into this category as it lacks a cognitive component (Wierzbicka 1999: 56). It is, however, more frequently encountered in the philosophical than in the psychological literature.

By contrast, those terms belonging to the "cognitive" category refer to feelings that arise as a response to a reflected appraisal. This does not imply that such feelings can be cognitively controlled, but merely that some cognitive capacity is a condition for a subject to experience such feelings. The emotional reaction will still be largely beyond the subject's willful control. Feelings of this quality are labeled "cognitive satisfaction". In particular, any global assessment of subjective well-being that involves more than just one's momentary mood will involve cognitive elements. "Happiness" clearly falls into this category, as does "satisfaction".

This distinction between purely hedonic and purely cognitive feelings is of course one between two polar cases on a continuum, and generally feelings will involve a combination of affective and cognitive qualities. Furthermore, as the survey items concerning life satisfaction are complete sentences designed to capture the respondents' appraisal of their lives as a whole (cf. p. 11), they usually will convey a slightly different meaning than a word such as "happy" or "satisfied" would in isolation. The responses may thus be expected to be less sensitive to the precise semantic nuances of the keywords ("happy", "satisfied", etc.) than to the wording of the question as a whole. This is evidenced by the fact that the correlation between the answers to a question involving the term "happy" and those to a question involving the term "satisfied" has been found to be close to the test-retest correlation (i.e. the correlation of two answers to the same question, once posed at the beginning and once at the end of the interview) of a third question about life satisfaction.[4] Nevertheless, some of the variance indeed seems to be due to the fact that questions mentioning the word "happy" are more correlated with measures of hedonic affect, while those mentioning "satisfied" were more correlated with measures of cognitive satisfaction (Diener 1984, 1994; Veenhoven 1991).

In sum, while one should not be oblivious to the distinction between the hedonic and the cognitive components of happiness, one can safely assume that, in general, SWB data do not depend critically on whether they include the word "happy" or the word "satisfied".

Apart from empirical evidence, hedonic affect and cognitive satisfaction seem to be closely interrelated on a conceptual level, too. My past record of affective balance is likely to have a major influence on my cognitive satisfaction with life, and, conversely, my cognitive evaluation of my life may be expected to be a major influence on my hedonic balance (Lazarus 1991, quoted in Diener 1994). The concept of happiness that matters when it comes to evaluating the goodness of our lives must certainly integrate both the hedonic and the cognitive dimension of well-being, as will be argued later on (ch. 4).

In order to appraise the usefulness of a measure of SWB – i.e. the internal consistency, meaningfulness, and the adequacy to one's research interest – we must obviously have some idea of what we expect from a useful SWB indicator. Ed Diener (1994: 106), psychologist and pioneering SWB researcher, has advanced three concrete criteria that should be met by such an indicator. These stipulate that a measure of SWB should (1) capture only *subjective* experiences, (2) require *positive* experiences, rather than only the absence of negative ones, and (3) include a *global assessment* rather than be limited to a particular life domain or time period. These three criteria demand some clarification and justification.

(1) The requirement that only subjective experiences be captured by a measure of SWB is of course already implied by the term "*subjective* well-being". It may nevertheless seem odd to a social scientist to consider subjectivity a virtue, perhaps even to the point that the entire enterprise of SWB research is discarded already at this point as unscientific, arbitrary, or impossible. Yet, such an attitude would fail to make the vital distinction between subjectivity in the generation of data, i.e. on the side of respondents, and subjectivity in the evaluation of the evidence, i.e. on the side of the researcher. The latter is clearly not desirable in the analysis of empirical data, even though it will always be, to some extent, inevitable. The former, however, may be altogether admissible and even desirable, namely when the research interest has a subjective dimension, such as

well-being or welfare. It is of course entirely possible and admissible to *objectively* analyze data that reflect *subjective* judgments, and it is only this kind of objectivity, i.e. objectivity by the researcher in the evaluation of (subjective or objective) data, that characterizes good empirical research.

Whenever empirical research concerns subjective phenomena, one must, from the beginning, take people's subjective perspectives as the yardstick for the adequacy of one's tools, methods, or theories. In contrast to research about purely physical phenomena, such as the forces of gravity, research about human well-being must rely to some degree on information that captures a subjective perspective (unless one takes the view that well-being is as objective a category as gravity). After all, the very understanding of a subjective concept, such as – to take a less complex example – pain, is only possible in a hermeneutic perspective that takes as its starting point the acknowledgment that pain is subjectively known before it can be explained. This implies, for example, that a person cannot be declared to be feeling pain with reference to objective evidence (such as a serious injury) when she credibly declares not to be feeling any pain (in fact, serious injuries often do not cause pain for hours or even days to the victim; Eich *et al.* 1999: 156). To put it simply, "by definition, the final judge of someone's subjective well-being is whomever lives inside that person's skin" (Myers 2000: 57).

One more reason why subjectivity is a desirable feature of a measure of SWB can be illustrated by reference to a morally inspired criticism against SWB measures. It is sometimes argued (Sen 1984a: 512; cf. p. 94 below) that SWB measures are biased to the degree that, for example, people living in extreme poverty without any prospect to better living conditions have come to accept their lot and, having adjusted their aspirations downward, report being satisfied with their lives (this objection will be taken up in more detail in ch. 4). A good indicator of happiness would therefore be one that truly reflects a person's objective well-being (cf. Tversky and Griffin 1991: 116–17). This view is problematic, however, because it ascribes more normative content to the idea of happiness than it carries in everyday language. If one defines happiness as referring to an objective state instead of a subjective evaluation, one will lose contact with common use of language and rob oneself of a meaningful concept. Instead of describing survey responses as biased just because they do not comply with the researcher's private definition of happiness that respondents do not share, one should take SWB data at face value and take seriously what they tell us about a person's life that objective data cannot. If we observe that people living in poverty report being satisfied with their lives, or people living in affluence unsatisfied, then this is valuable information and not a bias. Of course, this does not permit the *normative* conclusion that all happy people are leading good lives and that an unhappy person must be suffering from unjustified deprivation, but that is an entirely different issue (cf. p. 177).[5]

(2) Clearly, to get empirical clues of happiness, establishing the absence of negative experiences would not be enough: positive feelings must also be present. There seems to be no necessity to give this deeper justification than

hinting to the research interest – which happens to be happiness and not, for example, a sufficiency approach. Yet, saying that a measure of SWB should also capture positive experiences raises the question of how to distinguish positive from neutral or negative experiences. The terminology of "positive experiences" suggests that there must be some neutral zero point on the happiness scale. Psychologists and economists have debated this question rather controversially. Both sides of the debate seem to agree that, generally speaking, one can distinguish between two classes of labels used to describe subjective perceptions: absolute labels that are anchored in some natural scale with a natural zero point, and relative labels that depend on the context to convey meaning. An example of an absolute descriptive label would be "green", because a person will not reassign the label "green" to a color that is very distant from green just because the context has been manipulated. Even if a person can be induced in an experiment to describe a color as green that she would not normally describe so, then that person's perception itself has been manipulated, not the way she assigns labels to her perceptions. An example of a purely relative label is "big" or "large". The example of "a large mouse that ran up the trunk of the small elephant" (Stevens 1958: 633) makes clear that the meaning we ascribe to the label "big" or "large" (or "small") is inherently dependent on context, even if the point of reference will usually be only implicit (such as, in the example above, an average-sized mouse or elephant). Here we do in fact reshuffle the way in which we ascribe labels to our perceptions themselves.

With respect to happiness, some authors (e.g. Edgeworth 1881: 101; Ng 1978: 584–5) believe that happiness is an absolute label, while others (e.g. Helson 1964; Parducci 1968, 1995) think it is relative. Kahneman (1999: 21) takes an intermediary position by arguing that hedonic affect is an absolute label, while cognitive satisfaction is a relative one. However, this discussion seems to be largely irrelevant to the *concept* of happiness. As an emotion with the three dimensions mentioned above (feeling, cognition, and body; cf. p. 12), happiness does not seem to belong to either group of labels, i.e. it cannot be classified as either absolute or relative. The reason that labels such as "green" or "big" can meaningfully be classified as absolute or relative is that they are ascribed to concrete objects with corresponding perceptions (of color or size) with a specific sensory manifestation. The word "happiness", however, is ascribed to a complex emotion, not to a manifest perception of an object "out there", and since it relies to a large extent on a value judgment, it is inherently indeterminate, as will be argued below (ch. 4). In other words, the quality of an emotion such as happiness does not *exist* in the same, manifest way as does the quality of a visual perception of color or size (or of a pre-reflective feeling, such as the pleasure derived from stilling one's thirst). Rather, an emotion is to a considerable extent actively construed, rather than passively experienced, by the agent, and it is difficult to see how this process of construing the emotion can be separated from the process of ascribing a label to this emotion. In contrast to a visual perception, "happiness" is not ascribed to a given object but to the indeterminate *evaluation* of a subjective experience (cf. Diener 1994: 136).

To come back to the question of whether happiness is an absolute or a relative label, it will be of help to reconsider the case of the relative label "big". It is evident that "big" is relative with respect to, for example, one's visual perception. However, this does not mean that it does not have an absolute meaning in another space. In fact, for effective communication to take place at all, an absolute core in *some* space is altogether indispensable. In the case of "big", the anchor with respect to which "big" is absolute is a prototypical mouse, elephant, or whatever else the context suggests as the standard of comparison. Conversely, for any given label, one will probably be able to indicate some space in which its meaning is relative. It will therefore be more illuminating to identify the particular space with respect to which a given concept is absolute, rather than to classify it as either relative or absolute as such, without indicating the space with respect to which it is relative or absolute.[6] Happiness, then, is absolute with respect to the space of normative *judgments* about one's well-being and relative with respect to living conditions (and many other spaces), as will be analyzed in more detail below (ch. 4). Saying to be happy will always be a positive evaluation in the former space.

(3) As a third requirement, a measure of SWB should be global in two dimensions. In a temporal dimension, it should cover the entire lifetime from childhood to present, and in the dimension of life domains it should cover all life domains. Obviously, this requirement is highly ambitious and methodologically difficult to specify. It is not obvious, for example, when all life domains and life years are "correctly" aggregated and when one should say that one particular life domain is over-represented. However, while such a pure and balanced global assessment may remain an unachievable ideal (or, more precisely, an inherently indeterminate regulative idea with purely orientating function; cf. Ulrich 2008: 35, 84), SWB will usually be a sufficiently global assessment when it is not significantly influenced by current mood and when the questionnaire design takes care to prevent excessive response bias. That this is usually achieved will be shown in the next section.

Psychometrical qualities of SWB measures

The significance of SWB data is sometimes questioned because, it is argued, self-reports are subjective, arbitrary, unreliable, and imprecise and therefore contain no or very little relevant information. That this view is largely mistaken has long been established with the tools of the psychological sub-discipline of psychometrics.[7]

The adequacy of psychological constructs to quantitative empirical analysis, their psychometrical adequacy, is evaluated along the two criteria of *construct validity* and *reliability* (Figure 2.1). These criteria closely correspond to the general statistical concepts of unbiasedness and accuracy (low variance).

Construct *validity* refers to an indicator's quality to be roughly "on target" most of the time, i.e. to actually measure the (unobservable) construct it is supposed to measure, rather than being systematically biased, independent of the

High validity, low reliability

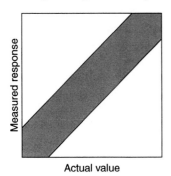

Low validity, high reliability

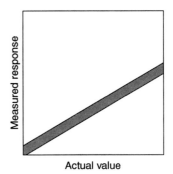

Figure 2.1   Construct validity and reliability.

Note
The shaded areas plot the actual values against the corresponding questionnaire responses. A measure with high validity will yield true responses on average. A measure with high reliability will yield a low variance in the responses corresponding to a given actual state.

presence of unsystematic measurement errors. Construct validity is established by observing whether the survey instrument correlates with factors it *should* correlate with on the basis of the shared understanding of the concept in question. For example, a measure of SWB should, over a large sample of respondents, correlate negatively with undernutrition, bereavement, loneliness, and anxiety, and positively with smiling frequency, goal-attainment, and self-esteem. A happiness indicator that fails to correlate with any of these factors would not have much validity.

This procedure has close resemblance in the way we give verbal definitions. Just as one can verbally define a theoretical construct only by spelling out the network of assertions that convey its meaning, the validity of an indicator has to be assessed by verifying if it satisfies certain statistical relationships (cf. Larsen and Fredrickson 1999: 44). For example, if we want to define a concept such as "intelligence", we will specify how it relates to other concepts with which we believe the audience is familiar, e.g. by saying that an intelligent person will understand abstract problems quickly. If we want to test a specific indicator of intelligence, then we must require that this indicator correlate with the speed with which people understand abstract problems.

Thus, it has been found that single-item self-report measures of SWB, i.e. those that elicit a numerical response to a single global life-satisfaction question of the kind quoted above (p. 11), correlate in the predicted way with subjective measures such as worrying frequency (correlation –0.25), negative affect (–0.31), positive affect (0.30), and number of life changes desired (0.44; all in Andrews and Withey 1976: 85). They also correlate with the evaluation of the subject's happiness by close relatives and friends (between 0.64 and 0.73; Diener *et al.* 1991: 47) and with objective measures such as smiling frequency (Diener 1984: 551) and brain wave patterns (Davidson 1992). The fact that the values of the correlations are rather moderate – well below the theoretical maximum of 1.00 (or minimum of –1.00) – should not be seen as weakening the validity of self-report measures of SWB, but rather as strengthening them. If the correlation between, say, smiling frequency and self-report measures of SWB were exactly one, SWB would be *nothing but* smiling frequency – which clearly is not the only aspect a measure of SWB should capture. Summing up, we can conclude that self-report measures are sufficiently valid to sustain substantive conclusions.

Multiple-item measures of SWB, i.e. compound indicators that are an arithmetical combination of a number of separate measures, have been found to have even higher validity, which should be expected since different sources of imprecision and/or bias that afflict each single measure will tend to cancel each other out. For example, for one eight-item indicator, a respectable validity value of 0.94 has been estimated (Campbell *et al.* 1976: 47). Yet, compound indicators have the disadvantage that they are less transparent and therefore more difficult to interpret because they conceal the underlying composition of the compound figure and do not correspond to a specific idea that can be expressed in a single survey question. The interpretation of single-item measures, by contrast, is straightforward and much less ambiguous.

The concept of *reliability* of an indicator refers to the idea that an indicator delivers identical values for repeated measurements of the same actual state, whether or not the values are actually on target. Reliability can therefore be approximated by a measure's test-retest reliability. Since SWB (i.e. the actual state) should not be very volatile during periods of a couple of minutes or hours, and certainly not during an interview session in which no significant life events should be expected, answers to the same question posed once at the beginning and once at the end of the same interview ought to be identical. Thus, reliability can be estimated by the correlation between these two survey items over a large sample of respondents. Andrews and Withey (1976: 78) did this for the question "How do you feel about your life as a whole? – delighted – pleased – mostly satisfied – mixed (about equally satisfied and dissatisfied) – mostly dissatisfied – unhappy – terrible", and their test-retest correlation for two separate samples yielded values of 0.68 and 0.71. To illustrate this for the case of the first sample, this means that, from 1,433 respondents, 54 percent gave two identical answers and 39 percent gave two adjacent answers, implying that less than 8 percent gave two answers that were more than one interval apart. Taking into account that a substantial portion of respondents may locate themselves on the border between two adjacent answer categories, the fact of checking two different answers for the same question does not, in all cases, have to reflect an instance of unreliability. Thus, while reliability is clearly not perfect, it is strong enough to sustain meaningful conclusions based on SWB data.

The psychometrical quality of SWB measures is also supported indirectly through the results of empirical studies that deliver a large set of robust, replicable, and highly significant statistical relationships with many different factors, as reported on the following pages. If SWB measures were not of reasonable psychometrical quality, we clearly would not be able to observe such patterns.

In conclusion we may state that, despite some limitations, single-item self-report measures of SWB are reasonably valid and reliable and hence contain a substantial amount of information. Allegations that such measures be arbitrary or unreliable can be safely dismissed. To be sure, the less-than-perfect degree of reliability and validity limits the comparability between individual scores, but as soon as large sets of data are statistically analyzed, this imprecision will largely cancel out, since little systematic bias seems to be involved (cf. Veenhoven 1996: 8).

Language and culture

An altogether different issue is the question of comparability across cultural or linguistic boundaries. Here we do, in fact, face very serious limitations of a more fundamental kind than those discussed so far. In order to understand the nature of these limitations, one needs to appreciate the fact that the concepts "happiness" and "happy" are not natural universals, but culturally, linguistically, and historically contingent constructs. There may be only a few, if any, languages that have an exact equivalent of the English concept "happiness", just as its meaning has shifted over time *within* the English language. Moreover, the domain of the adjective "happy" is considerably larger than that of the noun "happiness". When a person says, for example, "I am happy with the present arrangements" (Wierzbicka 1999: 52), this does not imply that the person is experiencing the same profound sense of extraordinary satisfaction implied by the word "happiness". This rather recent extension of the meaning of "happy" toward a weaker interpretation (the earliest quote in the Oxford English Dictionary for "happy with" is dated 1947; Wierzbicka 1999: 54) has not been accompanied by similar changes in other European languages. Thus, faces described in psychological experiments as *happy* by English speakers may not be described as *glücklich* by German, *heureux* by French, or *felice* by Italian speakers (Wierzbicka 1999: 53). Some languages, such as that of the Dani people of the New Guinea Highlands, do not even have remote matches for any of the six English-language emotions (including happiness) that Anglo-American psychologists once thought to be universal "basic emotions" (happiness, sadness, anger, fear, disgust, and surprise), as one of them later recognized himself (Ekman 1975: 39, reported in Wierzbicka 1999: 24–5). Over time, "happiness" has displaced "joy" in the English language, and "to be happy" has displaced "to rejoice". This is reflected by the fact that Shakespeare still used "happy" and "joy" in equal proportion, whereas in Bernard Shaw's works "happy" is seven times more common than "joy" (cf. The Victorian Literary Studies Archive 2010). This may reflect a tendency toward a more individualist and passive conceptualization of positive emotions, since "happiness" is much more restricted to one's personal life than is "joy", which can more naturally refer to shared reasons for positive feelings, such as "the joy of Christmas" (Wierzbicka 1999: 51). "I am happy" as an adjective construction has also lost the active meaning of the verbal construction "I rejoice". While the latter collocation indicates that the person is playing an active role in bringing about the positive emotional state, the former suggests that an external stimulus has moved the person toward a specific state. Notably, the closest counterparts to the English expression "to be happy" in a number of other European languages are active expressions (German: *sich freuen*, French: *se rejouir*; Wierzbicka 1999: 249). As this brief discussion of selected semantic evidence shows, almost any translation of a survey question such as "Taking all things together, would you say you are – very happy, quite happy, not very happy, not at all happy?" (World Values Survey; Inglehart 1997: 351) will slightly differ in meaning from the English original and, hence, may elicit answers that will not be exactly comparable to the answers given to the corresponding English question.

This semantic comparability problem has to be distinguished from a cultural effect that has already been touched upon above (p. 8). Apart from semantic differences between "happiness" and its (imprecise) translations into other languages, one culture may simply have a more optimistic and cheerful trait than another. Eva Hoffman, a writer who grew up in Poland and in the US, describes the contrast between an American and a Polish farewell ritual. While her American friends dwell on how great it was to have met her, her Polish friends express how sad they are about her parting. "This tone of sadness is something we all enjoy. It makes us feel the gravity of life, and it is gratifying to have a truly tragic event – a parting forever – to give vent to such romantic feelings" (Hoffman 1989: 78). To the degree that this anecdotal account may be generalized, it can thus be expected that Polish surveys will find lower SWB scores than American surveys, even if life circumstances were comparable, simply because cultures "play a key role in determining what types of information are chronically salient among their cultural members" (Suh 2000: 69), or, in other words, because Poles and Americans render different constructions of the world.

Even if cultural differences cannot be denied, however, it is important to understand that they do not authorize any value judgment. Finding that, under comparable circumstances, people in one culture tend to experience more positive feelings than those of another is simply a factual observation, not a value judgment, exactly as the observation that the average height of Swedes exceeds that of Japanese is no value judgment. If Poles find it more gratifying to look at the tragic side of the medal (the term "enjoy" in Hoffman's account cited in the previous paragraph is perhaps not adequate in this context since the very concept of "to enjoy" appears to be alien to the Polish language[8]), they *are* less happy, but to find this wrong, deplorable, or in any sense problematic would mean imposing on Polish culture a non-Polish value grid that could not make any claim to universal validity. Happiness (or, more universally speaking, the positive feeling experienced by a person when good things are happening to her; cf. Wierzbicka 1999: 52) is certainly a positive value in all cultures, but so are many other things, traits, and emotions (one may think of self-esteem, honesty, or authenticity), and it would seem preposterous to declare happiness the ultimate yardstick of a person's, let alone a culture's, success. Aaron Ahuvia brings this point out very clearly with respect to Asian cultures, which are generally held to be collectivist and to give higher priority than Western cultures to social status and the fulfillment of social obligations and lower priority to personal enjoyment:

> Claims such as "individualized society fits human nature better than collectivist society does" (Veenhoven 1999, p. 176) may go beyond what the data demands, by assuming that human nature always revolves around personal happiness. Defenders of collectivism give away the store when they allow Western psychologists to set the success criteria for a culture. If Western cultures may have the edge in producing happy people, Asian cultures may have the edge in producing people who value and meet their social obligations.
>
> (Ahuvia 2002: 31–2)

Starting from the presumption "the happier the better" would indeed have quite radical implications few would be prepared to embrace. At the limit, such a view would lead to the ideal of a culture whose members rejoice at funerals and delight in the face of human suffering.

While the semantic comparability problem is liable to create a genuine distortion between surveys conducted in different language communities because the scores may not refer to the same construct, the cultural effect does not in fact create a distortion (cf. Veenhoven 1987: 333). To the contrary, to the degree that cultures differ with respect to the status given to happiness (or related constructs), SWB surveys will capture a very valid source of variance that may be of great interest. A bias would only be involved in the space of normative assessments when, mistakenly, bare survey scores were given normative significance.

Finally, another related, but distinct, potential distortion needs to be addressed, to wit, social desirability. To the degree that a culture places positive value on appearing cheerful and on expressing that one is happy, or, to the contrary, on "portraying life as a pain in the neck", as Taylor (1977: 33) believes the French do (quoted in Diener 1994: 133), there is a possibility that people will over-report or under-report their SWB. What is meant here is not the cultural effect of people actually feeling more or less happy, as discussed in the previous paragraphs, but the effect that a person (mis-)reports a higher or lower degree of happiness than he is actually experiencing (in practice, these two effects may of course combine and be difficult to distinguish from each other). Psychometric studies, however, found only a negligible and non-systematic social desirability effect (Diener 1984: 551). Moreover, in a US study, respondents in face-to-face interviews did not give more positive answers than those in anonymous interview settings, as should be expected if social desirability played a role (Diener 1994: 114).

While these theoretical considerations suggest that semantic, cultural, and social desirability effects create difficulties for cross-cultural comparisons of

SWB surveys, empirical studies have so far only occasionally detected some minor effects. For example, to account for the relatively low SWB scores of the Japanese, Lane (2000b: 31) argues that the "Japanese are rarely very happy or very anything, for it is bad form to stand out", and a similar argument has been put forward by Iijima (1982: 5–6, reported in Veenhoven 1987: 331). Yet, these arguments are undermined by the observation that the Japanese do not make less use of the extremely *negative* option ("very unsatisfied") than Western European citizens ("not at all satisfied") do on average (Veenhoven 1993: 177–90). What is more, a number of studies could not detect a strong dependence of SWB on the respondent's language in multilingual countries, where living conditions should be rather similar across language groups. For example, no differences could be found between German-, French-, and Italian-speaking Swiss, nor between French- and Flemish-speaking Belgians (Inglehart 1977, quoted in Diener 1994: 113; Veenhoven 1987: 330). For Canadians, Blishen and Atkinson (1980: 31) found a somewhat higher level of SWB for French-speaking than for English-speaking respondents (8.91 vs. 8.64 when averaging across age groups, n = 3,288), but the variance explained by language (and age) was only 1.4 percent (and, assuming that the French-speaking Canadians are culturally closer to the French than are the English-speaking Canadians, the direction of the difference is the opposite of what might be expected on the basis of Taylor's conjecture quoted above). A later Canadian study, however, found no significant difference between English- and French-speaking Canadians (Tomes 1986: 433). Bruno Frey and Alois Stutzer (2002: 148), on the other hand, did find that Italian-speaking Swiss scored higher than their German-speaking compatriots, and the latter higher than their francophone ones, but the effect of speaking French (with German-speaking Swiss being the reference group) became insignificant (t = 1.32) after political participation variables were included, and the effect of speaking Italian was based on the data of a single canton and thus of little statistical significance. These results largely lend support to the hypothesis put forward above (p. 12) that questionnaire responses may not be very sensitive to semantic differences between the keywords *(happy, satisfied, glücklich, heureux*, etc.) because the context created by the wording of the question as a whole is likely to have a much stronger influence on the construction of the response than have the subtle connotations of the respective keywords in isolation.

While the role of culture shall be taken up again in some depth, and with a different focus, at the end of this chapter and will be revisited throughout the following chapters, the present discussion shall suffice as a preparation for the following section in which the most relevant findings of empirical happiness research shall be reviewed. The conclusion to bear in mind from the preceding analysis is that cross-cultural and cross-language comparisons of SWB data are admissible but limited. Differences of the order of magnitude of one standard deviation or more are perhaps large enough to justify the interpretation that people from two cultures really differ with respect to their experience of happiness, but such differences must not be interpreted normatively in the sense of reflecting a difference in terms of quality of life.

Empirical evidence on the correlates of happiness

Since about the 1950s, a vast number of academic studies and official surveys have gathered a plethora of data on SWB. Scientists from various disciplines, especially from psychology, sociology, and, more recently, economics, have subjected these data to statistical analysis from a large number of viewpoints. Our interest here is in particular the relationship between SWB and development variables in a comprehensive sense. The role of income and consumption is certainly of particular interest in this context, not least because it has been the theme of philosophical reflection, political ideologies, conventional wisdom, religious teachings, and parental advice for centuries, if not millennia.

It is interesting to note, however, that conventional wisdom with respect to the effect of income on happiness is divided. On the one hand, there is a rather widely held belief that "wealth is not good for you". Religious texts warn of the accumulation of worldly wealth and even describe it as an obstacle to divine blessing (e.g. in the Bible, Matthew 19:24). Philosophers and intellectuals have warned that wealth spoils the mind (e.g. Rousseau 1762/1922: I-58), and in legends as well as in literature, classic and modern, the modest who resist the worldly pleasures are portrayed as virtuous (and happy!) role models. On the other hand and quite contrary to this strand of thought, material wealth has always been an object of envy, and a reasonable fortune is held to be a sensible ambition within every sane person's plan of life. In some highly influential Protestant creeds, economic success (in terms of income, not consumption) even became the ultimate evidence of divine grace (as prominently analyzed by Weber 1975/1920), and a luxury car manufacturer could advertise his vehicles in the 1990s with the slogan: "Whoever said money can't buy happiness isn't spending it right" (Myers 2000: 58).

Whatever the normative stance as to what *should* be the status of material wealth, however, it can be observed that, as a matter of fact, most people do go to great lengths in order to attain, or maintain, superior consumption levels, sacrificing time and effort in the process. While this is probably no universal or "natural" phenomenon, material wealth appears to be a major ambition of people in many diverse cultures, and for many observers this ambition seems to be expanding in its cross-cultural reach as well as in intensity, for better (Porter 2000) or worse (Shweder 2000). From this behavioral pattern, therefore, we would expect a positive effect of income on happiness.

Before turning to the detailed picture of statistical correlations, let us step back and take a look at the broad picture of the quantitative evidence on SWB. It is striking that even all available "hard" variables, i.e. those easily observable and quantifiable by outsiders, taken together cannot "explain" (in the sense of "statistically account for") even 20 percent of the variance in SWB responses (Campbell *et al.* 1976). A study that included six demographic variables simultaneously (family life cycle stage, family income, age, education, race, sex) could explain a mere 11 percent of the variance in SWB, and none of these predictors alone could explain more than 6 percent (Andrews and Withey 1976:

141). When certain "soft" variables, i.e. those that cannot be easily observed and quantified by outsiders, are included, the variance that can be accounted for rises to 62 percent (ibid.: 135). Yet, since such percentages are attained by including degrees of domain satisfaction such as income satisfaction or family-life satisfaction (ibid.: 32), it can be argued that it is close to tautological to "explain" life satisfaction by these variables.

Restricting the analysis to observable variables, 80+ percent of variation remains unaccounted for and must consequently be ascribed to two general sources of variation: "soft", unobserved life circumstances and idiosyncratic characteristics (and measurement error of course). First, there is certainly some role for soft but nevertheless objective external influences, i.e. those life circumstances that are not readily measurable. For example, the objective quality of one's family life certainly has a sizeable impact on life satisfaction, yet it is usually not included in statistical studies because it would be extremely difficult to observe and even more difficult to quantify. One may therefore expect that hard and soft objective predictors together would account for well more than 20 percent of variance. Indeed, longitudinal studies that included both hard and soft *life events* as predictors (such as meeting nice people, quarreling with family, etc.) could account for 25 percent of variance (Headey and Wearing 1992, reported in Veenhoven 1996: 27).

The remaining variance that would be impossible to account for, even in an ideal statistical study of hard and soft life circumstances, must be ascribed to the person. Of two individuals under practically identical life circumstances, one may feel happy and another unhappy, simply because they are different persons. The deeper explanation for personal variation in this sense must fall, I believe, in one of three categories:

1   Neural compulsion. A person may be unable to experience a positive degree of subjective well-being due to strictly neural impediments, such as a major psychoneurotic disorder. For example, a person suffering from clinical depression will be altogether unable to experience happiness simply because the biological processes that underlie every experience of happiness are physically blocked. Conversely, it is conceivable that a specific drug or a direct stimulation of the brain makes a person feel euphoric no matter how dreadful the life circumstances. In cases of neural compulsion, the experience of subjective well-being (or the lack of it) is largely decoupled from the person's will and judgment. To the degree that a person is subject to neural compulsion, she will *behave* (in the sense of a mechanic stimulus–response program) rather than *act* (in the sense of autonomous choice).

2   Affective disposition (innate or acquired). Any given person can be seen as carrying with himself a "mental endowment" that is influenced by his genome, his upbringing, his cultural environment, etc. This mental endowment will never be neutral – if "neutral" has any meaning at all in this context – with respect to one's ability or inclination to experience happiness. In other words, each person has a stronger or weaker affective disposition to experience

happiness in certain situations. In fact, it has been found that genetic endowment is a relatively strong predictor of SWB. Comparing monozygotic and dizygotic twins, Tellegen *et al.* (1988; cf. also Lykken and Tellegen 1996) could explain 48 percent of the variance in SWB by genetic endowment and 13 percent by shared family environment. Similarly, as argued above (p. 21), people from different cultures may have different affective dispositions because they render different constructions of the world. As a consequence, people from one culture may be happier than those of another under basically the same life circumstances for reasons of cultural differences.

3   Free judgment. The idea of affective dispositions already implies the complementary idea of free judgment. The decisive difference between affective disposition and neural compulsion is that one's genetic endowment or cultural mindset does not compel a person to feel good or bad in any given situation, because, as any humanistic anthropology must assume, we have some degree of freedom to deal with our endowments – i.e. to make them manifest – in one way or another. A study of a group of 29 pairs of twin brothers (monozygotic and dizygotic), at least one of whom was jailed at the time of the survey, illustrates this freedom to affirm or to counteract one's dispositions. In that study, it was found that most of the jailed men had similarly unprincipled twin brothers. But of one monozygotic pair of twin brothers, one was a convicted criminal while the other was a criminal investigator (Lange 1929, reported in Frankl 2003: 55). One may imagine that the two brothers were disadvantaged by their upbringing, but that one succumbed to the ill influences of bad company while the other summoned up enough willpower to resist those influences he deemed wrong. Thus, even when, statistically speaking, 48 percent of variance in SWB can be accounted for by genetic heredity, this does not mean that people are 48 percent determined in their judgments of SWB. It just means that, on average, the free judgments of individuals with the same genetic endowment will be 48 percent less disparate than those of genetically unrelated persons.

The last point is of significance in a wider context – in fact, in all instances in which statistical tools are applied to human judgment (i.e. in most of psychology and much of sociology and economics). Whenever a phenomenon is (also) the result of a judgment, observed regularities must not be explained strictly in terms of cause and effect but have to be understood, at least to some extent, in terms of reasons and choice. For example, when it is observed that in 100 out of 100 cases in which people are asked what is one plus one, the answer is two, this does not mean that the human being is equipped with an (acquired or innate) stimulus–response pattern that makes her behave that way, but rather that any sensible person will normally think that this is the right thing to say, even if she could deliberately give a wrong answer. The predictability of choices owes itself (at least to some extent) to the non-arbitrariness of practical reason, not (only) to the determinacy of natural laws, and it has little to do with the predictability of, say, the weather. In Amartya Sen's eloquent words, "[t]he fact that statistical predictions can often be plausibly made on the ways ... freedom is likely to be used ... does not negate the fact that it is the exercise of ... enhanced freedom that is being anticipated" (Sen 1999b: 289).

As a last point, the question of causality needs to be highlighted. It is of course important to bear in mind that statistical evidence cannot demonstrate causality. Yet, the question is not only *whether* there is a causal link between two correlating observations but also in which *direction* causality might work. With respect to happiness, folk psychology might easily lure the researcher into regarding happiness exclusively as a consequence rather than as a cause. Empirical evidence suggests, however, that happiness is a matter of both bottom-up and top-down causality (Headey *et al.* 1991; Vendrik and Hirata 2003). It is therefore important to be careful in the causal interpretation of statistical evidence, in particular when regression models are designed with happiness as the dependent variable, as economists routinely do.

These general considerations (for a further discussion, cf. p. 000) shall suffice as an orientation for the minefield of statistical evidence on SWB that will be explored in the rest of this section. As an analytical grid, the evidence will be classified throughout as corresponding to one of four categories along two dimensions, the first being the *level of aggregation*, the second the *comparison perspective* (cf. Table 2.1).

Individual data would be unaggregated micro-data. The corresponding statistical results are to be interpreted as reflecting idiosyncratic variations or commonalities.

Group-average data are aggregated macro-data on the basis of micro-data. Typically, averages will be taken by country in order to compare aggregated key figures across countries, but other groups are possible as well (e.g. states, counties, districts, etc.). Since within-country variation as well as measurement errors largely cancel out in aggregated data, the percentage of variation that can be accounted for in macro-data can, for these methodological reasons, be expected to be much larger than that in studies of micro-data. Results from studies of group-averages can therefore not usually be compared with those from studies with an individual focus.

With respect to the comparison perspective, *cross-section* studies are the most frequently encountered. They make comparisons between different subjects or groups at a given point in time.

Time-series analysis compares the different values of the same subject (or group) over time.

Table 2.1 Classification of empirical happiness research

		Comparison perspective	
		Cross-section	Time-series
Level of aggregation	Individual	1A	1B
	Group-average	2A	2B

1A Studies with an *individual* focus in a *cross-section* perspective analyze differences between subjects at a given point in time. They examine the micro-data obtained from a sample of a usually geographically delimited population and investigate the relationship between the individual SWB scores and other individual characteristics, like age, income, or personality attributes.

1B Studies with an *individual* focus in a *temporal* perspective are the least frequently encountered. They rely on panel data, i.e. follow-up surveys of the same set of individuals over some period of time, making them rather costly and difficult to implement. A much more practical but somewhat less informative kind of analysis that will also be classified in this category is synthetic cohort analysis (cf. Easterlin and Schaeffer 1999; Easterlin 2001). In these kinds of studies, one identifies the same birth cohorts (grouped in brackets of a few years) across several surveys made at different points in time with samples that are not identical but drawn from the same population. Thus, one can follow, for example, the development of the cohort born in a given country during 1950–59.

2A *Cross-section* studies with a *group-average* focus examine differences between group averages, usually countries, at a given point in time. They do not analyze micro-data, but averages of SWB that are set into relation with other aggregate variables (GDP, political institutions). These levels and relationships are then compared to the averages of other groups.

2B Studies with a *group-average* focus in a *temporal* perspective examine the development of a nation's (or any another group's) average SWB and its relationship with other variables over time. The significance of such studies is limited, however, because a large number of potentially relevant independent variables is up against a quite limited number of SWB data points (SWB data for years before 1970 are available only for a small group of rather homogenous countries, and data from before 1946 are nonexistent). Nevertheless one finds quite a number of significant correlations.

The distinction between these different perspectives is vital because a relationship that holds in one perspective need not hold in another. The failure to recognize such differences can easily lead an observer to wrong generalizations.

On the following pages, I will present a compilation of statistical evidence on the relationship between SWB and other variables of interest in this context, beginning with socio-economic influences, continuing with demographic variables, and concluding with "soft" correlates. The data have been compiled from a large pool of sources, and every effort has been made to select the data in an unbiased way and to present a balanced picture of competing evidence. The interpretation of the results has been deferred to Chapter 3.

Income levels

The evidence on the relationship between income and SWB is not homogeneous, but it reveals some basic patterns that have been quite clearly established.

In a cross-section perspective with an individual focus (1A), the effect[9] of income on SWB is clearly and unequivocally positive: high-income earners have a higher degree of SWB than low-income earners within a given country at a given point in time, and this relationship is highly significant[10] in practically all studies. More specifically, the correlation is pronounced for the lower half of the income distribution (i.e. up to the median income earner) and weak or insignificant for the upper half, suggesting a curvilinear relationship that is consistent with diminishing marginal utility of income (in a cross-section perspective). See Figure 2.2 for an exemplary graph plotting household income against SWB.

In terms of magnitude, one study using an OLS regression (thus, imputing cardinality of SWB) on the natural logarithm of income (thus assuming that happiness rises in constant increments each time income doubles) and controlling for a number of other factors estimated that having twice someone else's income is associated with a SWB differential of 0.236 on an 11-point scale (Ferrer-i-Carbonell

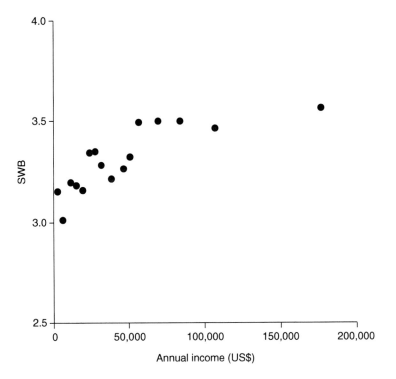

Figure 2.2 Individual cross-section evidence; income and SWB in the US in 2008 (source: US General Social Survey (www.norc.org/GSS+Website) (own graph)).

Notes
n = 1,209; income brackets with n<50 were consolidated with adjacent income brackets. Income data points are midpoints of income brackets (except for the highest income bracket which refers to "150,000 and over" in current dollars). Income is family annual income in constant 2000 US$. SWB was measured on a scale of 1 to 4 (1 = not at all happy, 4 = very happy).

and Frijters 2004: 647).[11] This would imply that, say, a person with an annual income of 100,000 can be expected to be about half a point higher on the 11-point SWB scale than a person with an annual income of 25,000 and otherwise the same characteristics.

Time-series studies of individuals (1B) have so far produced mixed results. The few real panel studies that have been done cover only short periods of time. One study (Brickman *et al.* 1978) found that those individuals who had won amounts between $50,000 and $1,000,000 in a lottery during the previous year did not report significantly higher levels of SWB than a control group (even though their average of 4.00 out of 5.00 was slightly higher than the 3.82 of the control group). A later study of windfall gains based on a large random sample did find a signific-ant and substantial positive effect of lottery gains in excess of £1,000 on SWB two years after the event (Gardner and Oswald 2007). Specifically, using the British "General Health Questionnaire" (GHQ), a multi-item-measure of SWB with a 36-point scale, they found that a windfall gain of more than £1,000 led to about a 1.4 step increase in the GHQ score (n = 10,365, among which were 3,059 lottery winners, about 96 percent of whom won amounts below £1,000). However, the study did not follow the respondents for more than two years after the windfall gain so that longer-term adaptation cannot be captured.

For the lack of panel data, Easterlin (2001) used synthetic cohort analysis in order to mimic panel data over a longer time span. He divided the sample into four birth cohort sub-samples spanning ten years each (all taken together cover-ing respondents born between 1911 and 1950) and analyzed their responses that were gathered over a period of 24 years (from 1972 to 1996). Even in the two younger cohorts whose incomes roughly doubled during the observed period, he could not find any effect of income on SWB over the life cycle (cf. also Easterlin and Schaeffer 1999).

Comparing national averages in the cross-section (2A) reveals a positive rela-tionship between income and SWB. The strength of the zero-order correlation between per capita purchasing power and average SWB has been found to be a highly significant $r = 0.58$ (Diener *et al.* 1995: 859) or even $r = 0.64$ (Schyns 1998: 15), implying that 34 percent or 41 percent, respectively, of the cross-country vari-ance in SWB can be accounted for by income alone. The magnitude of the relation-ship can be illustrated by two countries with rather typical SWB values for their income class: in 2007, Sweden scored 7.7 on a ten-point (1–10) SWB scale with a per capita income of $34,086, while India scored 5.8 with $2,600 (for the data sources, cf. Table 2.2). Assuming that SWB rises linearly for every doubling of income, an OLS regression on the data shown in Table 2.2 and Figure 2.3 results in the estimate that a doubling of income is associated with an increase in SWB by 0.4 on a ten-point scale, and this effect is highly significant. Using the even larger 2006 Gallup World Poll data set covering 132 countries, Deaton (2008: 58) finds that a doubling of income would predict an increase of SWB of 0.58 on an 11-point scale where income alone accounts for 69 percent of the SWB variance.[12]

Time-series studies with a group-average focus (2B) covering a significant period of time (i.e. a period during which there was a substantial rise in

Table 2.2 Cross-country evidence, 2005–08

Country	SWB	Income	Country	SWB	Income
Colombia	8.3	8,041	Peru	7.0	7,242
Mexico	8.2	13,307	Poland	7.0	15,655
Switzerland	8.0	37,595	South Africa	7.0	9,224
Guatemala	8.0	4,332	Indonesia	6.9	3,519
Norway	8.0	48,991	Malaysia	6.8	12,763
New Zealand	7.9	25,532	Iran	6.4	10,346
Finland	7.8	33,227	Hong Kong	6.4	39,958
Argentina	7.8	12,506	Ghana	6.1	1,285
Sweden	7.7	34,086	Mali	6.1	1,017
Brazil	7.7	9,146	Zambia	6.1	1,212
Uruguay	7.5	10,841	Serbia	6.0	9,509
Turkey	7.5	11,973	India	5.8	2,600
Cyprus	7.4	24,093	Egypt	5.7	4,762
Australia	7.3	35,184	Ukraine	5.7	6,547
Spain	7.3	28,510	Burkina Faso	5.6	1,062
Trinidad and Tobago	7.3	22,551	Moldova	5.5	2,562
Chile	7.2	13,055	Morocco	5.3	3,776
Slovenia	7.2	26,294	Bulgaria	5.2	9,924
Thailand	7.2	7,333	Georgia	5.0	4,444
Jordan	7.1	4,839	Ethiopia	5.0	740
Japan	7.0	31,669	Rwanda	5.0	877

Note
SWB data are from the fifth wave of the World Values Survey (www.worldvaluessurvey.org) conducted in 2005–2008. The question asked was "All things considered, how satisfied are you with your life as a whole these days?" with answers given along a ten-point scale ranging from one ("completely dissatisfied") to ten ("completely satisfied"). Annual income data are from the World Bank (data.worldbank.org) for 2007 and are expressed in international 2005 US$ at purchasing power parity exchange rates.

per-capita income) are only available for a limited set of countries, most of them high-income countries. The evidence is not homogeneous and its interpretation is therefore disputed. While earlier data pretty clearly suggested that there is no positive correlation between per-capita income and SWB or, almost equivalently, no positive time trend for SWB (Easterlin 1995), more recent studies often find evidence for a positive time trend. Ronald Inglehart, Roberto Foa, and colleagues (2008: 274ff.), for example, find that over a period of about 17 years, SWB[13] rose in 40 and fell in 12 countries, even though they do not report the statistical significance of these trends (which are in fact start-point to end-point comparisons, thus being sensitive to possible singular influences). In an OLS regression of SWB on time covering 14 countries, Ruut Veenhoven (2007: 1) found that over the period of 1973 to 2006, SWB had a significant (at 5 percent) positive trend in six and a significant negative trend in two countries, with the remaining six countries having no significant trend.

While time trends are certainly not irrelevant, they do not answer the question of whether there is a positive relationship between income and SWB over time.

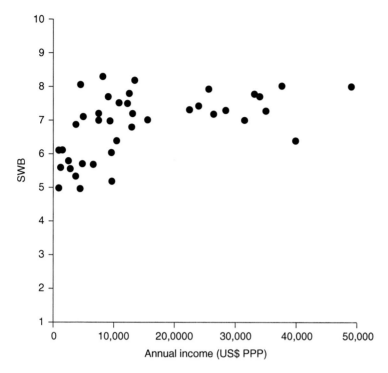

Figure 2.3 Cross-country evidence, 2005–08.

Note
See notes for Table 2.2.

To answer this question, one needs to check whether countries with a higher growth rate of income also experience a higher increase in SWB. This implies that, even if there is a positive SWB time trend for most countries, it is possible that countries with high income growth benefit less in terms of SWB than countries with lower income growth. In one such study, Betsey Stevenson and Justin Wolfers (2008) assembled considerable evidence for a significantly positive correlation between income growth and SWB over time. Using a different but no less plausible method (and a different set of data), however, Richard Easterlin and Laura Angelescu (2009) found no significant positive relationship between income and SWB. Thus, the time-series evidence is still mixed and appears to be rather sensitive to the sample selection and method used.

Income inequality

The evidence on the effect of income inequality on SWB is mixed. The (probably) first study on the relationship between SWB and income inequality found that Canadian men living in districts with higher income *equality* (measured as the share of income going to the poorest 40 percent) tend to score lower on SWB than those living in districts with more *in*equality (where coefficients were significant only at the generous threshold of 7.5 percent), but no such effect was found for women (Tomes 1986: 440).[14] On the other hand, when the income share of the richest 10 percent was used as a proxy for inequality, a more unequal distribution did have a negative effect on a person's SWB (at 5 percent in a probit regression but not in a linear regression; ibid.: 444). The results are therefore contradictory and highly dependent on the way income inequality is specified.

A later study (Hagerty 2000) of US data found that income inequality within a "standard metropolitan statistical area" had a negative effect on a given individual's happiness (controlling for a number of other variables). The study used several measures of inequality and found that skew (thinness of the right-hand tail of the income distribution), maximum income, and first (low income) and fifth (high income) quintile were significant at 5 percent (skew) or even at 1 percent in predicting an individual's happiness.[15]

A more recent study (Alesina *et al.* 2004) of US data found a negative effect of state inequality over time (as measured by the Gini coefficient and controlling for state-fixed effects) on individual happiness only for high-income individuals (defined as above-median income). For Europe, the same study also found a negative effect of inequality on happiness where, in contrast to the US, the effect became insignificant for the high-income group in isolation but stronger for the low-income group in isolation. In addition, the effect became insignificant for right-leaning Europeans but even stronger for left-leaning ones (ibid.: 2030). To reconcile these contrary results, the authors suggest that perceived mobility might mediate the relationship between inequality and happiness. If Americans believe that income mobility is higher than Europeans do, which appears to be the case (ibid.), then rich Americans will regard inequality as a potential threat to their status quo, while poor Europeans may regard inequality as a structural injustice (ibid.: 2034–5). Note that this interpretation relies on the *perception* of mobility, independent of whether the perception is accurate (for which there seems to be no conclusive evidence; cf. Graham and Felton 2005: 6).

Using basically the same data as Alesina *et al.* (2004) (but looking only at the states of the US), Blanchflower and Oswald (2003) find a moderate negative effect of income inequality on SWB. The effect is stronger among women and weak to insignificant among men. It is also stronger for people below 30 years of age, among workers, and among those with lower levels of education.

A study of British panel data over 11 years, however, found that people in regions with higher income inequality tend to score *higher* on SWB (Clark 2003). Here, too, the perception of opportunity might play a mediating role, because those who had experienced higher income fluctuations in the past were more positively affected by inequality (ibid.: 9–10).

Employment status

Employment status has emerged as a major correlate of SWB with some clear-cut results but also some more subtle interactions.

In a cross-section perspective with an individual focus (1A), study after study confirms that unemployment has a strong and highly significant negative effect on SWB, even after the loss of income is controlled for. The effect of the loss of income is dwarfed by that of becoming unemployed. The results of Blanchflower and Oswald (2004: 1382) suggest that the negative effect of unemployment on SWB is six times that of a $10,000 cut in one's annual income (where SWB is assumed to depend linearly on income). When the authors excluded income (and year dummies) from their regression, the coefficient of unemployment changed only slightly, from –0.8029 to –0.8321, and the associated t-statistic from 11.83 to 12.94 (ibid.: 1370, 1372), suggesting that the associated loss of income plays only a minor role in explaining the distress of the unemployed.

In panel studies (1B) investigating unemployment, the effect of unemployment is regularly found to be highly significant and of substantial magnitude. A pioneering study (Winkelmann and Winkelmann 1998) found that the effect of becoming unemployed on SWB is about seven times as large as that of a 90 percent reduction of one's income. Assuming, as the authors do, that life satisfaction rises linearly with each doubling of income, the compensating variation of unemployment (i.e. the amount of money needed to undo the loss in SWB from losing one's job) is an income increase by the stratospheric factor of 10,000,000. While one should not read too much into this kind of hypothetical interpretation, this figure illustrates the relative magnitudes of the unemployment and the income effect on SWB, clearly suggesting that "[t]he worst thing about losing one's job is not the drop in take-home income. It is the non-pecuniary distress" (Oswald 1997: 1821).[16]

Time-series data can also shed some light on the question of causality. For example, the study by Winkelmann and Winkelmann (1998: 6) referred to above also found that SWB is slightly lower not only for employed people who once were unemployed, but also for employed people who *will* become unemployed (later during the panel study, that is). This might reflect a causal effect from unhappiness (or rather, from below-average happiness) to unemployment – implying that people are more likely to lose their job if they are less happy than the average worker – but which could also simply reflect the fact that these people were less happy because they had a reason to fear losing their job. On the other hand, the panel data also show that SWB drops substantially after a person becomes unemployed, being consistent with the hypothesis that the causal effect from unemployment to unhappiness dominates the reverse effect.

In terms of absolute numbers, however, even the unemployed are, on average, above the middle of the scale (which ranges from 0 to 10). While all those employed in 1984 scored an average of 7.6 (n = 3,530), those unemployed scored 5.6 (n = 208) (ibid.: Table 1 and p. 6). By contrast, the average level of SWB for men (women are excluded in this study) who would become unemployed at some point in the future (between 1985 and 1989) was 7.3 in 1984 (n = 248).

This latter finding suggests that unemployment has a lasting negative effect on SWB, even after a person has been reemployed. Instead of providing a contrast experience against which employment is evaluated more positively ("a person who was once unemployed must value her job more than others because she doesn't take it for granted"), spells of unemployment appear to leave "scars" (Clark *et al.* 2001) on a person's SWB even after getting reemployed. The effect can reach such a degree that a person with a long unemployment experience will not see any SWB benefit from getting reemployed (ibid.: 230–1).

Education

Educational achievement, as measured in years of schooling, has apparently been investigated only in the cross-section and within nations. Without controlling for potentially intervening variables, the level of education correlates weakly but significantly with SWB in most studies, in the order of magnitude of $r = 0.10$ (Argyle 1999: 355). The correlation tends to be weaker in countries with higher per capita income (ibid.). When income and work status are controlled for, however, the effect of education is reduced (Blanchflower and Oswald 2004: 1372; Diener *et al.* 1993), disappears altogether (Argyle 1999; Ferrer-i-Carbonell 2005: 1009), or even becomes negative (Clark and Oswald 1996), which leaves the question open as to whether the positive zero-order correlation with SWB is not in fact mediated through the income effect. This would imply that education does not predict SWB because being educated makes people happy but rather because educated people have higher (relative) incomes, which in turn predicts happiness. Another explanation could be that education has positive returns to a certain degree (secondary education and apprenticeship) but negative returns beyond that, as Stutzer's (2004) data suggest (even after controlling for income and income aspirations).

Gender

Very few studies have found a significant difference in SWB between men and women (one exception is Russia where men appear to be happier; Graham and Pettinato 2001: 91), and this is true across cultures (Diener and Diener 1995). However, women have been found to report both more extreme positive and more extreme negative emotions when negative and positive affect are assessed separately (Frey and Stutzer 2002: 55). One study of US data also finds evidence that during the period from 1972 to 1998, women, but not men, experienced a significant fall in their SWB levels (Blanchflower and Oswald 2004). There also seem to be differences between the underlying patterns of factors influencing the SWB of women and men (Diener and Fujita 1995: 932). Unemployment, for example, has a stronger negative effect on men than on women, and working part-time rather than full-time has a negative effect on men, but a positive effect on women (Clark *et al.* 2001: 230).

Marital status

Marital status strongly correlates with SWB, albeit in a rather complex fashion (one exception has been found in a study of Russian data where no correlation materialized; Graham and Pettinato 2001: 91). In cross-section studies, married respondents are substantially and significantly happier than non-married ones (Blanchflower and Oswald 2004: 1370). However, time-series studies suggest that this effect has to be ascribed to the newly married because, after only a few years of marriage, the entire positive effect wears off (Clark *et al.* 2008: 234). However, this should not be interpreted in such a way that the effect of marriage on individuals is only temporary. A more detailed analysis shows that marrying is followed by lasting changes in the life satisfaction of the partners – but not necessarily for the better. Since marriages with positive and negative long-term effects more or less balance, this pattern disappears when considering only averages (Lucas *et al.* 2003). This observation also confirms the findings of earlier studies (e.g. Winkelmann and Winkelmann 1998: 13) that the causality seems to go mainly from marriage to SWB and not the other way.

Parenting

Having children has been found to be either unrelated to SWB (Blanchflower and Oswald 2004: 1371) or to have a negative effect (Diener 1984; Ferrer-i-Carbonell 2005: 1009), leading some scholars to talk of a "parenting paradox": while most parents seem to want children and in retrospect report being glad to have had children, they do not, on average, report being happier than childless couples (Marks 2004: 327–8). However, one study looking at the interaction between family income and number of children found that having children can have a positive effect on SWB depending on the household's income: the higher the income, the higher the number of children that would maximize SWB (Plug and van Praag 1995, reported in van Praag and Frijters 1999: 428). As a corollary, this suggests that having children reduces SWB for parents below that income threshold, probably because the costs of raising children reduce an already limited living standard, and that this indirect negative effect outweighs a possible direct positive effect from having children as such.

Age

The evidence of the effect of age on happiness is not uniform, but in any case it is not particularly large.

Cross-section studies (1A) have produced inconclusive results, including a negative correlation (Gurin *et al.* 1960, reported in Diener 1994), a positive, concave one, a U-shaped relationship if other factors are controlled for (both in Blanchflower and Oswald 2004), and a zero-correlation (Myers 1992, reported in Easterlin 2001).

Time-series data (1B) provide a conclusive explanation. Even though the extensive panel data that would be needed to do a neat time-series study of the age effect do not exist (we would need data for several decades in order to sepa-rate age effects from cohort characteristics), a synthetic cohort analysis (Easter-lin and Schaeffer 1999; Easterlin 2001) suggests that SWB is stable over the life cycle for any given cohort. Therefore, the age–SWB correlations sometimes found in cross-section analyses seem to reflect cohort characteristics (i.e. the coexistence of happier and unhappier cohorts) or the changing fortunes of differ-ent age groups, but they are unlikely to reflect an influence of age per se. More-over, since happiness appears to have a strong positive effect on life expectancy (Danner *et al.* 2001),[17] cross-section evidence will be positively biased for the elderly because the less happy tend to die earlier and therefore disappear from the data (Frey and Stutzer 2002: 54). Beyond levels of SWB, however, there seems to be a significant age effect on the composition of SWB. It has been found that young people experience stronger levels of both positive and negative affect and that they are also more likely to report being "very happy", whereas older people tend to be more satisfied with all life domains except health (Diener *et al.* 1985; Diener and Suh 1999: 445).

Personality traits

Among the "Big Five" personality traits – openness, conscientiousness, extra-version, agreeableness, and neuroticism – extraversion ("sociable, assertive, lively, and sensation-seeking" individuals; Diener and Lucas 1999: 218) and neuroticism (individuals being "anxious, depressed, emotional, and having low self-esteem"; ibid.) have been found to be those personality traits that correlate most strongly with SWB. Correlation coefficients range between 0.30 and 0.65 (Demir and Weitekamp 2007: 194) and normalized regression coefficients between 0.20 and 0.35 with SWB being the dependent variable (Cheng and Furnham 2001: 316, 321).

Self-esteem has been found to be a strong predictor of SWB in a number of studies of category 1A. Andrews and Withey (1976: 112), for example, com-puted a zero-order correlation between their measure of self-efficacy[18] and their SWB index of between 0.54 and 0.68, ranking among the highest they found among all variables. In a cross-cultural study covering 31 diverse countries, a correlation of 0.47 was found (Diener 1994: 115). Diener (1984: 558) reports that 11 studies found a relationship between self-esteem and SWB, but also reports of three studies in which the effect "has been weak or complex" (ibid.). He suggests that the causal relationship between self-esteem and SWB may be bidirectional since self-esteem might drop as a consequence of unhappiness (ibid.: 559).

Intelligence as measured by IQ tests has not appeared to be related to SWB. While in one representative study a positive correlation ($r = 0.18$, dropping to 0.13 when controlling for other variables) between interviewer ratings of intelli-gence and respondents' self-reported life satisfaction SWB emerged (Campbell *et al.* 1976: 368), Diener (1984: 559) lists six studies that found no significant correlation, three (including the one just mentioned) that found a positive one, and one that found a negative correlation. He adds, however, that the results so far are based on samples that are not representative.

Companionship

Studies investigating the relationship between personal ties on SWB found a clear positive relationship that was comparably large in comparison to other predictors. In an earlier US study, the number of a respondent's friends[19] was found to correlate stronger with SWB – no matter if other effects were (0.23) or were not (0.27) controlled for – than family income (0.14/0.17), intelligence (0.13/0.18), health (0.13/0.17), or education (0.10/0.10) (Campbell *et al.* 1976: 368). A later study found that among those reporting to have fewer than five friends, 26 percent said they were "very happy" compared with 38 percent of those reporting five or more friends (Myers 2000: 62). As always, these results do of course not establish the direction of causality.

Political and institutional conditions

Two obvious difficulties in establishing the effect of political and institutional conditions such as civil rights on SWB is that these constructs cannot be neatly measured and scaled and that these conditions themselves correlate strongly among each other and with per capita income, life expectancy, and other positive characteristics, giving rise to the problem of multicollinearity. Having said this, SWB has consistently been found to correlate significantly with several institutional conditions. For example, in one study (of type 2A) covering 55 nations, a measure of civil and political rights correlated $r = 0.48$ ($p < 0.001$) with a compound measure of SWB (Diener *et al.* 1995: 859). However, this correlation became insignificant once income, equality, or individualism (cf. the following section) was controlled for.

Another study (Frey and Stutzer 2002) investigating variations among the 26 cantons constituting the Swiss Confederation found evidence that the degree of democratic participation (through initiatives and referenda) and federal structure (local autonomy) correlated positively with SWB. More precisely, it was participation rights – rather than actual participation in political decisions or the outcomes of such decisions – that appeared to correlate with life satisfaction. The magnitude of this effect was considerable. Even controlling for a large set of possibly confounding variables (income, age, employment status, official language at place of residence, etc.), the predicted difference in SWB[20] between the average Swiss living in the canton with least participatory rights (Geneva) and one living in that with most (Basel Land) was larger than the expected difference between the lowest income category (<SFr 2,000 per month) and the highest one (>SFr 5,000), or about equivalent to the difference between married and divorced (and not re-married) respondents (Frey and Stutzer 2002: 188–9).

Culture

Culture is of course an extremely complex concept and defies quantification. What empirical studies investigate, therefore, is not the relationship between SWB and culture as such, or the difference between such problematic labels as "Chinese culture" and "American culture", but between SWB and socio-psychological constructs that reflect certain aspects that are commonly understood to be cultural characteristics.

Perhaps the most thoroughly researched cultural construct is the dimension of individualism/collectivism. Individualism and collectivism are two poles of one cultural dimension developed by Hofstede (1991, cf. also Triandis 1995).[21] Measures of individualism have been found to correlate strongly ($r = 0.77$ for a component measure of individualism, and 0.61 when Hofstede's measure was used only; $n = 55$) with nations' average SWB scores (Diener *et al.* 1995: 859). Interestingly, the same study found that individualism correlated even stronger with per capita income ($r = 0.80$ for the component measure) than it did with SWB (0.77). Individualism remained a highly significant ($p < 0.001$) predictor of SWB when income was controlled for, but income became insignificant when individualism was held constant. This would suggest that the "real" correlation (whatever the causality) is between individualism and SWB, whereas the correlation between income and SWB could be spurious. Measures of ethnic diversity, separatist movements, and cultural heterogeneity do not appear to be related to SWB (Diener and Suh 1999; Diener *et al.* 1995).

Another study (Rice and Steele 2004) showed that the SWB scores of Americans can be predicted fairly well by the average SWB in the country of which they are descendants. The correlation between the Americans' SWB score and the SWB average of their ancestral home was a respectable and highly significant 0.62. On the other hand, the variance among Americans was found to be smaller than that of the global sample (Rice and Steele 2004: 638), and earlier research had shown that second- and third-generation immigrants to America tend to be happier than first-generation immigrants (Beals 1985, reported in Rice and Steele 2004: 636). This suggests that the children of immigrants assimilate into their host country's culture, but that assimilation is incomplete even after a couple of generations, suggesting that culture maintains a substantive influence on a person's SWB.

A time-series study that looked into the role of trust as a cultural attribute found that the data were most supportive of the hypothesis that both SWB and a country's political stance (defined as the extent of welfare and redistributive policies) depend on trust rather than of the hypothesis that SWB depends on politics or that politics depends on SWB (Ridge *et al.* 2009: 281).

3 Relative income and happiness

The preceding presentation of empirical evidence on the relationship between subjective well-being and living conditions raises many questions. Of particular interest in our context is the question of how the inconclusive pieces of evidence on the relationship between income and SWB fit together and what mechanisms are responsible for the observed counterintuitive effects. It is clear from the presented evidence that a general statement like "more money means more happiness" or "happiness does not require money" will be inconsistent with either temporal or cross-section patterns. In other words, we must look for more subtle explanations for the observed pattern.

In interpreting the data, one must acknowledge the limitations of the empirical evidence. Most of the micro-data studies, for example, have been made with data from the US or Western Europe, meaning that they may be culturally colored or that they reflect patterns that would not be observed in low-income countries. Correspondingly, the range of countries covered by cross-country studies is also limited. Even though more recently, and in particular in the World Values Surveys,[1] SWB surveys have been extended to low-income countries (including, for example, Colombia, Moldova, and Rwanda; cf. Table 2.2), the almost complete absence of longer time-series data for low-income countries means that observations cannot be easily generalized, let alone extrapolated. The issue of translation (see also the discussion above on p. 19) should also be kept in mind, implying that, in comparisons between country averages, only substantive differences should be considered as being informative.

Furthermore, it should be obvious that one cannot, without further justification, infer causality or temporal trends from cross-section patterns, even though this is frequently done.[2] For example, the finding of a strong positive correlation between income and SWB across countries (cross-section) does not permit the conclusion that a country that moves from the lower end to the upper end of the income distribution would experience a rise in SWB.

Of course, even without having sufficient data, it is sensible to assume that additional income will make a positive contribution to the SWB of people with extremely low levels of material welfare. If additional income will allow a starving person to feed himself, for example, this will apparently raise his SWB. Moreover, a particular country may have maneuvered itself into such a situation

– for example, through the accumulation of international debt – that the only viable route to raise SWB levels is via economic growth. However, this would be a particular case with a specific reason why additional income is a prerequisite (but perhaps no guarantee) for raising SWB, and it would not allow the conclusion that the SWB of low-income countries without excessive debts would equally depend on income. Figuratively speaking, finding that a particular medicine heals a sick person does not mean that it will benefit a healthy one. The available data (Figure 2.3 and Table 2.2) clearly show that countries with a per capita GDP of only a fraction of the richest countries, such as Colombia, can be among the happiest countries. Anthropological research (cf. Norberg-Hodge 1991; Gasper 2004: 30) even suggests that some peaceful subsistence societies with hardly any economic exchange – i.e. with a GNP of little more than zero[3] – enjoy(ed) levels of SWB in the same order of magnitude as most of today's rich (and reasonably happy) countries.

The general conclusion from the evidence at this stage is simply that, within any given country, the rich tend to be happier than the poor and, across countries, the rich are not unhappy. Over time, a given person does not become happier even if income goes up, while this may or may not be true for a country as a whole. To look behind the surface of this general pattern and attempt a meaningful interpretation, this chapter will separately present three distinct mechanisms that can explain the evidence to a large extent. The first of these, the frame-of-reference effect, explains the societal mechanisms that can make individually prudent[4] behavior lead to socially destructive outcomes through negative effects on others' capacity to derive happiness from given living conditions. The second effect, direct externalities, refers to the well-known negative external effects that directly affect people's standard of living. The third effect, cognitive fallacies, shows that individually irrational behavior plays a part in feeding these societal mechanism and accounts for some other apparent inconsistencies.

The frame-of-reference effect

The frame-of-reference effect states that the degree of satisfaction (SWB) a person derives from a given constellation of living conditions depends considerably – albeit not exclusively – on a societal frame-of-reference. With respect to income, it accounts for the relative-income hypothesis, which states that SWB depends not on one's income in absolute terms, but on the relation between one's own income and that of some reference group. The relative-income hypothesis shall indeed be adopted here with some minor reservations, as shall be justified in the following.

The term "frame-of-reference effect" has apparently been coined by Robert Frank (1989), who subsequently developed it further (Frank 1997, 1999). The idea that the satisfaction derived from one's income (or rather from the things it buys) depends on the context and in particular on the average income in one's society or reference group is much older, however. Adam Smith, for example, already expressed this idea in his *Wealth of Nations*:[5]

With the greater part of rich people, the chief enjoyment of riches consists in the parade of riches, which in their eyes is never so compleat as when they appear to possess those decisive marks of opulence which nobody can possess but themselves. In their eyes the merit of an object which is in any degree either useful or beautiful, is greatly enhanced by its scarcity, or by the great labour which it requires to collect any considerable quantity of it, a labour which nobody can afford to pay but themselves.

(Smith 1979/1776: 190)

Writing 70 years later, Karl Marx described the role of the frame-of-reference as follows:

A house may be large or small; as long as the surrounding houses are equally small it satisfies all social demands for a dwelling. But if a palace rises beside the little house, the little house shrinks into a hut.

(Marx 1933/1849: 268–9)

Thorstein Veblen (1994/1899) famously described the life of the "leisure class" in terms of relative income and "conspicuous consumption". Arthur Cecil Pigou, too, thought that "a larger proportion of the satisfaction yielded by the incomes of rich people comes from their relative, rather than from their absolute, amount" (Pigou 1952/1920: I/VIII/3), and he approvingly quoted the Italian economist Eugenio Rignano who, writing in 1901, suggested that:

a man's desire to appear "worth" double what another man is worth, that is to say, to possess goods (jewels, clothes, horses, parks, luxuries, houses, etc.) twice as valuable as those possessed by another man, is satisfied just as fully, if the first has ten things and the second five, as it would be if the first had a hundred and the second fifty.

(Rignano 1901: 285, transl. A.C. Pigou)

Still in the same decade, George d'Avenel argued that, once the satisfaction of immediate subsistence needs had been secured, further material progress would not result in more satisfaction:

[We] so entirely ignore all that our immediate ancestors did for the advance-ment of our well-being that nobody even takes note of their achievements; therefore, nobody is happier because of them. Humanity is at bottom indif-ferent towards material progress.

(Avenel 1913: 63, transl. J.H.)

A couple of years later, Robert Michels (1918: 135) wrote that "the economic advance of one class does not reach into her conscience as long as it is not at least proportionate to the advance of the other classes" (quoted in Bruni 2001: 14, transl. J.H.).

While these statements were still based on introspection or intuition, later research has found empirical evidence that supported this interpretation. The (probably) first such contribution came from Duesenberry (1949), who convincingly showed that savings patterns that were hitherto considered behavioral anomalies could be explained under the assumption that people are more concerned with relative than with absolute income (cf. p. 51 below). In 1958, John Kenneth Galbraith published his highly influential book *The Affluent Society*, which, though differing in analysis from the aforementioned literature, gave new impetus and respectability to the idea of a frame-of-reference effect. Edward Mishan, for example, apparently alluded to Galbraith's book when he wrote:

> However, the more truth there is in this relative income hypothesis – and one can hardly deny the increasing emphasis on status and income-position in the affluent society – the more futile as a means of increasing social welfare is the official policy of economic growth.
>
> (Mishan 1979/1967: 161)

Richard Easterlin (1974: 116), in his seminal contribution, concluded that "it is hard to resist the inference that relative considerations play an important part in explaining the evidence presented here". In another path-breaking contribution, Fred Hirsch (1976: 6; see also the next section) showed that social scarcities put absolute limits to the availability to society of what he called *positional goods*, access to which "is determined in accord not with absolute but with relative real income".

The idea of the relativity of economic welfare, i.e. the notion that well-being depends on relative status and that, therefore, economic growth will not bring happiness, has sometimes been criticized as being a romantic indulgence, based on sentimental values, biased memories, and paternalistic attitudes. Objectively, it is claimed by these critics, we do have better lives than we did earlier (e.g. Beckerman 1975). My purpose here is not at all – to reemphasize what has been said already (ch. 1) – to argue that we are or are not living better than we did so many years ago, but to evaluate whether we are making wise and fair use of our productive potential. Yet, even if one agrees that much of the criticism at the benefits of economic growth is founded on particularistic values and unconvincing evidence, one can of course not conclude that other well-argued analyses which come to similar conclusions must therefore be wrong.

In the following, I will give an account of three underlying mechanisms that seem to be largely responsible for the frame-of-reference effect. While all three effects are related, there are some characteristics that distinguish them, and it will be worthwhile to appreciate these distinctions.

Positional competition

The term positional competition refers to the competition for positional goods and has been coined by Fred Hirsch who defined it as follows:

By positional competition is meant competition that is fundamentally for a higher place within some explicit or implicit hierarchy and that thereby yields gains for some only by dint of losses for others. Positional competition, in the language of game theory, is a zero-sum game: what winners win, losers lose.

(Hirsch 1976: 52)

How exactly would positional competition explain the observed failure of SWB to rise together with consumption levels? The basic idea is that many desires or preferences are directed toward socially scarce goods, i.e. goods the absolute supply of which cannot be expanded through technological innovation. Such goods include Rembrandt's masterpieces, residences with panoramic views, and social status itself, to name but a few.

Social scarcity can take one of two forms: a good can be absolutely scarce in a physical sense or suffer from congestion when mass consumption sets in. For example, the "Swedish Three Skilling Banco" stamp that sold for US$2.3 million in 1996 obviously derives its value from its absolute scarcity – it is the only known misprint of its kind (it was accidentally printed on yellow paper and slipped into circulation). On the other hand, to many people, a lonely beach will appear attractive for being quiet and for giving privacy, but as more and more people can afford to travel to remote places, its value erodes. The common feature of both cases is that only a minority can get the good desired, no matter how wealthy a society is. This is what is meant by social scarcity.

Importantly, for most visitors of lonely beaches, the fact that only a minority can afford that privilege may be an incidental feature rather than the reason for their valuation. Instead, they may like lonely beaches simply for their intrinsic qualities. Yet, whether people value lonely beaches because they want to feel exclusive or because they care for the intrinsic qualities, i.e. whatever *motives* people may have to value positional goods, the societal *effects* are the same.

It should be noted that a person caring for her relative position need not necessarily be moved by the desire to be better off than the others, i.e. to "surpass the Joneses". She can simply be moved by the desire not to be worse off than others, i.e. to "keep up with the Joneses" (Lichtenberg 1996). Yet, while the distinction between surpassing the Joneses and merely keeping up with them is ethically significant (and will, therefore, be taken up in ch. 5), it only makes a *quantitative* difference to the consequences of positional competition, not a *categoric* one. In other words, in a world where everybody merely tries to keep up with the Joneses (i.e. not be the worst-off individual), positional competition will be less intense than in a world where everybody tries to surpass the Joneses (i.e. be above-average), but even then positional competition will be present.

By definition, positional goods cannot be extended to everybody. No multiplication of everybody's income by whatever factor will ever enable the individuals at the low end of the income distribution to own a Rembrandt original or to spend their holidays on lonely beaches. This does not mean that nothing will change as a consequence of economic growth – and this is precisely the problem.

In the case of the Rembrandt paintings, their prices will be bid up infinitely. In the case of lonely beaches, increasing affluence will allow more and more people to reach remote coastal areas, but this of course means that formerly lonely beaches will become crowded. As an English middle-class professional remarked when cheap charter flights opened up a distant exotic country: "Now that I can afford to come here I know that it will be ruined" (Hirsch 1976: 167). The very rich will then be willing to further increase their holiday budget so as to reach one of those even farther beaches that the masses cannot yet afford to visit. In short, the same privilege will become ever more costly.

It might be objected that, in the case of Rembrandt paintings or the Swedish Three Skilling Banco, the price increase does not constitute any real expenditure for society as a whole, since the item traded is an asset. Therefore, the price would simply reflect the trade of liquid assets (money) against illiquid ones (paintings or stamps), not effort or resources sacrificed, and would therefore not be a social cost. This point is technically correct and not totally unimportant, but it does little to defuse the ill effects of positional competition. First of all, talking of "social costs" or "social benefits" in this sense of aggregated costs or benefits is fundamentally problematic, as will be discussed below (ch. 5). Even if it were not, however, it would be a long way from establishing that a change does not constitute a net aggregate loss in this sense to sanctioning this change as being ethically unobjectionable.

In this specific context, one problem might be, for example, that rising asset prices result in a biased development where benefits accrue predominantly to the already rich asset owners (e.g. the owners of real estate in attractive locations), leading to a rise in inequality that it would not be possible to justify by labor productivity, effort, or risk-taking differentials (whether either of these parameters would in itself justify inequality is another matter). Second and more importantly, assets constitute only a small portion of positional goods. Many, perhaps most, positional goods do require real productive activity, which is no longer available for the production of non-positional goods (it is just that Rembrandts and stamps make for didactically especially illuminating examples which is why they have been used to illustrate the principle of positional competition).

In most cases, positional competition involves the production of intermediate goods, the production of which does in fact use real resources. For example, if the ultimately desired positional good is status, watches might be one of these intermediate goods that can be transformed into status. As a society gets richer, a given person will realize that more and more people can afford his (what used to be a) luxury watch. To maintain his status (the good he is after), he will have to buy a watch that is more expensive than the one he is using. Yet, this means that additional real resources will be employed in the production of a fancy watch rather than for non-positional goods, while there is no net social benefit. The watch owner will have the *private* benefit of recapturing his former rank in the social hierarchy, but this effect is canceled out, from a social welfare point of view, by the adverse effect his new watch will have on the status of all others. In effect, a general upgrading of status symbols by everybody means that people's intention to climb up the status ladder will be frustrated. Only those who can upgrade their status symbols at a faster rate than all others will be able to actually improve their position, but then only at the expense of those who fall in the status hierarchy. Hence, on the benefit side, positional competition is a zero-sum game: whatever people are willing to sacrifice for positional goods, the total supply of these goods to society is fixed. As Hirsch says, "what winners win, losers lose". On the cost side, however, positional competition is a negative-sum game: people do actually sacrifice real resources for the intermediate goods they seek in order to maintain their position.[6]

The notion of positional goods is of course an ideal concept that will rarely be found in its pure form in the real world. Moreover, positionality is not "embodied" in a particular good. Rather, it is attached to a good when and to the degree that the qualities for which it is so widely valued depend on it being socially scarce. However, some degree of positionality seems to attach to a large number of goods in many contexts. It plays a role, to take some examples, to the degree that cram courses are attended to be better positioned for admission to top schools; luxury label clothes are worn to stand out from the masses; first-class tickets are bought in order to be shielded from crying children; or extra hours are worked to improve one's odds of being promoted to a contested position. The common characteristic of these goods is that access to them cannot be generalized: not every student can be admitted to top schools; not everybody can stand out by the quality of his clothes; not every traveler can be shielded from crying children; and not every employee can be a superior. In all these cases, attaining the positional good aspired means that there must be others who do not attain the same good. In this sense, the possession of positional goods is a form of "oligarchic wealth" rather than "democratic wealth" (Harrod 1958). Or, as Hirsch (1976: 5–6) put it, "what each of us can achieve, all cannot.... It follows that response to individual demands of this kind, whether in market processes or in public provision, cannot deliver the order".

We must distinguish, once more, between a systematic and a comparative perspective. When it is said that positional competition is a negative-sum game, this means that a social deadweight loss occurs in a systematic perspective, i.e. *with respect to* a hypothetical situation in which the same allocation of positional goods would be achieved without expenditures on intermediate goods. It does not mean that society is, in the process of positional competition, losing something it previously had. Moreover, in the presence of technological progress, well-being should rise despite the increase in the loss from positional competition because it would be implausible to assume that the productive gains from economic growth are spent entirely on positional goods. In other words, the growth-induced additional waste from intensified positional competition will, under reasonable assumptions, not completely crowd out additional consumption of non-positional goods. Therefore, positional competition alone cannot explain stagnant levels of subjective well-being. In the absence of other effects that make economic growth self-defeating, positional competition alone should still allow for a positive effect of economic growth on SWB, albeit a smaller one than would be predicted if positional competition did not exist.

Secondary inflation

Secondary inflation takes place to the degree that structural societal changes reduce the rate at which a given good can be transformed into functionings or, equivalently, to the degree that the costs of a given functioning in terms of inputs increase.[7] Just as (primary) inflation means an increase of money units required per good, so secondary inflation means an increase in the amount of real resources required per functioning.

The concept of "functionings" refers to the things a person can actually do with a particular good, what a person "manages to do or to be" (Sen 1985a: 10).[8] The underlying idea is that people ultimately purchase goods in order to do something with these goods. Often, these goods are perfectly exchangeable. For example, I do not buy a pen because I derive satisfaction from owning it, but in order to write with it, and many different kinds of pens will equally serve the same purpose. Conceptually, therefore, functionings are much more relevant to well-being than the underlying goods, which is why the exclusive focus on goods has been denounced by Marx (1887: I.1.1.4) as "commodity fetishism" (cited with approval by Sen 1985a: 28).

An example of secondary inflation would be the increasing necessity for car ownership. In Los Angeles, to take a famous example, the increase in car ownership driven by economic growth led to a deterioration of a formerly efficient public transport system: congestion due to increased individual traffic slowed public transport down, and wide car ownership reduced demand for public transport, leading in turn to a less dense public transport grid. In addition, widespread car ownership changed the shopping infrastructure: a large number of small grocery stores spread out across the city were replaced by a rather small number of giant supermarkets. This structural change meant that a functioning that used to be a matter of buying a bus ticket, such as doing one's grocery shopping, now requires ownership of a private car (Frank 1989: 82). In terms of commodities, car ownership of course means an improvement of one's living standard. In terms of functionings, however, the case is not that clear. Those people who bought a car for the *additional* functionings it offers (driving for the fun of it, for example) may be better off in terms of functionings. But those who bought one simply in order to maintain their former set of functionings (doing their grocery shopping) are now expending more resources than before without seeing any improvement in terms of functionings.

Secondary inflation may be quite a prevalent accompaniment of economic growth. To some degree, it indeed seems to be an almost built-in feature, such as in the case of the phenomenon pointed out by Richard Layard (1980: 741) that "in a poor society a man proves to his wife that he loves her by giving her a rose but in a rich society he must give a dozen roses". To the degree that an expenditure (also) serves to signal one's readiness to make a painful sacrifice – a typical feature of presents – the amount spent must increase along with an individual's and her reference group's purchasing power.

To which group exactly an individual compares her own living conditions is difficult to ascertain, and the limits of a person's reference group should be considered fluid and porous. While a poor person may not typically compare herself to the super rich, she will probably compare herself with those who are just a little better off – as Bertrand Russell observed, "Beggars do not envy millionaires, though of course they will envy other beggars who are more successful" (Russell 1996/1930: 73). Yet, those who earn a little more than the poorest will also compare themselves with those just above them in the income hierarchy, leading to an "expenditure cascade" (Frank 2003: 19) that only stops at the very top. Therefore, even the frame-of-reference of the poorest individuals will be indirectly affected by the consumption patterns at all income strata and, one might argue by extension, in places around the world. Thanks to cheaply available and globalized mass media, it may be expected that this effect has been intensified and accelerated on a global scale over the past decades (cf. Lichtenberg 1996; Lauterbach 1972: 276).

Moreover, defensive expenditures of individuals – i.e. expenditures made to fend off the effects of some deterioration in the environment – may generally be considered a manifestation of secondary inflation (cf. Hirsch 1976: 57). When increasing crime rates induce people to spend more on locks, fences, and alarm systems; deteriorating piped water quality forces people to buy bottled water; or increasing UV radiation obliges people to purchase more sun protection products, such additional consumption will look like a rise in welfare to the "commodity fetishist" (Marx), but is not an improvement in terms of functionings.[9] The next section (p. 48) will return to these issues.

The term "functionings" can of course be stretched to include a large variety of things, and depending on how far it is stretched, secondary inflation is prone to become a catch-all term for all kinds of frame-of-reference effects. At the limit, happiness itself could be called a functioning,[10] in which case it would become tautological to "explain" the failure of happiness to rise by the fact that the number of goods required per functioning has increased.

More specifically, when status is considered a functioning, positional competition becomes a special case of secondary inflation: due to other's increased expenditures on positional goods (in terms of time, money, or effort), more resources have to be expended by a given person in order to maintain her status. Yet, due to its additional peculiar features that set it apart from secondary inflation – to wit, social scarcity and status considerations – positional competition should be treated as a class of its own. This is also because, in contrast to positional competition, secondary inflation lifts the frame-of-reference in a way that still makes it possible for everybody to keep up in most respects. If in a rich society, it requires more roses to prove one's love than in a poor society, it is perfectly possible, in principle, for everybody to buy a dozen roses and to prove one's love (at least as long as "proving one's love" is not a matter of giving more roses than all others, which seems to be plausible). Depending on the good in question, this may require a rather egalitarian income distribution, but this is no systematic obstacle. In this sense, secondary inflation is consistent with democratic access to benefits as opposed to "oligarchic wealth" as in the case of positional competition (cf. p. 45).

Secondary inflation, therefore, remains a useful separate concept to capture social effects that are neither status-related nor psychological in nature. One may best think of secondary inflation as the devaluation of existing goods due to a changing social infrastructure, just as the value of yesterday's computer hardware is reduced by the increasing demands of the latest software. More specifically, secondary inflation can explain increasing material aspirations without having to recur to any psychological effects, as the third and last frame-of-reference effect does.

Adaptive aspirations

The effect of adaptive aspirations refers to the observation that the quality and/or quantity of stimuli necessary to make a person feel satisfied may vary over time as a consequence of exposure to above-average or below-average stimuli. More generally, however, adaptive aspirations are better understood as the manifestation of the contextual contingency of judgments.

In its most extreme interpretation, adaptation of aspirations would be absolute and, as a corollary, satisfaction would be entirely relative with respect to the space of stimuli. This so-called "setpoint theory" (Headey and Wearing 1992, reported in Lucas *et al.* 2004: 8) stipulates that the person experiences a person-specific intensity of satisfaction (the person's "setpoint") for a typical pattern of

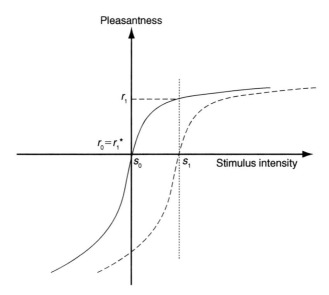

Figure 3.1 Setpoint theory.

Note
According to setpoint theory, a stimulus s_1 is perceived as pleasant only as long as a weaker stimulus such as s_0 is prevalent. Repeated exposure to s_1 will shift the response curve to the right (to the dashed line) so that s_1 will result in the original hedonic response $r_1^* = r_0$.

stimuli to which the person has been exposed for a sufficient period of time (where the setpoint itself will, for most individuals, be positive satisfaction rather than indifference). Deviations from this "normal" pattern lead, in the short run, to above-setpoint or below-setpoint experiences of satisfaction, but when sustained, i.e. in the long run, they lead to a new "normal" stimulus level and to a gradual return to the original setpoint level of satisfaction (cf. Figure 3.1). By implication, life events that lead to a sustained change in living conditions would only have a temporary effect on SWB.

Advocates of setpoint theory point to the large impact of genetic heredity on SWB (Lykken and Tellegen 1996; Tellegen *et al.* 1988) or to the surprisingly small long-term effects on SWB of major life events, such as a paralyzing accident or a lottery win (Brickman *et al.* 1978). Yet, since the impact of genetic heredity is still far from determining (cf. p. 25) and since the limited size of the SWB impact of major life events is "surprising" only from a prejudiced perspective (i.e. when one blindly subscribes to the popular view that lottery winners must be extremely happy and accident victims utterly desperate), while other life events (unemployment, marriage, friendships, etc.; cf. ch. 2) do have substantial and lasting effects on SWB, the extreme version of setpoint theory can be safely discarded (cf. Easterlin 2003).

Nevertheless, as we have seen above, adaptation clearly takes places with respect to certain living conditions, such as material comforts. We must therefore conclude that adaptation is important, even if it is selective, depending on more or less subtle distinctions. Some of these distinctions shall be made in the following.

In two similar, but apparently unrelated, strands of research, the complex and partly paradox interactions behind the effect of adaptive aspirations have been illuminated. On the one hand, Allen Parducci (1995) developed his range-frequency theory, which, in a nutshell, states that the pleasantness of a given experience depends on the distribution of the quality of previous similar experiences. In particular, an experience is evaluated more positively (1) the closer it is, relatively speaking, to the upper endpoint of the range, and (2) the more previous experiences fall into the lower part of the range. This implies that an experience that is more positive than any previous experience will be very pleasant, but it will also extend the range upward and thus reduce the pleasantness of any given future (or even past) experience. Even an experience that does not surpass the upper limit will have a negative impact on the evaluation of future experiences if it is rather positive with respect to previous experiences because it will "pull" the overall distribution upward. Parducci shows that, if his analysis is correct, the optimal tradeoff between the direct positive hedonic effect of an experience and its longer-term negative effect on future evaluations consists in a negatively skewed distribution, i.e. in a pattern of few very unpleasant experiences that extend the range downward (and provide a negative contrast) and many experiences toward the upper end of the range (yielding many positive evaluations). Thus, in order to maximize pleasantness, a person should try to avoid very positive experiences she knows she will not be able to repeat, but she should not necessarily avoid occasional rather negative experiences.

On the other hand, Amos Tversky and Dale Griffin (1991) came up with a closely related theory, making a distinction between a *contrast effect* and an *endowment effect*. Each experience, they argue, can add to a person's overall SWB through both of these channels. To the degree that an experience serves as a contrast for future (or retrospective) evaluations, it will enter with the opposite sign into a person's SWB – a positive contrast will make future experiences appear more negative, a negative contrast will make them appear more positive. Yet, an experience will of course also directly contribute to a person's overall SWB, and this is what Tversky and Griffin call the endowment effect – a positive experience will make a positive contribution, a negative experience will make a negative contribution. Depending on whether a person evaluates a given experience primarily through the contrast effect or through the endowment effect, it is theoretically possible that a very positive experience leads to an overall negative impact on her SWB.

What both of these theories suggest is that adaptation is largely, if not exclusively, a matter of contrast experiences that provide the frame of reference with respect to which a person evaluates her experiences. Both theories predict that a given experience will be evaluated more negatively the more positive her typical experiences are, i.e. the more she gets used to more positive stimuli. That these conclusions are reasonably well corroborated by experimental evidence will be shown below (p. 62).

As a basic distinction, psychophysical adaptation should be distinguished from cognitive adaptation. Psychophysical adaptation occurs when exposure to a given stimulus changes the sensory perception of that stimulus itself. A neat example of psychophysical adaptation is the eye's capacity to adapt to differences in luminosity intensity. For example, as one steps from a building into bright sunshine, a number of physiological adaptation mechanisms set in (pupil contraction, photochemical changes in the retina, and neural changes in particular areas of the brain), allowing a healthy person to see normally over luminance intensities that vary by a factor of over one million (Frederick and Loewenstein 1999: 302). The distinguishing feature of psychophysical adaptation is that the adaptation concerns the sensory response itself and is largely beyond the willful control of the person so that objectively different stimuli may really be perceived as exactly identical without the intervention of any cognitive evaluation. In the context of the happiness paradox, psychophysical adaptation may play a role in that people adapt to physical comforts brought about by economic affluence. We seem to adapt to such things as a hot morning shower, odorless drinking water, or air conditioning to such a degree that their sudden absence or deterioration triggers real bodily discomforts beyond the willful control of the person.

Cognitive adaptation, on the other hand, occurs when the hedonic evaluation of a given sensory perception changes as a consequence of exposure. For example, traveling business class quickly loses its initial thrill and soon becomes a routine experience (for an insightful fictional account, cf. Lelord 2002: 34ff.), not because business class comes to be *experienced* as economy class was experienced before (packed and noisy), but because business class comes to be *evaluated* as economy class was evaluated before – as the norm, lacking positive surprise and providing few substantive sensory pleasures.

Cognitive adaptation should be understood as an umbrella term for a number of different effects that arise from different sources, rather than as the exact description of a particular psychological mechanism. Moreover, it is perhaps more adequately described as a mental rather than a psychological effect because cognitive adaptation may involve moral judgment, transcending the psychological categories of "mechanisms" and "phenomena". In particular, social comparison and relative deprivation are two well-established concepts in psychology that can be considered specific variants of cognitive adaptation (cf., for example, Olson *et al.* 1986). *Social comparison* (Festinger 1954) basically means that life satisfaction depends, to an important degree, on how one's living conditions compare to those of "similar others", i.e. those persons with whom one interacts or relates in some important respect. The concept of *relative deprivation* (Stouffer *et al.* 1949) is closely related to social comparison but refers only to explicitly normative considerations and is typically applied to changes, not states, of entitlements. A person will experience relative deprivation when she considers herself deprived of a benefit others enjoy and to which she feels entitled. For example, an employee who sees her colleagues being promoted one after another without seeing a justification for herself being skipped will likely feel unsatisfied and experience relative deprivation.

The delimitation of "similar others" is often considered the major conceptual difficulty of models of social comparison since it may include everybody from one's brother-in-law to TV stars (cf. also the discussion of "expenditure cascades" above, p. 46). As will be suggested below, however (ch. 4), an even greater difficulty may lie in the (indeterminate) nature of human judgment itself (cf. Schwarz and Strack 1999).

Furthermore, the notion of a *demonstration effect* may be considered a major source of cognitive adaptation. The demonstration effect consists in the upgrading of aspirations as a consequence of the exposure to goods or lifestyles people feel are superior to their own. Christiaan Cornelissen already described this effect a hundred years ago, even if he did not use that particular terminology: "The new necessities of the non-working classes and the growth of luxury also affect the mass of the workers and instill in them an even clearer sense of deprivation" (Cornelissen 1908: 87, transl. J.H.).

James Duesenberry (1949: 26–7), probably the person who coined the term "demonstration effect", held this effect responsible for the failure of saving rates to rise with economic growth:

> In given circumstances, the individuals in question come into contact with goods superior to the ones they use with a certain frequency. Each such contact is a demonstration of the superiority of these goods and is a threat to the existence of the current consumption pattern … because it makes active the latent preference for these goods. A certain effort is required to resist the impulse to give up saving in favor of higher quality goods.

The demonstration effect is therefore not a social dynamic in the sense that the attractiveness of a good derives exclusively from the consumption patterns of others (as in the cases of positional competition or secondary inflation). Rather, a good's attractiveness is a matter of its inherent desirability and not necessarily dependent on prevailing consumption patterns, reflecting a match between the good's inherent features and an individual's existing (manifest or latent) desires, and the possession of superior goods by others within one's society is merely the trigger that "makes active the latent preference for these goods". The demonstration effect does not rely in a systematic way on the acquisition of superior goods by members of one's society. Demonstration could also take the form of television ads or product information on the internet, for example. A washing machine, for example, will quite naturally appeal to people because it liberates people from a disliked burden and not because changing living conditions make people learn to prefer it. The lack of a washing machine was not felt before it was invented, but the desire for it does not so much depend on one's neighbors having that good or not. Once a person has been exposed to it, the demonstration effect makes people experience an unsatisfied desire.

Later studies hypothesized that the demonstration effect must be at work in low-income countries as well and that an "international demonstration effect" (Nurkse 1953, cited in James 1993: 111) has a decisive influence on people's preferences (similarly, Lauterbach 1972: 276). It has been rightly criticized (e.g. by James 1993: ch. 6) that this "explanation" raises the questions of how exactly people come to regard some goods as superior, why in most cases these "superior" goods happen to be Western goods, and whether the underlying preference shift is autonomous (natural "latent preferences") or heteronomous (preferences acquired through social learning or cultural imposition). Yet, while in some cases (soft drinks, infant formula), the answer to such questions may make a difference, in other cases (washing machines, airbags), it seems beyond reasonable doubt that certain goods have quite a universal appeal independent of culture, addressing dormant desires that derive from universal values (avoidance of burden or bodily harm, safety) and which become a source of dissatisfaction once they are aroused but still unsatisfied.

Several authors have pointed out that adaptation is asymmetric (Figure 3.2). People quickly get used to better living conditions and adapt their evaluative frame of reference upward, but they take much more time to revise their evaluative standards downward when their living conditions deteriorate, and they may never return to their original level (Parducci 1995; Layard 1980).

This effect corresponds closely to the firmly established phenomenon of *loss aversion*, where people prefer avoiding a small loss to receiving a much larger gain (see Figure 3.3) (Kahneman 2003).

In contrast to the previously discussed frame-of-reference effects, adaptive aspirations are not primarily a social effect. Rather, what characterizes adaptive aspirations is that they arise out of an apparently universal predisposition to evaluate a given experience with respect to past experiences, expectations of the future, and the knowledge of alternatives. While in some cases the ordering of

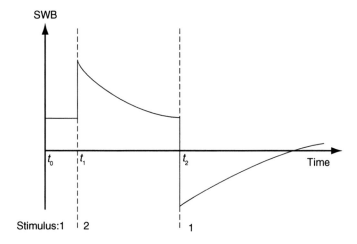

Figure 3.2 Asymmetric adaptation.

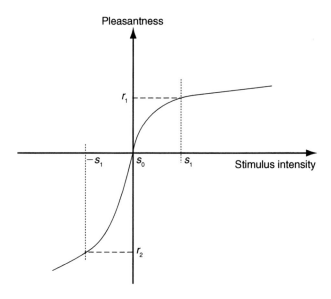

Figure 3.3 Loss aversion.

Note
Loss aversion means that the negative reaction r_2 to a negative stimulus $-s_1$ is larger than the positive reaction r_1 to a positive stimulus s_1 of the same absolute size.

the experiences along the scale of pleasant/unpleasant may be socially induced, it will often correspond to a preexisting, though latent, set of preferences.

Again it is helpful to distinguish between psychophysical and cognitive adaptation. While psychophysical adaptation is not subject to direct cognitive control

(I can perhaps *train* my body to like a cold morning shower, but I will not like it just because I *want* to), cognitive adaptation is no psychological mechanism in the strict sense. Rather, it is an observed social psychological tendency that any given individual can, upon reflection and within limits, find rational to affirm or to resist. For example, when I realize that I fail to derive satisfaction from a good meal because I have experienced superb meals in the past (cf. Parducci 1995), I might, to some degree, regain the original enjoyment by a conscious change of attitude (more on this below, p. 91). While it is conceivable that rare experiences of intense happiness may have a negative overall effect on life satisfaction of nostalgic dreamers (Parducci 1995: 5), "a few glorious moments could sustain a lifetime of happy memories for those who can cherish the past without discounting the present" (Tversky and Griffin 1991: 117).

Taking a step back, we can now see how and to which degree the three frame-of-reference effects here discussed can explain the contradictory evidence on the relationship between income and SWB (Table 3.1). Generally speaking, all three effects work through a change of the frame of reference that constitutes the necessary "solid ground" for any evaluation. The frame of reference can be constituted by others' status goods (positional competition), the social infrastructure (secondary inflation), or one's familiarity with available consumption goods (demonstration effect).

More generally, the frame of reference appears to affect a person's SWB to the degree that it affects the set of functionings she thinks that she should be able to enjoy. Saying "should" is clearly a normative requirement and can refer either to a social or personal norm or to a likelihood. For example, a person may feel dissatisfied when she does not enjoy a benefit *most others* enjoy as a matter of fact (heteronomous norm) or when she feels she is *entitled* to a benefit she does not enjoy (autonomous norm; both cases are normative counterfactuals). An example for the former would be a poor person who cannot afford to buy fashionable clothes (even if she does not believe that she is morally entitled to do

Table 3.1 Three frame-of-reference effects

	Positional competition	*Secondary inflation*	*Adaptive aspirations*
Benefit	Oligarchic	Democratic	Democratic
Motivation	Not falling behind others, status, or exclusive benefit	Maintaining a given functioning	Maintaining satisfaction
Cause for dynamic spiral	(Threat of) advance of others	Changing environment: more commodities required per functioning	Changing reference for judgment

so); an example of the latter would be an employee who was the only one not to get a pay rise and thinks this is unfair. A person can also feel dissatisfied for not enjoying a benefit she expected to receive (likelihood counterfactual), e.g. when her lottery ticket number was wrongly announced to be the winning ticket (which may generate unhappiness), or she can feel satisfied for being spared a likely disadvantage, e.g. when she survives a plane crash (which may generate happiness).[11] Apparently, we are satisfied when reality matches and very satisfied when it exceeds our aspirations, which in turn are based on normative and likelihood counterfactuals. Put boldly, "what we understand to be normal is critical in determining our chances of happiness. Few things rival the torment of the once-famous actor, the fallen politician or, as Tocqueville might have remarked, the unsuccessful American" (De Botton 2004: 55).

The three frame-of-reference effects presented should not be taken as parallel, additive effects but rather as distinct but overlapping perspectives on the same reality that differ primarily with respect to a person's cognitive construction and the underlying motivation. Adam Smith's account of the necessity of linen shirts and leather shoes illustrates this complex web of effects:

> By necessaries I understand not only the commodities which are indispensably necessary for the support of life, but whatever the custom of the country renders it indecent for creditable people, even of the lowest order, to be without. A linen shirt, for example, is, strictly speaking, not a necessary of life. The Greeks and Romans lived, I suppose, very comfortably, though they had no linen. But in present times, through the greater part of Europe, a creditable day-labourer would be ashamed to appear in publick without a linen shirt, the want of which would be supposed to denote that disgraceful degree of poverty, which, it is presumed, no body can well fall into without extreme bad conduct. Custom, in the same manner, has rendered leather shoes a necessary of life in England. The poorest creditable person of either sex would be ashamed to appear in publick without them.... Under necessaries therefore, I comprehend, not only those things which nature, but those things which the established rules of decency have rendered necessary to the lowest rank of people.
>
> (Smith 1979/1776: 869–70)

The change in preferences toward linen shirts and leather shoes may be motivated by a concern for superior status (positional competition), by the desire to maintain the functioning of being able to appear in public without shame (secondary inflation), by comparison with the possessions of one's peers (social comparison), by a feeling of being unfairly left behind others (relative deprivation), by some inherent attractiveness of those goods (demonstration effect), or by any combination of these and other considerations. That the tendency observed by Adam Smith is still relevant today is suggested by surveys in which Americans were asked "What is the smallest amount of money a family of four needs to get along in this community?" (cf. Frank 1999: 73–4). Over the 36 years during which the survey was repeated (1950 to 1986), the amount of income respondents deemed necessary to "get along" rose at practically the same rate as the actual average income, remaining at a constant proportion of about two-thirds of average income (Rainwater 1990: 5). While this observation does not provide any information as to the underlying effects of this relative-income effect, it would suggest that the frame-of-reference by which people evaluate their standard of living rises by one percent each time the average income grows by one percent, thus entirely offsetting any direct SWB benefits economic growth might deliver.

It should be noted, however, that an increase in material aspirations may appear in a morally different light depending on the precise interpretation of the underlying mechanism. In particular, an increase in material aspirations does not necessarily have to reflect greed, envy, or status-mindedness (Lichtenberg 1996). These ramifications will be taken up in more detail below (ch. 5).

While this discussion of intervening effects makes no claim to completeness and, moreover, raises further questions concerning the precise nature of the processes underlying the effects sketched here, this account of frame-of-reference effects makes some important characterizations and distinctions that will go a long way in helping us understand, in the remainder, the intricate relationship between economic well-being and happiness and the ethical implications.

Direct externalities

The effects presented in the preceding section can all be interpreted in terms of negative externalities[12] of consumption on some frame of reference (Frank 1997, 1999, 2003). In other words, they constitute a specific case of externalities that interfere with the transformation of commodities into functionings and/or of functionings into satisfaction.

This section, by contrast, will investigate whether "ordinary" externalities may also help to explain the happiness–income paradox. Such externalities affect advantages directly rather than the rate at which these are transformed into satisfaction, and they leave the frame of reference unaffected. In other words, these externalities belong to the conventional, well-known class of negative externalities that are well-established in economic theory. The classic example of such externalities would be the economic damages resulting from environmental pollution (as pioneered by Pigou 1952/1920). Negative externalities are defined in economics as costs (or benefits, in case of positive externalities) that arise from a particular decision but that are not borne by the person who takes the decision (but effects transmitted through the price mechanism are usually excluded). I will refer to the former type of externalities (as discussed in the previous section) as *frame-of-reference externalities* and to the latter type of externalities (to be discussed here) as *direct externalities*.

I shall not go very deep into the possible sources of direct negative externalities from economic growth since there is a host of candidates and the task of evaluating their effect would lead us too far away from the interest of the present investigation. Rather, what is of interest in our context is the systematic role of direct externalities and their implications for frame-of-reference externalities in light of the empirical evidence. I will turn to these two issues after a brief presentation of the major lines of arguments with respect to direct externalities.

Accounts of direct externalities

The literature on direct externalities[13] of economic progress (whatever that means precisely)[14] is vast and heterogeneous. The contributions range from personal narratives based on introspection and anecdotal evidence (e.g. Norberg-Hodge 1991) to impassioned statistical analyses (e.g. Meadows *et al.* 1972). While both types of accounts may lead to valuable insights, the discussion here will continue to rely on theoretical argumentation and quantitative (and statistically significant) evidence, all the while recognizing that no quantitative analysis will ever be – nor needs to be – "objective" or "value free" in any strict sense and that most contributions will lie on a continuum between the two extremes.

Perhaps most accounts of the direct externalities of economic progress are concerned with social pathologies of various sorts. It has been pointed out, for example, that loneliness has increased and that family ties have suffered as a consequence of modern economies' demand for geographical mobility and their encouragement of individualism (Lane 2000a; Putnam 2000). The secular increase in clinical depression rates and in alcohol abuse, especially among youth, have also been linked to economic progress (Layard 2005: 35–7). The multiplication of options (Gross 1994) combined with an erosion of traditional moral codes probably confronts people more violently than before with existential questions and challenges their faculty of judgment. Obesity (Mokdad *et al.* 1999) and crime (Layard 2005: 37) also show clear upward trends over the last half of a century or so. It has also been argued that economic progress systematically erodes commitment to social norms (Hirsch 1976: 117ff.; Frank *et al.* 1993).

The second major group of direct externalities consists of those that affect the *environment*, natural or otherwise. The externalities of environmental pollution are perhaps the most salient negative externalities in the public perception. Environmental degradation of various forms – global warming, species extinction, etc. – has clearly been a consequence of modern economic activity. Yet, environmental deterioration is only registered on the radar screen of the happiness perspective to the extent that it affects current human happiness. In other words, the happiness perspective leaves out effects on the natural environment that do not affect human beings' subjective well-being (such as some instances of species extinction) or do not affect it today (such as the long-term repercussions of the greenhouse effect). This does not imply that these effects are irrelevant from an ethical point of view, of course. To the contrary, this points to an important limitation of the happiness perspective for ethical purposes that will be discussed below (p. 117).

Effects on the environment in a larger sense include more than just the natural environment. They also include effects on urban, cultural, etc. environments. It is evident, for example, that economic progress has triggered a dramatic increase in urbanization and major changes of urban environments that many people experience as threatening or alienating. Edward Mishan (1979/1967), for example, argues that the spread of private automobiles and the corresponding city planning (or its absence) are responsible for "uglifying" (ibid.: 110) cities to an extent that exceeds the benefits of private transport (and he shows, in the appendix, how this can be demonstrated as a possibility even in strictly welfare economic terms).

Some authors, however, argue that economic progress (in particular, economic growth and full employment) has positive externalities as well. Benjamin Friedman (2006: 15ff.), for example, shows that there are good reasons to believe that economic growth is a prerequisite for tolerance toward minorities, fairness, and dedication to democracy.

Inevitable vs. incidental externalities

The systematic role of direct externalities and, in particular, their normative implications depend critically on whether they are *inevitable* or *incidental* consequences of economic progress. A consequence would be inevitable if economic progress could not take place without it. It would be incidental if it follows from particular activities or changes that are not indispensable for economic progress. Again, most real-world examples will fall on a continuum somewhere between the two poles.

The reported externalities of monetization – such as weakening of social ties and erosion of civic virtues (Rhodes 2000: 91–2) – would be close to being inevitable consequences of economic progress, since monetization is practically inseparable from modern economic activity. On the other hand, certain forms of environmental externalities (e.g. fish stock depletion) are arguably the result of poorly managed economic progress, rather than an inherent consequence of economic progress as such.

This distinction is of huge importance for the questions at issue. To the extent that negative externalities of economic progress are inevitable, economic progress will be partly or wholly self-defeating in terms of SWB. We would have to accept that when we want economic progress, we can only get it in a package with the corresponding negative externalities. Whether such a "package" is worth the while would then be a question of the tradeoff between costs and benefits and of whether the gains of the winners justify the losers' losses. To the extent that externalities are incidental, on the other hand, there is scope for "cherry picking": by devising ways to reduce or even avoid negative incidental externalities, societies can get the benefits of economic progress without having to put up with its side-effects (cf. p. 64).

Implications

If we now recall the empirical evidence underlying the happiness–income paradox, the invocation of direct externalities has the curious implication that economic growth per se must after all have a positive effect on SWB. Even if one reads from the evidence that SWB has been stagnant, it follows that, *if* economic growth has negative direct externalities, which, seen in isolation, subtract from SWB, then some other effect, presumably increased consumption or enlarged choices in general, must add to SWB to offset the negative externalities. As a corollary, if the supposed negative externalities are claimed to be large, so must the positive isolated effect of economic progress. Moreover, if both direct and frame-of-reference externalities are present, then the frame-of-reference externalities cannot be so large as to *entirely* offset the SWB payoff of economic progress, and vice versa (net of positive externalities). Algebraically speaking, if the net effect on happiness is zero, the three components – frame-of-reference externalities, direct externalities, and the direct effect of economic progress – must each be either zero or positive and negative in corresponding magnitudes so as to cancel each other out. Even though this additive metaphor is of course limited (cf. the remark on p. 55), it should give a valid idea of the implications of the various hypotheses.

To the degree that direct externalities are *inevitable*, this observation merely makes a difference in terms of distribution and accounting (where "merely" is of course not meant to imply that distributional questions are unimportant). It would simply show that stagnation is a result of gains and necessarily corresponding losses, rather than of stagnation across accounting domains. However, to the degree that direct externalities are *incidental*, the claim that economic progress has negative direct externalities carries with it the positive message that economic progress can, after all, be reconciled with rising SWB once the externalities are reduced or altogether eliminated.

Cognitive fallacies

The previous two sections have shown how (part of) the happiness–income paradox may be explained in terms of externalities, i.e. by showing that social outcomes suffer from the unintended side-effects of individual decisions. This view rests on the silent assumption that, from the perspective of the respective actor, choices are individually rational in the non-technical sense that the decision taken is in fact conducive to one's own well-being. The negative social effects were, therefore, not a result of individual irrationality, let alone of malice, but of the interplay of individually rational choices that lead to socially deleterious outcomes (as in the prisoner's dilemma).[15] This section will deal with the question of whether behavior is in fact always rational and, if not, what this may mean for happiness and economics.

Empirical happiness research provides probably the first quantitative instrument that permits an objective assessment of the goal-conduciveness of satisfaction-oriented behavior because it taps satisfaction directly. So far, and especially in the revealed preference approach[16] of economics, intentions were derived from behavior, making it impossible – or, more precisely, tautological – to assess goal-conduciveness of behavior: when the purported goal is derived from behavior, then behavior is, by definition, goal-conducive.

This section will briefly present and cite evidence for three particularly significant cognitive fallacies identified by empirical happiness research and then offer some deeper reflections on the relationship between goals and choice.

Unanticipated adaptation

When people are asked about what would make them happy or how satisfied they would be with particular changes, they systematically mispredict their satisfaction. As a consequence, to the degree that expected satisfaction plays a role in people's choices – whether as the dominant objective or as one consideration among others – a person's choices are liable to work against her intentions. In other words, not knowing that or to which degree we adapt to changing life circumstances will interfere with our ability to take decisions that are conducive to our intended purposes.[17] The consequences of unanticipated adaptation may often be trivial, but when it comes to predicting satisfaction with major acquisitions, career choices, or other major live events, they may be very significant.

Empirical evidence strongly suggests that people frequently and substantially err in anticipating adaptation. Often they fail dramatically. For example, when healthy people are asked to predict how satisfied a person they would be if they had a particular serious disease, their estimates are far too pessimistic when compared with people who actually suffer from that disease. Correspondingly, healthy people also state a lower willingness to undergo life-extending treatment than those actually facing the choice (Loewenstein and Schkade 1999: 92). Furthermore, when in a "cold" state, people tend to mispredict how they will behave in an emotionally "hot" state (ibid.: 93). A smoker, for example, will typically be unrealistically optimistic about his ability to quit smoking as long as he is not actually experiencing the symptoms of craving.

There are also instances of overprediction of adaptation, however. The most remarkable case is that of noise. People usually think that they will adapt to consistent background noise, such as that from a busy highway in front of their home. However, empirical evidence shows that people do not adapt. Sometimes even the contrary is true: instead of adapting, people become sensitized and show more symptoms of noise-related stress the longer they are exposed to the noise (Frank 1999: 81; Loewenstein and Schkade 1999: 90).

Unanticipated adaptation (or the overprediction of adaptation) can of course have fundamental consequences on choice. In fact, any satisfaction-oriented choice is ultimately based on an attempt to anticipate one's satisfaction in a future situation. Hence, any unanticipated adaptation will distort this anticipation and potentially lead to unwanted outcomes.

Focusing illusion

Apart from mispredicting the degree of satisfaction a particular change will generate, people tend to overestimate the weight of a particular domain satisfaction (e.g. financial satisfaction) in future global life satisfaction as soon as their attention is drawn to it. This *focusing illusion* (Schkade and Kahneman 1998) apparently arises because, when comparing one's current state with an alternative, the characterizing differences of the states in question are brought to awareness without, at the same time, being set in proper relation to common background features or less salient differences. For example, when students of a Midwestern and of a Californian university were asked to estimate average life satisfaction in the two regions, both groups predicted that Californians would be more satisfied, but in fact no difference emerged, even though Californians did in fact report greater domain satisfaction with climate (ibid.). The respondents apparently focused on the more agreeable Californian climate without being aware that climate as an influence on SWB is negligible in comparison with other factors that will essentially be the same in the Midwest and in California.[18] Similarly, able-bodied individuals who affirm that they would prefer not living at all rather than being confined to a wheelchair may focus on the distinctive negative aspects of being handicapped, thus failing to realize that some of the most essential sources of SWB and meaning, like friendship and self-esteem, are still available to para- and quadriplegics.

A specific case of the focusing illusion consists in the overemphasis of changes vis-à-vis the subsequent enduring state (Kahneman 1999). When contemplating a particular decision, the transition to the new state and the new state's initial affective quality are much more salient than the prospect of being in that state for a longer period of time. For example, when predicting one's life satisfaction as a paraplegic, one's judgment may be overproportionately influenced by the idea of an (assumed) painful experience of *becoming* paraplegic (e.g. by an accident) and on the initial desperation at one's misfortune, rather than being based on the state of *being* paraplegic. Similarly, the happiness from owning a new car will usually be overpredicted because the initial excitement and the thrill of novelty receive excessive weight in one's judgment, whereas habituation, the increased anxiety about petty damages, and the equal immobility in traffic jams are understated or even entirely neglected.

Memory bias

The described tendency to overemphasize the initial phase of an episode in *ex ante* judgments stands in stark contrast to the observed bias of remembered satisfaction. When giving an overall affective rating of painfulness or pleasantness, people's responses are almost exclusively based on the peak and the end affective value of the episode, rather than on the initial experience or on the duration. For example, patients undergoing a colonoscopy, a rather painful diagnostic procedure, rated their experience of pain significantly more favorably when the treatment was extended by one minute of only mild discomfort (cf. Kahneman 1999). The same paradoxical valuation has been observed in experiments exposing subjects to unpleasant noise and cold water. After being exposed to two painful trials, the second of which was identical to the first except that it was prolonged by a slightly less painful period, most subjects preferred to repeat the second (prolonged) rather than the first trial, even though they had rated it as more painful by a real-time rating method (Kahneman *et al.* 1997).

This phenomenon has been found to conform to a simple formula of peak-end evaluation. The average of the peak and of the end affective intensity accounted for a substantial amount of variation of the retrospective evaluation (up to 45 percent in the colonoscopy study and up to 93 percent in other experiments; ibid.). This implies that the retrospective evaluation is not a temporal integration of the painful experience, but rather a two-moment evaluation based solely on the peak and the end intensity, which is why Daniel Kahneman (1999) talks of a phenomenon of *duration neglect* because the duration of the experience had almost no influence at all. The peak-end rule implies not only that the retrospective evaluation of pain is inaccurate, but also that monotonicity is violated (i.e. more pain is not always evaluated as worse). As a consequence, the welfare criterion of the temporal integration of instant (dis)utility, as proposed explicitly by Edgeworth (1881) and accepted implicitly in most welfare economic texts, will yield a different ordering than observed choice. As Kahneman (1999: 20) put it in an allusion to Bentham, "the sovereign masters that determine what people will do are not pleasure and pain, but fallible memories of pleasure and pain".

Beyond cognitive fallacies

So far, this discussion has been consistent with, though not dependent on, the idea of *psychological hedonism*, i.e. the idea that decisions are ultimately motivated exclusively by the desire to maximize the balance of pleasure and pain (more on this below, p. 000). This idea was famously championed by Jeremy Bentham (and, as a precursor, by Thomas Hobbes) and refined, rather than qualified, by Daniel Kahneman and others. After all, what they show is merely that expectations or memories of pleasure and pain will often be inaccurate, but that does not invalidate the view of psychological hedonism that decisions are *motivated* by pleasure maximization. This view will be challenged in this section.

To be sure, any hypothesis concerning human motivation must remain beyond falsification as one can always invoke unobservable factors to save one's hypothesis (cf. Thielemann 1996: 112ff.). Nevertheless, empirical happiness research has come up with intriguing evidence that goes a long way, I will argue, in shifting the burden of proof on the defenders of psychological hedonism.

Consider an experiment in which subjects were presented with the choice of either working for an annual salary of $35,000 when one's equally qualified colleagues receive $38,000, or receiving $33,000 when one's colleagues earn $30,000. When asked which of the two jobs they would *choose*, 84 percent of the subjects (27 out of 32) said they would prefer the $35,000 job, but when asked in which job they would be more *satisfied*, 62 percent of another group (21 out of 34) gave preference to the $33,000 job ($p < 0.01$) (Tversky and Griffin 1991: 114–15). Parducci (1995) showed that, in more general terms, people systematically are guided in their decisions by a desire for objective success, but that they actually feel more satisfied with relative success (be it relative with respect to others or relative with respect to one's own past experiences). In other words, wanting (choice) is not identical with liking (happiness). Indeed, it has even been found that wanting and liking arise from two different neural systems (Berridge 1999), giving rise to the behavior of wanting without symptoms of liking, and symptoms of liking without the behavior of wanting.

These results do not, of course, say that expected happiness is not an important motive in decision-making. They do, however, suggest quite forcefully that decisions are motivated by much more than maximizing happiness. In particular, people seem to use learned heuristics of socially established criteria of success that receive much more weight than would be warranted in terms of happiness. Loewenstein and Schkade put it this way:

> In fact, ... many decisions involve little conscious deliberation. People decide based on rules..., habits..., and gut feelings, none of which involve explicit predictions of future feelings. The most common source of experimental surprise could therefore be the absence of an explicit prediction in the first place.
>
> (Loewenstein and Schkade 1999: 100)

Refining the perspective

So far, the analysis and interpretation have been largely confined to statistical relationships that have been identified in SWB data. Of the evidence presented thus far, two remarkable basic insights into the happiness–income paradox shall be highlighted.

First, even if people often take poor decisions as judged by their own intentions, what lies beneath the happiness–income paradox is not primarily human irrationality but rather the cumulative effects of individually rational decisions. From the perspective of each individual, it often makes perfect sense to invest time and effort in improving one's standard of living, to work extra hours and consent to all kinds of additional demands from one's employer in order to get that pay rise and to be able to move to a better – and more expensive – neighborhood. The individual concerned will typically not even think of such a choice in terms of relative position because she only cares about the absolute functionings she can achieve. The fact that such decisions also affect her relative position will not typically be understood or, even then, be seen as a means to the end of a better standard of living, rather than as an end in itself.

Second, the negative cumulative effects of individually rational decisions are not the result of particularly selfish motives. Even in a society of mindful and benevolent citizens who take care not to inflict undue harm on others, the pursuit of legitimate plans of a good life would still be liable to negatively affect the frame of reference. Expecting from people to stop bettering their lives whenever this raises the frame of reference would be asking far too much, namely to forsake a very substantial part of one's idea of a good life. As Richard Layard noted in the context of positional competition in the workplace, "it is not clear just how a person observing the social contract would know when to stop work" (Layard 1980: 744). Even the circumspect, legitimate pursuit of one's self-interest seems to come with a good deal of positional externalities.

These two observations have the significant implication that neither self-help advice nor moral betterment – in isolation or in conjunction – on an individual level will be sufficient to overcome the happiness–income paradox, even if they are perhaps not entirely futile. Instead, one will have to turn to institutional arrangements that take these effects into account. These implications will be discussed in more detail in Chapter 6.

Apart from these general observations, the statistical findings reported should be put into context and complemented by a perspective that regards people as agents, rather than reducing them to carriers of a deterministic behavioral program that can be deciphered by means of statistical observation. In such a perspective, it becomes clear that statistical analysis can only be a starting point for understanding human behavior and the resulting cumulative effects. In the following, a few insights that can be gained from this perspective shall be discussed.

Lasting gains

The evidence on the happiness–income paradox can be quite discouraging when looking at macro trends. It appears that SWB is largely unaffected by economic growth. After all, even over periods of substantial economic growth, the effect on life satisfaction is hardly discernible. So should we discard economic growth as a way to increase subjective well-being?

As a more differentiated analysis of the data reveals, we do not need to go that far. Even though the overall effect of income on SWB has been nil or at best tiny over time, it appears that specific living conditions have a lasting effect, positive or negative, on life satisfaction, while others are subject to almost complete adaptation. Commuting to work, exposure to consistent noise, or being unemployed are examples of conditions that have a lasting negative impact on a person's SWB and to which adaptation is incomplete or inexistent. Reducing exposure to such conditions therefore has a lasting positive effect on life satisfaction. On the other hand, the number of holidays, physical exercise, time spent with family and friends, and having autonomy at the workplace contribute positively and lastingly to SWB (Frank 1999: 80–9). If economic growth was used to invest in such lasting sources of SWB, it might after all make a clear positive contribution to SWB.

The fact that societies *have not* transformed economic growth into increases in SWB does not mean that they *cannot* do so in the future. Once we understand what exactly prevented societies from raising SWB and what does and does not contribute to lasting increases in SWB, we are in a better position to evaluate the question of whether economic growth, or indeed any other condition, can contribute to enhancing SWB.[19]

Culture

One puzzle of the happiness–income paradox consists in the coexistence of a positive correlation between income and SWB across countries at a given point in time and a non-correlation or a much weaker correlation between income and SWB over time for any given country. The hope, inspired by the cross-country evidence, that economic growth will eventually raise SWB is discouraged by the time-series evidence.

Culture has been suggested as holding one possible solution to this apparent contradiction. As reported above (p. 000), one empirical study found that individualism was a more robust predictor of SWB than income. While this result should be interpreted with considerable caution,[20] there are additional reasons that lend plausibility to the hypothesis that the cross-country correlation between income and SWB is spurious and that the causal effect in fact runs from culture to SWB (and, possibly, from culture to income as well). Ahuvia (1999, 2002), for example, argues that people in individualistic cultures tend to experience more positive affect because they have been taught to pursue their own goals rather than fulfill expectations of their family or their community (even though one's own goals and others' expectations may of course coincide for a given person). The individualist's liberation from "networks of social obligation" (Ahuvia 2002: 30) increases the individual's liberty to make choices that cater to his intrinsic needs, rather than choices geared toward meeting external expectations. In addition, as the work on self-determination theory of Edward Deci, Tim Kasser, Richard Ryan, and colleagues (Deci and Ryan 1985; Kasser and Ryan 1993, 1996; cf. also Kasser and Ahuvia 2002) shows, those who pursue intrinsic goals tend to score higher on SWB than those who pursue extrinsic goals. In economic terminology, this would roughly mean that the individualist's behavior is dominated by those preferences that are most rewarding in terms of utility – namely intrinsic desires – rather than by preferences that are imposed on the independent individual and, hence, yield a lower happiness payoff. The upshot of this theory is that "the direct pleasures of consumption play little part in this phenomenon" (Ahuvia 2002: 30), i.e. that the high consumption standards of individualist societies are an accompanying feature, but not the cause, of the high SWB levels of these societies.

Nothing of this is to say, to reiterate an earlier proviso (p. 20), that happier cultures are the better cultures or that a happier life is necessarily a better life. Just as life in a collectivist culture may seem unattractive from an individualistic perspective because it is less conducive to SWB, the constant cheerfulness of individualistic cultures can seem unattractive to collectivists and strike them as a form of "self-suppression" (Hoffman 1989: 271).

Idiosyncrasy

The objective of correlational or regression analysis is of course to single out the *common* variation within a sample and not to explain the "unexplained" variance. As has been pointed out, the share of the SWB variance that remains unexplained in *micro*-data studies is very large, between 40 percent and almost 90 percent, depending on which predictor variables are admitted into the analysis (cf. p. 23). For *macro*-data, this share is much smaller because much of the unexplained micro-level variation cancels out in the macro-data (cf. p. 29). Yet, one should not get carried away with high r-square figures. First of all, "explaining" in a statistical sense really means "accounting for". When a statistical model "explains", say, 50 percent, this merely means that it can predict 50 percent of the variation within the sample. Whether or not this prediction also describes a causal effect is an entirely different question.

Second, even with a high r-square, one should still take an interest in the unexplained variance and, in particular, in outliers. Considering cross-country evidence, for example, one can observe that a couple of countries do not fit the broad trend for poorer countries to have lower SWB than richer countries (cf. Figure 2.3 and Table 2.2). In particular, the poorest countries are not among the lowest on SWB, and the happiest countries are not all among the richest. In fact, in the fifth wave (2005–08) of the World Values Survey, the country that scored highest on SWB (Colombia with 8.3 on a ten-point scale) had not even a quarter of the per-capita purchasing power (US$8,041 vs. US$37,595) of the third-highest placed country (Switzerland with 8.0). And some of the countries lowest on SWB (Ukraine with 5.7 or Bulgaria with 5.2) still had comparatively large incomes (US$6,547 and US$9,924, respectively), at least well above some countries that are economically backward but rather high on SWB, such as Guatemala (US$4,332/8.0) or Indonesia (US$3,519/6.9).

One can of course not build a theory on outliers alone, but outliers do put the burden of proof on incumbent theories. Sometimes outliers can plausibly be explained by variations of control variables or by contextual influences (such as in the case of an extremely low level of SWB in the Dominican Republic in 1962 that was apparently due to political turmoil in that period). When they cannot, however, they challenge the meaningfulness of the statistical regularities found. If Indonesians are pretty satisfied with their lives, earning US$3,519 on average, but Bulgarians are dissatisfied with their lives, despite having almost three times as many goods at their disposal, how meaningful is it really to say that SWB depends on consumption? I am not suggesting that the answer to this question should be "not at all", but rather that the context, and in particular what has above been called the frame of reference, may have a much larger influence on SWB than consumption itself. If this were not so, we would have to conclude that people in pre-industrial societies could not have lived happy lives and that people in subsistence societies today cannot be high on SWB. Yet, while subsistence societies are certainly not always characterized by high degrees of SWB, many cases of generally satisfied subsistence societies have been documented (e.g. the Masai people in Africa, in Diener and Seligman 2004: 10, the rural population in Bhutan, in Pankaj and Dorji 2004, and the population of Ladakh in India, in Norberg-Hodge 1991).

Indeterminacy

Analyzing human behavior and social trends by means of statistical methods is a delicate exercise and prone to misinterpretation. The formality, rigidity, and objectivity of quantitative analysis easily inspire a misplaced confidence that the observed social patterns are governed by inherent quasi-natural laws that are being laid bare. Such an objectifying view, however, is at odds with the way individuals go about making decisions – and after all, society is made up of individuals. Human beings act upon *reasons* rather than being compelled by *causes*. Thus, when interpreting statistical evidence, we need to *understand* more than we need to *explain*. In other words, our approach must ultimately be hermeneutic.

To illustrate what this means concretely, consider the statistical observation that, at a given point in time, life satisfaction is negatively correlated with the income of others. In an analytical, causal perspective, this would imply that there is some psychic mechanism that heteronomously causes a given individual's satisfaction to fall when others' incomes go up. In this perspective, the individual is doomed to passively watch her aspirations rise with her reference group's income. In a hermeneutic perspective, however, the same observation merely implies that people tend to have less reason to judge their life positively when their income falls short of some comparison income, and understanding the phenomenon would require understanding these reasons. Whether or not a person's life satisfaction is negatively influenced by the income of others would then depend on the specific reasons a person has for being satisfied. These reasons, in turn, are not dictated by the circumstances. Rather, it is the individual that constructs these reasons as an autonomous agent. But if we admit that human beings are endowed with at least a minimum of personal autonomy, i.e. freedom of will, then we cannot adequately describe happiness in strictly causal terms. Moreover, since freedom of will places human choices under the duty of moral justification, the phenomenon of happiness cannot be duly apprehended without due appreciation of its ethical dimension. It is this dimension that will be the subject of the following chapter.

4   Happiness and ethics

The case for studying the ethical dimension of happiness is twofold. The first has been touched upon at the end of the previous chapter: if human beings have a free will and if happiness has to do with a person's judgments, then happiness must have a moral dimension. The second arises out of the underlying motivation of most happiness research: even though few authors explicitly say so, practically all the literature on subjective well-being is ultimately motivated by a concern for good development, and this is clearly an ethical concern. We may therefore expect that, by discussing ethics explicitly, we will come to a more comprehensive, more human, and, therefore, more adequate conception of happiness, as well as understand the appropriate role and limitations of happiness in a conception of good development.

This and the following chapter will address these issues. To begin with, the precise understanding of ethics adopted here will have to be specified. This will prepare the ground for the development of a normative conception of happiness, as well as for the discussion of the relationship between happiness and good development. I will not, however, discuss in depth the classical philosophical question of the relation between happiness and morality ("Is happiness a matter of being a virtuous person?") since this would go beyond the scope of the present study.[1]

Living well and living righteously: ethical questions require ethical answers

Most research in the social sciences still aspires toward the ideal of objective, value-free analysis. Normative research is thought to be subjective and arbitrary and, therefore, unscientific. Yet, this dualistic division between "good" and "bad" research, besides being normative itself, rests on a lack of differentiation and on a misconception of ethics. To be sure, it would be inappropriate and of little scientific interest to simply postulate and prescribe some specific values or practical measures and demand their observation. Yet, this is not what ethics is about. Rather, the business of ethics is the reflection on the ends and principles that should orientate the way we make use of our freedom.[2] Given that we have freedom and that we share it with other free human beings in a social setting, we cannot help but experience an obligation to justify our acts and decisions before ourselves (in terms of meaningfulness) and before others (in terms of justice). One major task of ethics is to raise this obligation to a higher level of consciousness, to investigate the nature of this obligation, to spell out what it means concretely, and to reflect on its implications for practical purposes and especially for situations where interests conflict (either within a person or between persons).

Ethics should not remain purely descriptive, though. Describing and comparing different ethical schools or observed moral codes may be interesting in itself, but that is not what ethics ultimately is about because a purely descriptive approach fails to deliver ethical orientation. Ethical orientation, in turn, specifies the *perspective* in which the meaningfulness and legitimacy of actions and decisions needs to be evaluated, in contrast to moral prescription, which *anticipates* this evaluation of actions and decisions. The specification of this ethical perspective cannot be neutral in the sense of being indifferent with respect to the admitted values, but its norms will refer only to the way evaluations are made, not to their content as such. Moreover, most of these norms need to be accepted as the basis of rational discourse (academic or else) anyway, such as truth-telling, sincerity, respect for discussion partners, etc. (cf. Apel 1973; Habermas 1983). In other words, adherence to these norms is not simply a volitional act in the sense of an innate or acquired taste for or against these norms that cannot be further motivated, but rather in itself a (consciously or unconsciously) rational commitment that can be validated by ethical reflection and without which any meaningful discussion about norms would be impossible.

The job of "area ethics",[3] such as business ethics or development ethics, to which the present investigation may be said to belong, is therefore not to prescribe particular kinds of behavior, derive moral codes and lists of values, or recommend specific political measures (even though any of these may be evident derivative "spin offs" of ethical critique). Rather, their dual task is the critical examination of the normative content of incumbent theory and practice, as well as the breaking down of general ethical principles into more contextually relevant principles addressing the respective discipline's specific ethical challenges.[4]

The weight of ethics comes to bear most heavily where conflicts between different individuals' interests are concerned, but its scope is wider than this and extends to conflicts of interest or principles *within* a given individual. What is more, ethics comes into play before an individual even *has* well-defined interests that can conflict. Whenever a person asks herself what she really wants to do in her life, she is (also) asking the question of what would be *good* to do in a noninstrumental sense. This is clearly an ethical question, even though it does not need to involve – at least not inherently – the interests of others.

We can thus make a major conceptual distinction within the domain of ethics between (1) the meaningful determination and mapping of a given individual's interests, and (2) the determination of legitimacy in the presence of conflicts of interest *between* individuals. These two tasks of ethics are best conceptualized as two distinct but nevertheless related dimensions of ethics. Figure 4.1 (adapted from Ulrich 2008: 107) visualizes this relationship as one between two orthogonal dimensions. The vertical dimension represents dimension (1) and is concerned with evaluative questions addressing the problem of what makes a given person's life a *good* life. It is therefore about the prudential, rather than moral, question of the contents of a good life. This dimension is the *teleological* dimension. The horizontal dimension represents dimension (2) and is concerned with moral questions addressing the problem of how to live together with other human beings without violating their moral rights. In particular, it is about the question of one's rights and duties in the face of conflicts of interest. It is therefore about the moral question of righteous action by the criterion of legitimacy. This dimension will be called the *deontological* dimension. Table 4.1 outlines the major differences between the two dimensions.

In the following, these two dimensions will be explicated somewhat further and then discussed jointly to pave the ground for the development of a normative conception of happiness. It should go without saying that this treatment must remain regrettably selective and that it may not be satisfying for the reader who is unacquainted with the ethical literature referred to. Nevertheless, it should do to describe the understanding of ethics adopted here, to clarify some key concepts, and to position the present text with respect to some key debates of the ethical literature.

Leading a (so-called) "good life"

In the social sciences, human beings are typically portrayed as rationally (in the sense of "efficiently") pursuing given preferences. Even though economics continues to attract the most massive criticism for its "*homo oeconomicus*" model of

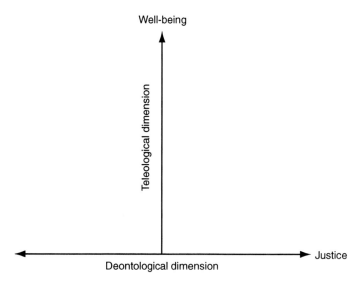

Figure 4.1 Two dimensions of ethics.

Table 4.1 Two dimensions of ethics

	Teleological dimension	*Deontological dimension*
Unit of reference	Individual person	Society
Primary virtue	Well-being	Righteousness
Currency	Interests	Rights and duties
Ethical category	Good	Legitimate
Question	What do I really want?	What shall I do? What may I do?
Locus of judgment	Volitional rationality	Public reason

human rationality as utility maximization, the other social sciences are arguably in the same boat as long as they portray human rationality in terms of *given* preferences, as most of the literature appears to do. When preferences are taken as given, the human being is reduced to a stimulus–response machine, a "bundle of preferences that happen to coexist inside a single skin" (Schwartz 2000: 81), devoid of any human individuality, simply executing deterministic behavioral programs. The very concept of the person becomes alien under such a conception (cf. Frankfurt 1971). The *homo oeconomicus* model is perhaps particularly vulgar about human motives in that it explicitly describes them as egoistic, but then egoism is an inbuilt feature of any deterministic desire satisfaction account of human motivation. More precisely, deterministic desire satisfaction accounts should be described as *solipsistic* rather than egoistic since, for want of conceivable alternatives, egoism becomes indistinguishable from altruism and therefore an unintelligible concept when preferences are given (Hirata 2001b). Solipsism, by contrast, indicates that the horizon of possible intentions is restricted to the inner life, namely the given preferences, of the individual in question.

The upshot is that the question of what a good life consists in does not arise at all under a deterministic conception of human motivation and behavior. Rather, what the good life consists in is already determined through the preferences. The only prudential challenge that might appear to remain would be to efficiently satisfy these preferences, i.e. to effectively maximize desire satisfaction ("utility maximization"), but this would then merely be an informational problem, not an evaluational one. Yet, if preferences – and this of course means *all* preferences – are really given, this means in the last analysis that even informational problems will not pose prudential challenges, since information seeking and processing behavior can again be factored down into mechanical stimulus–response behavior, as *all* behavior can. Consequently, evaluational or ethical problems could impossibly arise. Put simply, there is no role for ethics where the free will is supplanted by a deterministic account of motivation and behavior (cf. Hirata 2004).

For ethics to have any place at all, some degree of rational (in the sense of "guided by reason") autonomy of human beings, i.e. a free will, must be acknowledged. If this is so, the human being is inescapably confronted with the existential question of how he *wants* to live. Being unable to recur to a complete set of given preferences, he must make up his mind about what he *wants* to value and who or what he should like to be and to do. As the philosopher and economist Frank Knight once said:

> life is at bottom an exploration in the field of values, an attempt to discover values, rather than on the basis of knowledge of them to produce and enjoy them to the greatest possible extent. We strive to "know ourselves," to find out our real wants, more than to get what we want.
>
> (Knight 1964: 1)

The issue is not whether we start our quest for a good life in empty space, free from any restrictions, innate desires and points of reference – we certainly do not. Rather, the issue is whether we are subject to natural law-like determinacy or whether we have some scope to autonomously affirm or revise the preferential predispositions into which we are born and raised. The fact that nature and nurture, in whatever combination, endow us with a number of unchosen preferential predispositions and limited behavioral repertoires does not deny the possibility that it is ultimately the person who autonomously molds her values and preferences out of this endowment by virtue of volitional rationality, rather than the other way round (Frankl 2003: 56). "For the self is prior to the ends which are affirmed by it; even a dominant end must be chosen from among numerous possibilities" (Rawls 1999/1971: 490–1). The freedom we have in choosing our preferences transpires into every individual decision we take. It would be paradoxical to say that we can choose our preferences and from there on they determine our choices, or that we choose our meta-preferences, which then determine our first-order preferences (as in meta-preference theories). One cannot derive deterministic results from an indeterminate basis. If our preferences are indeterminate, so must be our every choice.

The free will, and indeterminism in general, is of course a challenge to science, or rather to the worldview that dominates most of science and that has been appropriately described as "the scientiphical metaphysic" by Peter Unger (1999, 2002). According to this view, anything existent, including human beings, is a result of the strictly causal interaction of purely physical forces. Indeterminacy has only relatively recently been admitted into physical theories, but then in the form of chance (random) on the level of subatomic phenomena (e.g. the phenomenon of quantum superposition) rather than in the form of a free will. While indeterminacy plays a marginal role in physics, being limited to quantum mechanics, it is still practically banned from other disciplines.

This ban on indeterminacy seems to be an almost inevitable consequence (or cause?) of the prevalent conception of rationality in the (Western) sciences. This concept requires consistency with general rules of natural law-like rigidity. The paradigmatic question driving science takes the form of "why", and that very question is biased in that it demands an "explanation" in causal terms. When asking "Why did person X do Y?", a scientist expects an answer that shows the causal links that inescapably lead to X doing Y. In other words, subjecting human behavior to scientific inquiry is practically equivalent to imputing causal determinacy. Within this conception, one cannot defend the idea of a free will because this defense can impossibly take the admitted form. To defend it, one must transcend this "scientiphical metaphysic" and adopt a more encompassing concept of rationality – one, by the way, that need not be unscientific.

If human behavior is determined by (quasi-)natural laws, and if it is intentional at all, then it will be perfectly coherent in the way it pursues the intended ends. The only model that can satisfy this condition seems to be a model of a *dominant end*, i.e. a model in which all apparent ends, except for one, are in fact means to a single dominant end. Economic theory has perfected such a model and formalized it as a model of utility maximization, but an essentially identical model must underlie all deterministic conceptions of intentional behavior. Under utility maximization, all behavior is exclusively aimed at increasing expected utility. Thomas Hobbes illustrated this idea when he explained that he gave alms to a beggar outside St. Paul's Cathedral because it pleased him to see the beggar pleased rather than for altruistic or ethical motives.[5] This position of *psychological hedonism* (cf. p. 62) is a particular case of a dominant-end conception of behavior where the dominant end is pleasure. It was famously defended by the spiritual father of utilitarianism, Jeremy Bentham, when he said that:

> Nature has placed mankind under the governance of two sovereign masters, pain and pleasure. It is for them alone to point out what we ought to do, as well as to determine what we shall do ... They govern us in all we do, in all we say, in all we think.
>
> (Bentham 1907/1789: ch. I.1)

Under psychological hedonism, "helping the beggar" would not be accepted as an intrinsic intention. Supposing deterministic decision algorithms, a proponent of psychological hedonism would always demand that the reasons for giving alms be perfectly commensurate with the reasons for using one's budget (of money, time, or else) in other ways. In particular, he would claim that a person gives alms exactly to the extent that this generates more pleasure than alternative uses of her money, since otherwise behavior would be irrational or arbitrary. In this perspective, there must be some highest-order intention, the dominant end, to which the lower-order intentions contribute to varying degrees, and it must be these contributions that determine the behavior of a person.[6]

This is not the place to rearticulate the criticism that has been raised against this conception.[7] The point to note here is that any model of human decision-making that assumes causality and intentionality must also imply perfect commensurability, perfect coherence, and a dominant end. The widely objected habit of economics to express all sorts of values, including that of a human life, in terms of money is nothing else than giving a label to the metric of commensurability. If one dislikes this practice of putting money values on human lives, one must argue against determinism of evaluation and behavior as such, rather than against the label chosen for the metric of measurement or against particular preference orderings. In doing so, however, one must be aware that one is also arguing against perfect commensurability and coherence. Trying to uphold any one of these five features – determinacy, commensurability, perfect coherence, dominant end, or monetization of values – while rejecting any other feature would be self-contradictory. The claim here is of course not that behavior is chronically incoherent or wholly incommensurable or that there is no hierarchy of ends at all. It is claimed, however, that preferences are not simply given and that therefore there is no perfect coherence and no perfect arithmetic commensurability of ends and no single dominant end.

A recurrent problem is that even philosophers' conceptions of the good life overlook these dependencies and stipulate the necessity or the existence of a dominant end and of a coherent teleological concept of the good life. Aristotle was probably the first and still the most prominent thinker to articulate such a view:

> Every art and every investigation, and likewise every practical pursuit or undertaking, seems to aim at some good: hence it has been well said that the Good is That at which all things aim.... If therefore among the ends at which our actions aim there be one which we will for its own sake, while we will the others only for the sake of this, and if we do not choose everything for the sake of something else (which would obviously result in a process *ad infinitum*, so that all desire would be futile and vain), it is clear that this one ultimate End must be the Good, and indeed the Supreme Good.
>
> (Aristotle 1934: 1094a)

Later philosophers developed similar conceptions of the good life, often supposing that it requires a conscious design or discovery of a coherent life plan, characterized by a well-ordered hierarchy of intermediate ends culminating in one dominant end. With the renaissance of teleological ethics during the last 15 years or so, such accounts have gained wider currency among contemporary philosophers. Julia Annas, for example, argues that:

> If [an agent] just has [two] aims, both of which are sought for their own sake, and no established way of giving one of them priority, he will have no rational way of choosing between them when he has to do so.... Once I start reflecting at all on the end-directedness of my single actions, there is nowhere to stop short of a single final end.
>
> (Annas 1993: 32–3)

> ...once we recognize, even if at an indeterminate level, that we have a final end, questions and problems about happiness now occupy exactly the right place. Coming up with the proper specification of our overall goal in living will make us happy.
>
> (Annas 2004: 48)

There are several problems with such an account of a good life, in addition to the implications involving the free will that have just been discussed. To begin with, there seems to be little independent evidential warrant for any systematic coherence of a person's intentions, simply because there seems to be no independent way to observe motives and intentions apart from fallible introspection. The case for coherence apparently rests on the implicit *premise* that intentions (i.e. value systems) must be coherent, rather than being a result obtained from unprejudiced analysis. If this is true, the "result" of coherence would of course be a tautology. A classical argument for coherence and for a dominant end (invoked by Annas in the preceding quote) goes that only a determinate decision algorithm with a corresponding ultimate end can save human behavior from arbitrariness. The corresponding ultimate end need not be a concrete, explicit end for which we have a single expression. It can simply be the implicitly encoded maximand of the decision algorithm that is supposed to solve all decision problems (and in economics, this maximand has come to be called *utility*). But why should rational choice be perfectly unambiguous and coherently goal-directed in the first place? What, apart from an ad hoc premise of coherence or, equivalently, determinacy, demands that rationality be restricted in this way? This premise appeals because it guarantees a neat, well-ordered system of values that can be analyzed by means of quantitative models and that generates solutions to all teleological problems. Yet, it would be problematic, to say the least, to force human rationality into a conceptual straightjacket just because we want to analyze it with the same quantitative rigor as the laws of nature. It is indeed astonishing "how easily the learned give up the evidence of their senses to preserve the coherence of the ideas of their imagination" (Smith 1980/1795: 77). That problem was already familiar to Aristotle, who found it necessary to emphasize that:

> it is the mark of an educated mind to expect that amount of exactness in each kind which the nature of the particular subject admits. It is equally unreasonable to accept merely probable conclusions from a mathematician and to demand strict demonstration from an orator.
>
> (Aristotle 1934: 1094b)

Even religious thinkers apparently have got carried away with these nice properties, such as Ignatius of Loyola (a sixteenth century saint and founder of the Jesuits), who held that serving God was the dominant end that alone conferred value to health, a long life, friendship, or any other conceivable desideratum (cf. Rawls 1999/1971: 485). Indeed, as Ahuvia (2002: 30–1) observes, it is easy to proclaim any one of a number of goods as the ultimate intention of all human striving (e.g. happiness, social recognition) and build a neat model around it, but there is no compelling reason other than culturally colored introspection or folk psychology to single out any of these goods and put it above all the others.

Apart from methodological considerations, however, there are more substantive reasons to reject the idea that the good life consists in the accomplishment of a single grand objective. When the good life is thought of in terms of intentions, there is a certain danger of conceiving intentionality in terms of a means–ends dichotomy, which then demands justification in terms of the end pursued (in the form of "in order to"). Intentionality, however, is not restricted to such an instrumental Humean understanding (cf. Schmid 2005: 52). It may also be understood in the sense of acting upon reasons rather than pursuing goals. In this understanding, actions would be motivated by the reasons one has, rather than the ends one pursues. For example, I may want to congratulate a friend on his birthday simply *out of* friendship, or cast my vote *out of* a sense of duty rather than *in order to* achieve any higher-order goal (even though, just to anticipate a natural objection, some such goal may *also* motivate me in addition to the cited reasons).[8] Such actions are of course still intentional, but rather than being motivated by desire, they are motivated by a *commitment* for which one has a reason (ibid.; see also the other contributions in the same volume). Even Aristotle, in contradiction to his stated views on the ultimate end (cf. Hardie 1965: 279), describes "the perfect form of friendship" as marked by the absence of instrumental considerations (cf. also Spaemann 2000/1989: 97).[9]

The point is that instrumental explanations reduce all possible intentions, except for the dominant end itself, to *purely* instrumental and perfectly exchangeable means serving a single end, depriving the person of her individuality and her purposes of their intrinsic value. Labeling these means "intermediate ends" would be misleading without making any difference. As long as perfect coherence is demanded, there can be only one dominant end with respect to which all other purposes are derivative. It is again John Rawls who put the problem this view raises most succinctly:

> Human good is heterogeneous because the aims of the self are heterogeneous. Although to subordinate all our aims to one end does not strictly speaking violate the principles of rational choice (not the counting principles anyway), it still strikes us as irrational, or more likely as mad. The self is disfigured and put in the service of one of its ends for the sake of the system.[10]
>
> (Rawls 1999/1971: 486)

All this does, of course, not mean that talking of "the good life" becomes meaningless. It does mean, however, that we must think of "the good life" as a formal concept rather than as a substantive end. Or in the words of Hardie (1965: 279), we must distinguish between an *inclusive end* and a *dominant end*. Whereas a dominant end is thought to be a particular, substantive good with respect to which all other possible intentions are derivative and without intrinsic worth, an inclusive end is a "secondary end" (ibid.) in the sense that it consists in the desire to achieve a plurality of irreducible primary (substantive) ends in a rational way. In this latter perspective, the relationship between one's substantive purposes and the good life is not like that between means and end, but rather like that between the parts and the whole, just as the different voices of a choir are not *needed* to *make* the music – they *constitute* the music (cf. Spaemann 2000/1989: 23). "The good life" then becomes a label for a terminological place-holder for an unfinished idea that helps us to order our thoughts and make communication more economical, and it is only in this limited sense that it may be thought of as an objective that is pursued. It must not, however, be taken to reflect a harmony of subordinate intentions that are coherently ordered to serve a single, grand dominant end. "[O]ur various and particular drives do not, of their own, integrate themselves into a life which turns out well. Human beings have to 'lead' their lives, and this has to be learned" (Spaemann 2000/1989: vii).

So does philosophy have anything at all to say about the good life, apart from the insight that it is a formal concept in this sense? One can identify basically three different positions on this question around which philosophers can be grouped. The first position would simply deny that possibility. In this view, people naturally know what is best for them, and philosophers are neither able nor entitled to give their advice on that question. This position is a corollary of psychological hedonism (cf. p. 000). When human beings are entirely "governed" (Bentham) by pain and pleasure, it is difficult to see how philosophical reflection could possibly add anything to our understanding of the good life. At most, factual information about the human psyche could help people make "better" choices in terms of maximizing the net balance of pleasure by providing knowledge about the actual sources of pain and pleasure, but the collection of such information would fall into the domain of psychology and neurology rather than into that of philosophy. Even though few philosophers seem to defend this view, most economists appear to continue to adhere to it (e.g. Edgeworth 1881; Becker 1976; Kirchgässner 2000/1991), with many alleging somewhat obscurely that questioning preferences would be equivalent to forceful interference and thus illegitimate (e.g. The Economist 2005; McMahon 2005a).

The second position would assert that philosophy can, in principle, identify a set of substantive ingredients of a good life with universal validity. The most prominent proponent of this view is probably Martha Nussbaum, who offers a list of "central human functional capabilities", which includes in its latest version (1) life, (2) bodily health, (3) bodily integrity, (4) senses, imagination, thought, (5) emotions, (6) practical reason, (7) affiliation, (8) other species, (9) play, and (10) control over one's (political and material) environment (Nussbaum 2000: 78–80, 2006: 393ff.). Nussbaum does not claim that this list is definite or the only possible one, but she does argue that philosophical reflection can and should, in principle, substantiate such a list, however debatable or tentative it may be. She explicitly builds upon the works of classical and modern philosophers, such as Aristotle and J.S. Mill, who also proposed specific contents of a good life (Nussbaum 1992, 2004), and her views are largely shared by a number of contemporary "neo-Aristotelian" philosophers (cf. the contributions in Steinfath 1998).

Between these two positions one finds a continuum of philosophers who believe, in contrast to the first position, that philosophy has something to say about the good life, but that it is not possible, against the second position, to specify substantive contents of a good life. Rather, they believe that philosophical reflection can, to a greater or lesser extent, narrow down some *formal* aspects of a good life. Martin Seel (1999/1995), in an elaborate essay on "the form of happiness", argues that, starting out from the uncontroversial premise "that it is important for any being ... that not few of his wishes become fulfilled" (ibid.: 78–9, translation J.H.), philosophical reflection can explicate certain conditions of the form of a good life. The conditions Seel proposes are formal in the sense that they do not specify *what* a person should want in her own interest, but *how* she should want whatever she wants (ibid.: 75).[11] He argues that a good life is one that is led in self-determination that is receptive with respect to the world in which the person lives (orig., "*in welt-offener Selbstbestimmung*", ibid.: 178).

John Rawls, too, gives a formal account of the human good (Rawls 1999/1971: 372ff.). He argues that, in general, "a person's good" consists "in the successful execution of a rational plan of life" (ibid.: 380). The successful execution of a rational plan of life in turn invariably requires, according to Rawls, a number of "primary goods", such as rights, liberties, opportunities, income, wealth, self-respect, health, vigor, intelligence, and imagination (ibid.: 54; cf. also Rawls 1982). Even though Rawls specifies the primary goods, his account should be considered formal since he proposes these goods as mere means to ends, which he leaves unspecified, and he does not suggest any set of rules by which to prioritize and evaluate these primary goods.

Criticizing Rawls's account for its blindness toward interpersonal differences, Amartya Sen (1983/1979) proposes yet another formal account of the good life. He argues that a good life depends (among others) on *capabilities*, the substantive freedoms to realize functionings one has reason to value (Sen 1999b: 75). Since different people value different functionings and since, in order to achieve a given functioning, they require commodities in different quantities, Sen argues, it is more informative to assess a person's freedom to achieve functionings, rather than her endowment with commodities. In contrast to Nussbaum, however, Sen does not specify any particular capabilities as ingredients of a good life because he argues that any concrete list must be historically, culturally, and personally conditional.[12] While he is not opposed to unpretentious attempts to draft tentative lists of capabilities as such, he "stand[s] up against a grand mausoleum to one fixed and final list of capabilities" (Sen 2004a: 80). He believes that, while drawing up capability lists would not be illegitimate, it could not be accomplished within the methodological confines of "pure theory" (ibid.: 78). Rather the specification of capabilities would require "general social discussion or public reasoning" (ibid.: 77).

This brief presentation of different formal accounts of the human good is by no means exhaustive, but it should suffice to provide a fair idea of the major positions on the potential of philosophy to make statements on the good life. The present investigation falls into the last group of positions. However, as my concern here is on the relationship between happiness and the good life, it will be convenient to defer the further discussion of the concrete conception of the good life adopted here to a later point where the concept of happiness will already have been discussed.

It should be noted already at this stage, though, that the good life might not be everything we care about. A person may care about many other things – his parents' health, his participation in political elections, the bequest he leaves for his children, etc. – that cannot be subsumed under his "good life" (or where doing so would overstretch that concept). We therefore should not, from the outset, limit the question of happiness to a question of the good life, and neither should we believe that the good life could be thought of as a matter of happiness alone.

Whatever the precise conception of the good life, the simple fact that human beings live together in communities and societies raises the problem of the vulnerability in terms of the good life. However, in contrast to the vulnerability that arises from natural hazards, such as natural calamities or disease, the vulnerability that arises from within a society does not, or does not only, depend on chance and nature, but on the will of other human beings. In other words, it depends on the way other human beings make use of their freedom. This is the essence of the deontological problem of morality (the horizontal dimension in Figure 4.1) to which we shall now turn.

The symmetry of human dignity

One can talk of a *problem of morality* on at least three different analytical levels. In a rather trivial sense, morality is a problem because, as we will see presently, its lack means unjustified and unnecessary harm (the problem of harm). Second, morality is a problem in the sense that it poses a number of conceptual and theoretical questions that are the object of continuous discord despite – or perhaps because of – millennia of sophisticated discussion (the specification problem). In a third sense, morality is a problem because, while being by definition desirable, its demands do usually not perfectly harmonize with people's preferential dispositions, and people may more or less often betray their own moral convictions as they succumb to their personal preferences (the execution problem).

The first problem is not of much relevance in this context as we are concerned with conceptual issues rather than the specific real-world problems to which the concepts under scrutiny pertain. While real-world problems may aid ethical reflection by *illustrating* conceptual issues, the *practical* problems they pose – in particular their evaluation, the ascription of specific rights, duties, and responsibilities, the recommendation of change or solutions – are basically *political* problems, downstream the division of labor between ethics and politics. To do any of this, one already needs to have a conception of morality that is grounded in ethical reflection. The conclusive evaluation of any specific real-world setting will then require the actual exercise of value judgments, going beyond the domain of ethics as a scientific discipline (cf. p. 84).

The specification problem of morality, by contrast, is at the heart of ethics, and it will occupy us for some while before turning to the execution problem. A major characteristic of the specification problem is that, while everybody seems to intuitively understand what morality is basically about (namely about what one ought to do, or not to do, for non-strategic reasons, cf. Ulrich 2008: 13), there is wide disagreement with respect to the nature of the obligation implied by this "ought". It is contentious whether there is any absolute obligation (categorical imperative) or only a conditional one (conditional imperative); whether there are any universal (cross-culturally valid) moral principles or only culturally contingent ones; and whether morality should be defined in terms of an agent's maxims or in terms of her acts' (foreseeable) consequences, to mention just a few debated issues.

Let us begin by recalling the simple fact that people with competing conceptions of a good life live together in communities and societies where each person's action (or inaction) has the potential to be conducive or detrimental to others' lives. In such a world, we simply cannot evade the question of how the effects of our actions on other people's lives should influence our behavior. Here, we basically have the choice between two possible modes of seeing other human beings: the communicative (or ethical) and the strategic mode, to stick with Habermas's (1981) terminology (cf. Ulrich 2008: 216). In the communicative mode, other human beings are seen as equally dignified subjects whose moral rights (i.e. needs and interests that can be justified; their legitimate claims) deserve to be respected for no other reason than the subject status of their bearer. Respecting others' moral rights in turn means being, in principle, prepared to let good reasons influence one's decisions, even if this does not further one's interest. The communicative mode forbids in particular regarding another person merely as a means and not also as an end (Kant 1977/1785: 61).

The alternative to the communicative mode would be the *strategic* mode. In this mode, other human beings are seen as mere objects without any moral rights. A strategically rational actor would take other persons' needs and interests into account only to the extent that they are strategically (i.e. instrumentally) relevant to his own interests. When the interests of strategic actors conflict, these conflicts of interests will be settled by the principle of "might is right", rather than by good reasons (Ulrich 2008: 216).

While this distinction may be criticized as a foundation of morality for being very formal and therefore imprecise and permissive with respect to the concrete behavioral implications that follow from it, it seems to be the only way to describe a *rational* moral point of view, i.e. a conception of morality that is grounded in reason, rather than being derived from a particular moral authority or tradition. Moreover, being formal does not mean being arbitrary or empty with respect to outcomes. Restricting the form in which actions must be justified is quite a substantive requirement. Demanding more than this, such as specific commandments or prohibitions, would be more than may be expected from a rational conception of morality. In a way, it would actually be much *less* since such a value-list conception of morality would fail to describe general maxims that alone can provide orientation in cases where competing values conflict or where the postulated values themselves are being questioned.

Yet, the question remains, "Why should one adhere to the communicative mode of interacting with others?", or simply, "Why should I commit myself to morality?", or simpler yet, "Why should I care about others?" There are again two different ways in which such a question can be asked. If it is asked, "What is *my advantage* if I commit myself to morality?", the question itself positions the asking person outside the moral playing field, making it impossible from the outset to argue in favor of the moral point of view. By positing "my advantage" as the ultimate and exclusive point of reference, the person is ruling out listening to reasons that do not further his private advantage. It is this readiness to be receptive to good reasons, however, that is a prerequisite of morality. The question must therefore be, "Why *should I want* to commit myself to morality?" since this form of the question allows the answer to be put in terms of arguments that address the asking person's reason rather than his private advantage. "One cannot demand to hear reasons why one should listen to reasons" (Spaemann 2000/1989: viii) because a person who sincerely enters a rational discourse is already, by definition, listening to reasons. Conversely, someone who does not listen to reasons in the first place is out of reach of any rational discourse (cf. also Tugendhat 1995: 85, 89; Ulrich 2008: 15–16).

The question of why I *should want* to commit myself to morality, therefore, implies that the asking person is in principle prepared to listen to good reasons, i.e. to arguments that convince by their intersubjective reasonability rather than by addressing private advantage. Now, given that the person is prepared to listen to good reasons, it is possible to show that he cannot deny his duty to respect all other human beings in the sense described above without becoming insincere and inconsistent.[13] First of all, any sincere and sane person will recognize that he has an interest in a good life (he has a concept of a good life, and he wants his life to succeed in terms of this plan) and that this good life is, in principle, vulnerable to the actions of other people. Second, he will acknowledge that he has the ability to recognize this same vulnerability (and the corresponding interest in a good life) in other human beings. He is able to "put himself in the shoes" of other persons and to empathize with their interests. As Adam Smith already observed:

> By the imagination we place ourselves in his [our suffering brother's] situation, we conceive ourselves enduring all the same torments, we enter as it were into his body, and become in some measure the same person with him, and thence form some idea of his sensations [...].
>
> (Smith 1976/1759: 9)

This ability to take the role of another person (i.e. empathy) means that I understand that my vulnerability is shared symmetrically by all other human beings, and that my need for protection of my human dignity is felt equally by all others. I can therefore not deny the dignity of any one person without denying my own dignity and becoming cynical, i.e. without losing my integrity as a person (Ulrich 2008: 35, 143–4). At the same time, empathy allows me to understand that the specific desires and vulnerabilities are not identical for each person, just as my own desires and vulnerabilities can change over time. Since I can impossibly know every person that may be affected by my actions, while at the same time I know that all of them share the same human dignity that I claim for myself, I understand that I must respect not only (but also) specific persons and their respective conceptions of a good life, but also the *freedom* of all human beings to pursue any legitimate conception of a good life (cf. the discussion of Sen's capability approach, p. 78). The admitted scope of a *legitimate* conception of a good life is already implied by the symmetric reciprocity of this respect: I must respect all those conceptions of a good life that do not disrespect other respectful conceptions of a good life. In other words, my claims must be universalizable in the sense that they do not violate equally universalizable claims of others so that they can be conceded to every other person at the same time. In keeping with a solid body of ethical literature, I shall call this principle of morality the *universalization principle* (e.g. Habermas 1983: 127; Ulrich 2008: 36).

We thus have a conception of legitimacy that is not contingent on any particular traditional authority (religious or otherwise) but independently substantiated. It is based on, but not reducible to, the two anthropological constants of an interest in a good life and the ability to empathize. Yet, there are basically three different philosophical views on what exactly a theory of morality needs to, and can, show. Kant as the major proponent of the first view thought it necessary, and possible, to show that moral obligations are what he called a "categorical imperative": we *must* conform to them, full stop. He believed that one can deduce such a categorical imperative from pure reason alone so that it would be true independently of experience. The second view holds that morality is a matter of factual convictions within a given community. Since it can be observed that different communities have different norms, and since there would be no way to decide which community's norms should be used to evaluate these differences, there would be no independent way of establishing the truth of norms. Their validity would therefore be relative with respect to a specific social context. What is good depends on what the community has established as good. The third view is less radical than either of the first two. In keeping with the conception of morality outlined above, it holds that one can rationally demonstrate the universal validity of a key principle of morality, but that there is no way to demonstrate that we *must* be rational and obey this principle in an *a priori* sense. What can be shown is that a person who engages in moral discourses at all must abide by the specific principle of morality outlined above. He could not get away by simply referring to local norms (even though local norms may be *part* of a justification, which in turn needs to satisfy the universalization principle). Yet, when it is said that such a person must abide by the principle of morality, this "must" is a conditional "must" in the sense that the person would otherwise commit an inconsistency. It would not be possible to convince a person who never engaged in moral discourse that he must do so in the same way as, say, he could be convinced that he has to agree that $1 + 1 = 2$ (cf. Tugendhat 1995: 88, 92).

However, it is not easy to live a life without, from time to time, engaging in moral discourse, and it is not necessarily an attractive option. Whenever a person argues in terms of good and bad, judges other people, expresses indignation, or in any other way expresses the wish that people should use their freedom in certain ways and not in others, she implicitly acknowledges the universalization principle, as discourse ethics has shown (cf. Apel 1973; Habermas 1983). Its validity can simply not be argumentatively denied without invoking this very principle, thus leading to a performative contradiction (Habermas 1983: 140). Still, the person can acknowledge to be inconsistent and then say that she does not care about being inconsistent. Again, it would not be possible to show that she *must* be consistent in any absolute sense, but her answer would strike us as nonsensical and deeply inhuman and it would place her outside the moral playing field. A person who does not care about being consistent with her (implicitly) stated convictions cannot really have these convictions in the first place and would lack identity as a key characteristic of a person.

A person who never engages in any moral discourse and who does not want to be member of the moral community, on the other hand, would not be inconsistent, and the only way one could try to make him opt back into the moral community is by showing why he might *want* to recognize it. The person must therefore *want* to be good before she can understand what it means that she *should* act in accordance with the universalization principle. This third view therefore proposes a specific duality between those (very rare) persons who do not participate in moral discourse at all and for whom there can be no moral imperative, and those who want to be member of the moral community and for whom the universalization principle can be shown to follow from this attitude. In this view, people decide freely whether to be in the game of morality or out of it, but once in the game they cannot cherry-pick the rules as they prefer as this would again be inconsistent with the universalization principle.

Recognizing that one should act in accordance with certain norms, however, does not guarantee that one will do always do so. This leads us to the last of the three problems considered here, the execution problem. In a nutshell, it consists in the competition between the intent to be a good person and other motives and drives, in particular with deeply ingrained preferential dispositions (cf. the analogous concept of "affective disposition" on p. 24). It is once again due to our free will that this problem exists at all. If our behavior was determined, the influences on our behavior would result in one single possible course of action and it would be meaningless to say that a person could be acting differently than she is acting. The existence of a free will forces a person to make up her mind in situations where her motives conflict. When I know I should, say, reject a bribe but end up accepting it because I get carried away by the prospect of living a life in material luxury, then the problem is not that I do not recognize the validity of the universalization principle, nor the lack of the intent to be a good person, but the weakness to execute what I recognized as being right in the presence of competing motives that address my personal advantage.

One may think that the execution problem may sometimes in fact be a case of moral demands being too heroic (or "unrealistic") for ordinary earthlings to meet them. Yet, this interpretation would reflect a misunderstanding of what morality demands. When it is said that a demand is too heroic, this means that it cannot be justified, i.e. there are reasons that justify why one may *legitimately* fail to fulfill it. As an unjustifiable demand, however, it can, by definition, not be a moral demand. If I accept a bribe because that is the only way for me to get the money for a life-saving medicine for my child, then this may be a universalizable justification to break a rule that should *not usually* be broken, just as a situation of self-defense may legitimize homicide. Yet, in contrast to specific norms for which one can always construct a scenario in which one may break them, legitimacy represents the highest-order idea of morality that has to be referred to when justifying specific norms (or their violation) and its violation can therefore not itself be justified. It would thus be wrong and self-contradictory to say that I am justified to override a moral demand. Either what I do is justified and therefore moral (i.e. legitimate), or it is not. The idea of morality must already take into account that the sacrifice that sometimes needs to be made when honoring moral commitments must be commensurate with the reasons that can be advanced for that commitment (cf. Ulrich 2008: 141).

This brief account of the deontological (horizontal) dimension of ethics shall suffice to outline the scope and relevance of this particular dimension. In fact, much of the philosophical – and even more of the non-philosophical – literature refers to this dimension alone when talking of ethics, omitting the teleological (vertical) dimension. As the following section shall make clear, the deontological dimension of ethics (i.e. morality) cannot be thought independently of its teleological dimension and is intricately intertwined with it.

Legitimacy, public reason, and the indeterminacy of ethical judgments

The basic relationship between the teleological and the deontological dimension of ethics has already been touched upon above (p. 80), but it needs some further refinement in order to avoid misunderstandings and to prepare the ground for the elaboration of a normative conception of happiness. It has been said that morality (i.e. the deontological dimension of ethics) is about respecting other people's freedom to a good life. Yet, this relationship must not be misunderstood as a *functional* dependency: it does not mean that morality is reducible to the mutual enhancement of a good life in the sense of being instrumental to a higher-order purpose. Rather, the role of a good life is *constitutive* for an independent role of morality: we understand the principle of morality (if we understand it) *because* there is something as a good life, but not (or rather, not only) *in order to* enhance the good life. Without something as a good life, the notion of morality would simply lose its significance, but this does not mean that morality is *nothing but* the enhancement of a good life. Once we understand this, the idea of morality takes on a significance of its own: we respect the other for the sake of respecting him, i.e. because of his dignity, not in order to realize an ulterior purpose. An example where the difference between these two perspectives, functional and constitutive, is particularly apparent is the case of a promise given to a dying person. After her death, there is obviously nothing I could do that would enhance or compromise her life, but I could still violate her dignity (i.e. instrumentalize her) by opportunistically breaking my promise. If I keep such a promise, then I will do so *out of* respect for the deceased person and her conception of the good life, and not *in order to* further that person's good life, i.e. out of commitment, rather than in order to achieve a substantive end.

A purely functional conception of morality can in particular lead to a utilitarian conception of ethics with all its problems,[14] the gravest perhaps being that it puts human beings in the service of a greater good (to wit, social welfare), substituting the derivative value of an individual's instrumental contribution to world utility for the intrinsic dignity of the individual. As Adam Smith already remarked:

> The concern which we take in the fortune and happiness of individuals does not, in common cases, arise from that which we take in the fortune and happiness of society. [...] our regard for the individuals [does not] arise from our regard for the multitude [...]. [Rather] our regard for the multitude is compounded and made up of the particular regards which we feel for the different individuals of which it is composed ... when a single man is injured, or destroyed, we demand the punishment of the wrong that has been done to him, not so much from a concern for the general interest of society, as from a concern for that very individual who has been injured.
>
> (Smith 1976/1759: 89–90)

Thus, the deontological dimension cannot be reduced to the teleological dimension. Whether people within a society live *good* lives and whether they are leading their lives *in a legitimate way*, i.e. in accordance with the demands of morality, are two categorically distinct questions. The first is a question of the evaluation of goods, the second is a question of the justifiability (i.e. universalizability) of actions where the consequential effects on the lives of others (and of myself) play an important but not exclusive role.

Similarly, the teleological dimension cannot be reduced to the deontological dimension. The good life is not simply the virtuous life, as, for example, Plato has Socrates argue on several occasions (Plato 1998: 507c; cf. also Seel 1999/1995: 18). Such a view would once more force a heterogeneous reality into a conceptual straightjacket, imposing a harmonious worldview where there is only limited harmony to be found. Of course it would be possible to say that the perfectly virtuous life is "good" in the sense of being commendable (even though, depending on the meaning of "virtuous", even this view might be criticized). However, a "good" life in the sense of being a life that a person has reason to like will not naturally coincide with a perfectly virtuous life.

On the other hand, saying that a good life will usually not be a *perfectly* virtuous life does not mean that morality is *systematically* antagonistic toward the good life. Often, moral commitments may produce manifest personal advantages, such as a good reputation, or they may correspond to rather natural preferential dispositions, such as a mother's care for her child, and there is no reason why the presence of such advantages would make behavior less moral. In other words, morality does not necessarily involve sacrifice, as Kant's account of morality is sometimes said to imply. It may be especially heroic to honor moral commitments at a high cost to one's self-interest, but this does of course not imply that the presence of a benefit spoils the nobility of moral behavior. Indeed, a person who internalizes a particular norm (say, collecting one's garbage after a picnic) to such a degree that he feels good about observing it, and suffers from a bad conscience if he fails to do so, should arguably deserve more rather than less praise than someone who grudgingly obeys it as a self-imposed duty. Moreover, as far as friendship is concerned, we even *want* our friends to experience our presence as something enjoyable and to be friends *also* for reasons of self-interest (Spaemann 2000/1989: 102), even though at the same time we want them to care about more than their personal payoff and to be faithful to our friendship also when, occasionally, it comes at a cost to them.

Morality, in short, is a matter of respecting others' dignity rather than of being selfless. Whether one enjoys or detests doing what morality demands is of little relevance. It is also of little relevance whether moral considerations or self-interest is the motivating force of behavior as long as other people are not instrumentalized in the process, i.e. as long as one is sincerely committed to not violating anyone's moral rights.

Only in a very specific, constitutive sense can one consistently speak of a self-interested origin of morality (Seel 1999/1995: 150ff.). In this line of reasoning, even the pre-moral person would recognize that a commitment to morality adds unique value to one's life, in particular the ability to experience mutual friendship and, in general, communicative interaction as such. If a person considers this benefit to outweigh the associated costs, she may opt for morality out of strategic reasons. Once opted into morality, however, her perspective changes from the strategic to the communicative mode, and she will commit herself to morality for intrinsic rather than instrumental reasons. In hindsight, she will find the strategic motivation of her decision for morality contemptible. Again, this scenario is not meant to describe a real process but rather a way of reasoning by which one may argue that morality has (also) a constitutive origin in self-interest.

So far, the criterion of legitimacy has remained largely unspecified. "Not violating anybody's moral rights", "respecting other people's dignity", etc. are admittedly imprecise formulations of a principle of morality. Indeed, proponents of competing conceptions criticize this ambiguity and claim that a conception of morality must provide a more concrete criterion of righteousness. Utilitarianism, for example, claims that morality consists in maximizing (sum-total or average) utility, and even though utility cannot be precisely quantified, this criterion would provide reasonably specific guidance toward optimal decisions based on the best estimate of the unknown utility values.

One problem of such a view follows directly from what has been said above about the good life and the impossibility of utility maximization even within a person. If it is true that, for want of *given* preferences, the individual just cannot maximize his own utility, then, by logical extension, one cannot talk of maximizing the sum of different individuals' utilities. Furthermore, there is also no independent warrant for stipulating such a neat, coherent principle of morality. Again, the well-behaved moral system of utilitarianism appears to rest on the *premise* that the principles of morality must be determinate, coherent, and precise, just as the laws of nature. By believing, figuratively speaking, "that there is a book in heaven that contains the answers to all moral challenges" (Tugendhat 1995: 332, transl. J.H.), utilitarianism creates a seemingly scientific substitute for the lost moral authority of religion (ibid.).

Instead of imputing to morality specific properties that we would like to see because they allow us to deploy our convenient analytical tools, we should restrict ourselves to what we can independently substantiate. As argued above (p. 82), this is the universalization principle in all its abstractness and ambiguity. One may deplore its lack of precision, but then there is no alternative. "Enriching" ethics with additional arbitrary rules to improve its precision would sacrifice its standing as a universally defensible explication of the moral point of view – clearly too high a price to pay. The imprecision of the universalization principle is therefore no embarrassment, but a reflection of the inescapable indeterminacy of morality (cf. Apel 1973: 435; Sen 1995: 48–9; Ulrich 2008: 85).

The ambition of this conception of ethics is therefore different from that of precise conceptions. It attempts to specify the *ethical point of view* from which evaluational and moral problems can be judged, but it does not specify, as utilitarianism does, how exactly such judgments are to be made. It provides *orientating* for how to deal with ethical problems, but no instrumental knowledge for how to solve them (Mittelstrass 1982).

When it comes to practically dealing with ethical problems – i.e. to make judgments and take decisions – there is no other alternative than to make "public use of one's reason" (Kant 1977/1784), i.e. justify one's interest before a critical public and conscientiously heed the reasons that are then brought forward by any of the (potentially) affected individuals. The resulting judgment will still be contestable, but, if it is the result of conscientious deliberation, it will not be immoral. For the larger context of social institutions and arrangements, this principle implies a form of *deliberative democracy*, as will be discussed later on (ch. 6). For the time being, the point to bear in mind is that the role of ethics is to provide *orientation* for judgments that ultimately remain the contestable exercise of practical reason.

A normative conception of happiness

So far we have been talking of happiness without providing a detailed account of that concept in the hope that the ordinary meaning of that term in everyday language would be sufficiently unambiguous to make the discussion intelligible. Indeed, as will be argued presently, the everyday understanding of happiness goes a long way in establishing some firm ground for a refined conception of happiness.

It is often said that happiness is relative, that it is something different for each person, and that it is "subjective". Such claims do hint at some important limitations with respect to the extent to which happiness can be specified, but they would be misconceived if they were to imply that one cannot make any universally valid statements about happiness. Of course happiness is relative in the sense that different individuals experience different degrees of happiness under given life circumstances (or require different "inputs" to obtain the same degree of happiness; cf. p. 15). However, it does not follow from this that the thing these different people call happiness is also different.

The reason why we can be assured that the understanding of happiness across people of the same language community will converge is the non-arbitrariness of language. Language allows us to communicate effectively (including about emotions) precisely because the meaning of words is largely fixed within a language community. We first pick up their meaning by hearing them used in social interaction or familiar verbal contexts, thus learning how to use them to convey the intended meaning (Wierzbicka 1999: 9). A dictionary makes use of precisely this embeddedness of each word in a network of assertions to explicate it (cf. p. 000). Ultimately, its role is to *reflect* a language community's use of words, not to *prescribe* it. That is, we do not understand the meaning of happiness because some dictionary or scientist has defined it for our language community, but because we have understood, through social interaction and verbal accounts, the common idea people around us intend to transmit when using that word (and sometimes we refer to a dictionary to reassure us of that use).

There is still a difference, though, between, on the one hand, having an intuitive understanding of a concept and, on the other hand, being aware of it, understanding its implications, its relationship to other concepts, and its limitations. It is therefore not superfluous to explicate commonly understood concepts, especially when they are as complex as happiness. Moreover, to the degree that the concept at hand is ambiguous, its precise interpretation needs to be specified. After all, the fact that there is one common idea associated with each word does not mean that there cannot be various mutually exclusive interpretations beyond that common core. This is also why a dictionary offers various glosses for most entries ("1. ... 2. ..."). Since each of these interpretations may be in itself coherent, the question is not, as Haybron (2000: 216) points out, which one is "correct", but rather which one is relevant and meaningful for the specific purpose at hand (ibid.: 217). Relevance must of course not override the common understanding of a concept. If a term is arbitrarily tailored to one's needs without conserving its commonly shared core, its resulting use will be unintelligible at best and misleading at worst. As long as one's specification respects the commonly shared core of a concept, however, the selection of an interpretation by the criterion of relevance may be expected to contribute additional insights.

What does relevance require in the present context? As we are concerned with happiness as a policy objective, and since we are taking an ethical perspective, the concept of happiness we should be looking for can be described as *happiness that matters*. More specifically, the type of happiness that interests us should matter to the goodness of people's lives, to their well-being. This means, for example, that quantitative precision should not be sought when it comes at the expense of normative relevance. As usual, we should prefer "to be vaguely right than exactly wrong" (Read 2005/1901: 320).[15] On the other hand, however, we should not seek a conception of happiness that is identical with the notion of a good life or well-being because that would add nothing to our vocabulary. Moreover, such a definition would most likely be at odds with the commonly shared understanding of the term, besides leading to even more formidable philosophical and conceptual difficulties as pointed out above (p. 70).

An additional issue is the problem of languages and culture. As indicated above (p. 19), we must not expect that any two language communities each have a word for exactly the same concept. The dictionary glosses given for happiness will therefore not refer to exactly the same concept. In fact, different languages might express the same experience by means of entirely different grammatical constructions. For example, in a situation in which an American says "I am happy", a speaker of German might prefer to use an active verbal construction *("ich freue mich"*, grammatically corresponding roughly to "I rejoice"), whereas a speaker of Spanish or Portuguese must choose between two different translations of the copula *to be* (conveying either a long-term characteristic – "I am a happy person" – or a transient state – "I am feeling happy"). Moreover, it is important to keep in mind that different functional forms of the same stem, such as *happiness* and *happy*, are often not equivalent in their use (cf. p. 19).

What all this means is that there will hardly be any two words in two languages (such as "happiness" and *"Glück"*) whose domains of use are exactly the same. It has already been pointed out, however, that any given explication must usually be selective and cannot cover the entire domain of a word without becoming inconsistent. From this, it follows that a particular explication of happiness might happen to capture exactly that part of its overall domain that overlaps with the domains of concepts from other languages.

To give an example, consider the English-language term "tube". Its domain differs between British, American, and Australian language sub-communities. Both the (American) Merriam-Webster Online Dictionary and the Cambridge Advanced Learner's Dictionary offer five glosses for their respective territory. In the UK, but not in the US, the (capitalized) word "Tube" may refer to the subway of London; in the US, but not the UK, a tube may be a piece of clothing; and in Australia (according to the Cambridge Dictionary), a tube may be a can or bottle of beer. Clearly, the domains of "tube" differ across language communities. However, if a person were to refer to squeezable toothpaste containers, she could rely on a definition of "tube" that is shared by all three language communities, despite the different domains of that word.

As concerns happiness, it might thus very well be possible to come up with a conception that would be valid across a large number of language communities, but to establish this would require extensive linguistic research. Since this would clearly lie beyond the scope of the present study, no claim will be made here to universal validity of the terminological distinctions. All that is claimed is that the proposed conception is meaningful in English and relevant to the purpose at hand, and the reader may privately evaluate the hypothesis that the presented concepts apply equally to her own language community.

Happiness between psychology and ethics

Happiness clearly involves a subjective perspective. To know whether a given person is happy, we must know something about her subjective experience, be it through explicit verbal testimony or through gestures, facial expressions, etc. that convey information about her subjective state. On the other hand, happiness is not about subjective experience alone, as will be demonstrated presently. Put in psychological terms, happiness is neither about stimuli alone, nor about the corresponding experience alone, but about the interaction and correspondence between stimulus and experience. What is more, however, happiness goes beyond purely psychological categories, involving an ethical dimension as well.

When analyzing complex concepts, there is always a strong temptation to make an attempt at a clear definition that expresses the essence of the concept at hand. Such a definition typically takes the form of "concept x is a case of y with the special properties $a, b, c \ldots$" (e.g. "a dream is an imagined experience occurring during sleep"). Such a definition effectively narrows the concept in question down to a single higher-order category (y) and by implication excludes the possibility of concept x also, occasionally, being an instance of another category than y. A definition of this form is, of course, not necessarily wrong. Rather, the danger consists in starting out on the premise that one's concept be amenable to such a definition, becoming blind to the possibility that one's concept is in fact heterogeneous. In other words, one might wrongly believe that the meaning of the concept at hand falls entirely into the domain of a single higher-order concept provided by the respective language's lexicon. We will thus have to consider the possibility that happiness is not a homogeneous concept in this sense but a heterogeneous one.

Our analysis of the different aspects of happiness will proceed as follows. I will make a first-level distinction between subjective and objective aspects of happiness (I will say more on these terms presently). Within the subjective aspects, a further distinction will be made between psychological and ethical aspects. What can be said at this point already is that happiness involves all three (sub-)aspects, i.e. psychological and ethical subjective aspects, as well as objective ones. In other words, all three categories matter to happiness.

That happiness involves subjective aspects is probably too obvious to merit an elaborate justification. What still deserves some analytical effort, though, is an explication of the precise role of the subjective dimension of happiness, as well as the concept of "subjective" itself. In the social sciences, subjectivity is typically used with pejorative undertones, imputing arbitrariness and meaninglessness. As has been argued above (p. 13), however, one has to distinguish between subjectivity *in the data* (i.e. data reflecting subjective judgments) and subjectivity *in the interpretation* of data (i.e. subjectivity on the side of the researcher). Whereas the latter is potentially problematic, the former is just a particular type of data, namely those that have been solicited by asking people for their subjective evaluation of something. Now, someone's subjective evaluation, in turn, will not be arbitrary or meaningless. Taking the case at hand of asking people how happy they are, their subjective evaluation will reflect, among others, a judgment that is based on specific reasons. When it is said that the evaluation is subjective, it is not implied, therefore, that the person will give a random answer or that her answer will be determined by some momentary mood alone. Rather, subjectivity means that only the respective person is competent to ascertain her degree of happiness, not only because outsiders lack information, but also because happiness is a matter of sovereign judgments that, by definition, cannot be entirely objectified. For example, whether I find the winning of a gold medal by a particular athlete uplifting or depressing is entirely a question of my personal judgment.

We can now make the sub-distinction between psychological subjective aspects and ethical subjective aspects of happiness. The psychological aspect of happiness refers to the fact that happiness requires positive affect. A person who describes herself as happy must simply feel good. Of course, a person's momentary feelings can be complex and ambiguous. One can experience negative and positive affect simultaneously, for example, when a person learns that she got the desired job and at the same time is feeling the pain of a bee sting. The most convenient manner to "solve" the question of happiness in such ambiguous situations would probably be the Benthamite approach, to say that a person is happy if the balance of pleasure and pain is positive (cf. the quote of Bentham on p. 73). Yet, such a "solution" would not do justice to the complexity of happiness, and it would reduce happiness to a purely psychological phenomenon. Instead, one should look for a further refinement of the idea of happiness in the domain of ethics. For the time being, it should be kept in mind that happiness also requires some positive affect, whether or not negative effect is also present.

The ethical aspect of happiness can be further subdivided into an evaluational (teleological) aspect and a moral (deontological) aspect. The evaluational aspect directly connects with the psychological dimension of happiness. Describing happiness as a matter of positive affect raises the question of what brings positive affect about. Within a purely psychological approach, the causes for positive affect would probably be located within the domain of human nature, including innate needs, acquired tastes and habits, subconscious desires, etc. Yet, while all of these may be relevant, and occasionally sufficient, to explain why a person does or does not experience positive affect, the psychological perspective alone cannot do justice to the complexity of positive (or negative) feelings because of their dependence on ethical evaluations in the light of a conception of the good (cf. Haybron 2000: 209). Apart from rare instances of immediate, pre-reflective pleasure (as when stilling one's thirst or taking drugs), positive affect is mediated by the cognitive evaluation of something that matters to me. A situation or an event is not in itself positive or negative for a person – it is the person who evaluates it as such. To make sense of the idea of "enjoy" or "benefit" at all, one must already have some idea of what one really wants, i.e. one must have a conception of the good life. As in the example of a particular athlete winning a gold medal, the evaluation of something by a person always occurs against the backdrop of a teleological conception of the good.

The way such an evaluation is typically made has already been described above (p. 52) in the context of the frame-of-reference effect. A person will judge her experience against what she observes happens to be normal in comparable situations within her society, against what she believes she is entitled to, and against likely alternative outcomes. The outcome of this judgment cannot be predicted because the person is ultimately free to give different weight to the different aspects or even to defy the suggested evaluation heuristic altogether (such as a happy ascetic monk). The second consideration, what a person believes she is entitled to, is particularly complex and interlinks with the moral aspect of happiness that will be discussed shortly.

Not every positive evaluation will manifest itself in positive affect, however. A great many things that I will evaluate positively will not make me feel distinctively positive. For example, when I learn that the central bank maintained the interest rate at a level I endorse, I will approve of that decision, but it would appear strange if I experienced positive affect as a consequence. In order to experience positive affect and, therefore, happiness, one must not only desire something and approve of it, but also, as Harry Frankfurt (1999: 157) suggests, care about it. In addition to considering something valuable with regard to one's conception of the good, a person must also be "*committed* to his desire for it" (ibid.: 161) rather than being "prepared to give the desire up" (ibid.). This of course implies that the fulfillment of just any desire a person happens to have does not necessarily lead to happiness. Only if a person also cares about the object of her desire does its fulfillment make her feel happy (and this is most certainly not the case with the central bank's interest rate). This aspect will be discussed more fully in the following section (p. 96).

The moral (deontological) aspect of happiness refers to the fact that, in order to experience happiness, a person must also approve of the thing or the situation that makes her feel happy. Put simply, she must find it good that she feels good. This may sound trivial or even tautological at first, but it clearly is not. For example, a religious vegetarian who enjoys a meal he believes is vegetarian will suddenly feel unhappy upon hearing that his meal in fact contains meat. What has changed in this scenario is not the sensory perception or any subtle psychological influence, but the moral judgment of the person. A person who disapproves of the reasons or the circumstances for her feeling good will not feel happy. Even if a person truly likes something, she will not feel happy about it if she believes that others had to pay too high a price for her benefit, or that she is violating an ethical principle she cares about. Recalling what has been said above about normative counterfactuals, and in particular about the assessment of reality against what a person believes she is entitled to, we can now say that a person will fail to be happy not only when she gets *less* than she feels she is entitled to, but possibly also when she gets *more* than she feels she is entitled to.

Saying that happiness requires a person to approve of the reasons for her happiness does not mean, however, that only noble moral considerations qualify as reasons for happiness. Rather, it means that, overall, the person does not find it wrong to feel happy about whatever makes her feel positive. The reason for her happiness may be quite a self-centered motive (e.g. a new car), but as long as she does not disapprove of that motive and the circumstances of her happiness, we should call her happy.

In fact, the reason for a person's happiness may even be malicious and illegitimate. The question is whether the person approves of her happiness, not whether it is legitimate in an absolute sense of being justifiable from an impartial point of view. It just means that the respective person does not see sufficient reason to disapprove of it. This of course implies that we may have to call a person happy even if her happiness derives from things most would find despicable (e.g. the car thief's happiness for his newly stolen car). Yet, restricting happiness to intersubjectively legitimate (rather than subjectively approved) reasons for happiness would burden the concept of happiness with too much ethical substance. It may be tempting to define happiness as "legitimate pleasure", but that would be inconsistent with the way this word is commonly used. Not only would such a definition raise the problem of having to specify what is legitimate (i.e. one could not call a person happy before one has decided about her happiness's legitimacy), it would also fail to do justice to the subjective dimension that is inherent to the idea of happiness. Nevertheless, as we will see shortly, a somewhat less radical ethical condition indeed appears to characterize our understanding of happiness.

Previously, it has been said that for a person to approve of her happiness, she must not believe that she is violating an ethical principle. Put this way, this condition is somewhat too rigid, however. It would be quite a radical position to say that a person cannot feel happy as soon as she slightly violates her ethical principles. Instead, the condition of not violating an ethical principle should be a matter of commensurability in the sense that a minor violation of one's ethical principles may not spoil one's experience of happiness if a significant benefit is at stake. For example, if a person finds a concert ticket for her favorite singer on the sidewalk, she may keep it and feel happy about it, even though she believes what she is doing is wrong and that she has a moral obligation to return the ticket to its legitimate owner. This would not be a case of her benefit *justifying* the violation of a norm. If she believed that the particular situation justifies an exception to the norm of returning lost items, she would in fact feel morally entitled to keep the ticket and would not be breaching an ethical principle in the first place. What is meant here is that, even though the person does not believe her conduct can be justified, she does not consider her violation of an ethical principle to be so grave that it would end up spoiling her happiness. This case is meant to be included by the requirement that a person approves of her happiness: the person does not need to consider her happiness to be perfectly justified, but she must also not feel that her happiness involves a violation of ethical principles that is out of measure with her benefit. This is entirely analogous to the relationship between virtue and the good life outlined above (p. 85), where it has been argued that a good life will typically not be a perfectly virtuous one. Put more succinctly, happiness is not reserved for those with a pure conscience, but neither does it go well together with a strong sense of guilt.

From an ethical perspective, "subjective happiness" (i.e. happiness as it has been discussed so far in this chapter) is clearly relevant because it indicates to what degree people approve of their lives. Yet, happiness does not give unambiguous information about the *goodness of a person's life*. For example, a given person's unhappiness may be simply due to envy with respect to people who are deservedly better off, but it may also be due to unfair treatment. We might deplore the envious person's failure to take a more positive attitude, but her unhappiness does not mean that she is leading a bad life or that she is the victim of injustice that needs to be rectified. As Amartya Sen rightly points out – but wrongly describes as a shortcoming of the happiness perspective rather than of utilitarianism or welfarism – people tend to adapt to privileged or abject living conditions. As a consequence, their evaluations of their lives "can take a deeply biased form", being negative despite a high standard of living because of snobbish expectations or positive despite miserable living conditions because people "adjust their desires and expectations to what little they see as feasible" (Sen 2009: 283). Happiness and unhappiness can provide first clues to the presence of undeserved misery or injustice, but unhappiness (or inequality of happiness) is not illegitimate, or a sign of illegitimacy, as such (ibid.: 276–7).

The dependency of happiness on a person's ethos provides another ethical insight. It suggests that, rather than being antagonistic toward morality, happiness is inclusive of it. Once an individual has internalized specific norms, she does not derive happiness from breaking them. This is not to say that people are not also seducible and that they will not sometimes feel happy despite having violated their norms, but when they are truly concerned about the moral rights of others, knowing that their acts do no illegitimate harm to others will tend to make them happier rather than unhappier. In other words, a person's ethos will feed back into her judgment of happiness.

Saying that people derive happiness from moral integrity does not mean that they are concerned about moral integrity *in order to* be happy. Such a reading would presuppose that all behavior is motivated exclusively by a desire to maximize happiness (the view of psychological hedonism criticized above, pp. 62, 72). The view of happiness as a judgment sketched here, however, is incompatible with such an interpretation. If happiness really is (also) a judgment, its normative status cannot be that of a dominant end as these two categories are incompatible (cf. p. 73). What the status of happiness should be instead shall be discussed below (p. 95).

In addition to purely subjective criteria, happiness appears to require some objective criteria as well, where objectivity is not to be understood as precise measurability (or ascertainability), but rather as independence from a person's subjective feelings and evaluations. More specifically, a subjective feeling of happiness that meets all of the subjective criteria discussed above might not actually be happiness, or it may be significantly diminished, if it is not based on a reasonably authentic, well-informed, and reflected judgment. If a person wants, and cares about, something because of indoctrination, wrong information, or poor reasoning, one may find it inappropriate to call that person happy even if she declares to be happy. A cuckold wife who does not suspect that her husband betrays her, for example, may declare to feel happy, but since she would not call herself happy if she knew about her husband's escapades (and, what is more, if she affirmed that she cares about her husband being faithful), then we would probably not call her a happy person (cf. Haybron 2000: 209), or at least not as happy as she would otherwise be. Similarly, it would appear odd to call a person happy who has been indoctrinated to believe that dying as a suicide bomber is the most rewarding purpose to which to dedicate one's life.

Of course, what exactly counts as unauthentic, indoctrinated, or poorly informed is a matter of another imprecise judgment, and different legitimate points of view may arrive at different judgments. Yet, for an investigation of happiness that never claimed to come up with a determinate, homogeneous conception of happiness, this openness as such is no embarrassment. The significance of this objective aspect of happiness does not depend on any objective verifiability. Rather, it consists in spelling out the idea that happiness is not a matter of being in line with just any conception of the good life, but with a (minimally) rational conception of the good life (cf. Rawls 1999/1971: 358ff.)[16] and that one's evaluation of one's life must (minimally) correspond with reality.

This also reconnects to Sen's critique reported above (cf. p. 94). Sen is right to point to the problem that self-reported happiness may be biased in the sense of being unauthentic, poorly informed, or unreflected (i.e. the problem that SWB may not coincide with happiness for these reasons). However, from this it does not follow that people with a low standard of living cannot be truly happy and that they must be victims of their disadvantaged situation if they describe themselves as happy. This is not to say, to repeat an earlier remark, that social injustice or discrimination is fine as long as its victims are truly happy. Rather, the point is that, if we want to know whether a person is leading a happy life, we cannot from the outset limit the admitted set of answers according to some material conditions concerning her standard of living. Rather, whether we should accept self-reported happiness as true happiness is a matter of formal conditions, like the ones specified (authenticity, adequate information, and reflection). Moreover, one should distinguish between happiness and subjective well-being, and rather than discarding SWB information out of a concern that the response may be biased, one should admit it as a valuable piece of information on that person's subjective evaluation of her life.

It should be clear that the objective component of happiness is an additional (necessary) criterion and not a sufficient one. A person must always also feel happy (i.e. experience positive affect and approve of her experience) in addition to being free from illusion or indoctrination. One cannot declare a person happy against her subjective perception. This also implies that purely performance-oriented accounts of happiness must fail. When happiness is conceptualized as a matter of realizing a particular plan of life, for example, one would have to call a person whose life is going well but who is suffering from a depressive disorder as happy.

In essence, then, the objective dimension of happiness means that happiness is not exclusively a matter of a subjective evaluation, but also a matter of whether this subjective evaluation is minimally rational and of whether it corresponds to reality. This latter aspect shall be the subject of the next section.

Happiness as a self-transcendent phenomenon

When happiness is considered a person's dominant end and ultimate motivation of all behavior, then this means that the person is concerned only about her inner state of mind that results from her experience. All other considerations will become purely instrumental, turning the person entirely indifferent with respect to both (1) the reasons that bring about these inner mental states, and (2) anything that does not become part of her experience (and hence does not influence her inner mental state). Other people's well-being and the respect for their rights enter her "felicific calculus" (attributed to Bentham) only if and to the extent that they have an impact on her own happiness. Such a view shall be called a *solipsistic* conception of happiness. It is the view of economics (*homo oeconomicus*) in particular and psychological hedonism in general.

This conception is squarely opposed to the real concerns most people care about. This becomes clear as soon as one spells out some of the implications of the solipsistic conception of happiness. To begin with the second type of indifference (2), a person would not care about what people do behind her back as long as it does not have any consequences on her affective experience. A wife would not care about her husband's faithfulness as long as she does not learn about it. A person would not care about the health of a friend as long as it does not affect his affective state. People would not care whether a friend was just being nice in order to reap a personal benefit rather than out of sincere friendship. In fact, in a world of solipsistic pleasure maximizers, every so-called friend would only be nice out of a cold calculus of advantage. Real friendship would be inexistent.

Robert Nozick (1989: 104) suggested the following thought experiment to test the concept of solipsistic happiness. Imagine a machine that can give you pure and unlimited pleasure for an arbitrarily long period. What is more, this machine generates not just blind pleasure but the perfect illusion of happiness. The person connected to this machine will experience a perfect illusion of friendship, love, good music, delicious food, etc., being entirely unaware of being locked into the machine. There would be no negative side-effects of using this machine and its use would not imply any costs. If you choose, you can remain in that machine until the end of your life. Would we want to get plugged to such a machine, and would we call that experience happiness?, Nozick asks us.

Nozick was probably not aware that his thought experiment was not even that far removed from reality after all. Already in the 1950s, neuroscientists had identified a pleasure center in the brain of rats which allowed them to motivate the animals by administering targeted electric pulses directly into the brain to do whatever the researchers wished them to do (Olds and Milner 1954). Similar experiments involving human patients with severe neural conditions showed that electric stimulation of particular areas of the human brain could make severe depression or chronic aggressiveness give way to spontaneous enthusiasm as if by magic (Hooper and Teresi 1992) and induce liking of a particular experience by making a patient feel pleasure during the experience (Moan and Heath 1972).

Economist Yew-Kwang Ng is enthusiastic about the possibility to make widespread use of pleasure engineering. "The possibility of intense pleasure without diminishing marginal utility opens up a tremendous avenue for increasing our welfare by a quantum leap" (Ng 1997: 1849). Genetic engineering would be an even more welfare-enhancing technology "in the far future" (ibid.). Apparently, Ng would choose to get plugged into Nozick's happiness machine.

Perhaps he would not go that far if he contemplated what really matters to a good life. As it seems, people really care much more about various aspects of their life beyond their affective experiences, and even about aspects of the world that have no influence on their lives at all. Spouses actually care about their partner's faithfulness much more than about their knowledge of it ("if you make sure I will never get to know about it, feel free to cheat on me"). People care about the well-being of their friends, independent of their affective reaction, and they care about whether their friends are just being opportunistic or whether they are committed to a friendship beyond a calculus of personal advantage.

Of course, as long as she does not know about it, a cuckold wife does not *feel less happy* when her husband cheats on her, but her *happiness* will be diminished because she is not indifferent between these two states of the world. A person who really cared only about his subjective experience of happiness would pay any price for a happiness pill that slightly increases his personal happiness. Any person who refused to accept a deal by which, to take a drastic example, one thousand strangers would have to die (and where taking the pill would make the person forget about this part of the deal) in order for him to get a minimal increase in subjective happiness would thereby prove to care about more than just solipsistic happiness.

In short, people seem to (also) have self-transcendent values about which they care, rather than being limited to a solipsistic horizon of values and intentions. Whether I want to be faithful to my spouse; help a blind person across the street; visit a sick friend; or go all the way to the ballot box to cast my insignificant vote; in all these cases my motives are transcending the limited horizon of my own psyche. All of these intentions, once realized, may make a person feel happy, but this does not mean that this is what the person cares about. Rather, the resulting happiness is merely an incidental consequence of the materialization of a valued state of the world and therefore merely a *symptom* for the presence of a *reason for* happiness, albeit an enjoyable one. "Do I then strive after happiness? I strive after my work" (Nietzsche 1988: IV/408, transl. T. Common).[17]

It may be tempting to criticize such a concept by asking whether one would still care about one's friend, helping a person over the street, or casting one's vote if all this did not also trigger happiness, or if it triggered unhappiness. Yet, putting the question this way would be a paradoxical use of the word "happiness". It would wrongly suggest that the reasons for one's happiness and the resulting emotional response were separable. It would be somewhat like asking if one still wanted to cast one's vote if one came to believe that it is wrong to do so. It would be a gross misconception of morality to suggest that feeling good about doing a moral duty spoils the morality of an act. As argued above (p. 90), being happy about something routinely includes approving of it, and it does not make sense to ask if one would still approve of something if one no longer approved of it. In short, the event that makes me happy is not a detached and substitutable *cause* of my happiness but its irreplaceable *content* (Spaemann 2000/1989: 38; cf. also Forschner 1998: 156–8).

Nothing of this is to deny that happiness is *also* desirable in its quality as a psychic experience. Just as we seek to be comfortably warm or as we seek to avoid boredom, we prefer to experience happiness rather than unhappiness for reasons of our personal well-being. Philosophically speaking, the experience of happiness as such is one natural content of a good life among many others. This does not mean that a person will desire the experience of happiness with no regard to the underlying reasons. If a person's unhappiness is due to some manifest reason – something is going wrong in her life or in those of her loved ones – she will be concerned about this unfortunate state of the world, as just described, and will seek to change this state of the world, rather than try to make her unhappiness go away with substitutes. Yet, if she is just having a bad day and feels unhappy for no apparent reason or simply because some trivial event that she does not care about and cannot change either – e.g. bad weather – has a negative impact on her mood, she might be concerned about changing her mood itself. She can do that directly – eating chocolate, listening to her favorite music, taking a happiness pill – or indirectly, bringing herself into a situation she expects will provide a real reason for happiness – visiting a friend, doing a favor for her sick neighbor. Both ways may be effective as long as she does not delude herself (and will be legitimate as long as other individuals are not being instrumentalized).

The problem of the happiness pill, therefore, is not its occasional use to relieve a bad mood but its use to manipulate one's assessment of reality, leading to an indifference toward reality and, therefore, toward values one is actually having (probably without being aware of it). Still, even the occasional use of a happiness drug could be problematic since one might want to be obliged to endure a bad mood occasionally. One might even want to live in a world without a happiness pill, eliminating the need to have to make a choice between taking and not taking it (cf. Elster 2000; Schwartz 2000, 2004). On the other hand, however, "happiness pills" (albeit imperfect ones) are of course already existing in the form of anti-depression drugs. Yet, to the extent that these are used to compensate for physical defects of the biological system that provides the physical preconditions for the experience of happiness, their use should not be considered to be interfering with the happiness that matters to people, but rather as curing a pathological interference with our happiness. Moreover, a person in a situation of emotional distress that she is unable to change may well be happier under the illusion of happiness brought about by a happiness pill than in the reality of depression, and it would be preposterous for an armchair philosopher to condemn such a choice as imprudent before knowing the alternatives. For example, there are good reasons to judge the illusion of a happy life to contain more happiness than the reality of being locked up in a maximum security prison – at least that is what 87 percent in a student sample would choose (De Brigard 2010, quoted in Angner 2010).[18]

To conclude this chapter, let us wrap up the conception of happiness that has emerged from these reflections. As careful linguistic analysis shows, the term happiness involves basically three aspects: positive affect, normative approval, and a minimum of rationality. If positive affect is a spontaneous, pre-reflective experience, it has to be complemented by an approval of that experience in order to constitute happiness. However, positive affect can also be a consequence of a positive judgment, namely when a person's positive judgment refers to something she cares about. This judgment, in turn, must be minimally rational and largely free from illusion.

Moreover, happiness is a self-transcendent phenomenon in the sense that the approval it expresses may be largely independent of the effects of the approved event or state on one's personal well-being in general and on one's affective experience in particular. In other words, being happy does not necessarily mean that something good is happening to oneself; it may also mean that something good is happening to someone else. This implies that the object of concern is the event or state that is approved of rather than the resulting affective state. The fact that the realization of one's desires, values, and intentions triggers happiness is merely incidental. In other words, desiring, valuing, or caring about something naturally implies that one will feel good about its realization, but this feeling is not necessarily the motivating objective.

We now see that happiness is not only a matter of a good life, even though so far, to keep matters simple, we have pretended that it is. Rather, happiness is also a matter of the good life of others or, more generally, of a good state of the world. Everything I truly care about can become the content of my happiness, but since I can care about much more than my own good life, my happiness, too, will extend beyond my good life. For example, if I am happy about my friend passing an important exam, then I am happy for something that is part of her good life, not mine. Of course one can define the good life as comprising everything I care about, but this would not correspond to what we ordinarily understand by a good life, and it would risk being misunderstood in an instrumental sense ("I am happy *because* my friend's success enhances my own life"). With such an understanding of the good life, we would have to say that my life is going worse because my friend did not pass the exam – probably not an intelligible way to express that I care about my friend's success.

Another remark is at place in this context. We have assumed all along that happiness is generally desired by people and that it is a good thing to be happy. However, this is not true without qualifications because of the self-transcendent nature of happiness. If we really do not, or not only, care about being happy for the sake of being happy, but care about certain things (states of the world), then being happy is not unconditionally better than being unhappy. For example, if I attend a funeral, I will not prefer being happy to being sad because that is not what I care about at that moment. Rather, I care about my feelings being authentic and about making my reverence to the deceased. Apparently, being always happy is not something a person can reasonably want, and it is probably not consistent with the idea of a good life (cf. p. 120).[19]

Thus, happiness has a dual role as a *symptom* for the presence of reasons for happiness and as a *content* of a good life. In its first role, it indicates whether reasons for happiness are present, i.e. an event or a state of the world that we judge favorably and that we care about. In its second role, the experience of the affective aspect of happiness is intrinsically valuable as something that is simply enjoyable and therefore subject to a favorable judgment as long as there are no reasons to disapprove of that experience. In this sense, pre-reflective pleasure should not be discarded as an illegitimate content of happiness. As long as such a kind of pleasure does not interfere with one's conception of a good life and neither with the moral rights of others, there can be no ethical case against it.

5 Happiness and good development

The recent boom of academic and popular interest in happiness is certainly not mere curiosity for a psychological phenomenon. Rather, this interest appears to spring from a disappointment with the effects of economic progress on our well-being. Apparently, economic growth has not been accompanied by human betterment. Human betterment (a term I take to be most general and which I am borrowing from Boulding 1972), however, is a complex and contentious notion. In a development ethical text, a more elaborate discussion of the idea of human betterment is obviously not out of place. In this chapter, therefore, I shall develop a concept of good development, clarify the distinction between principles and procedures of good development, and synthesize these ideas into an unfinished conception of good development, giving particular emphasis to the role of happiness therein.

The idea of good development

Good development is the implicit normative standard for political debates. Whenever a condition, a project, or a change is criticized as not being the best available alternative for society, it is actually criticized that something is not conducive to good development, or not as conducive as it could and should be. In other words, the (usually implicit) claim of all political proposals is to be the best available alternative by the standard of good development.

As such, good development is a regulative idea (cf. p. 16) rather than a substantive goal, even though it can of course be claimed that good development *consists* in one particular substantive goal (such as the maximization of a society's gross national product). As a regulative idea, it is an idea that represents a principle, or a set of principles, that shall regulate the overall evaluation of societal states and societal change in terms of their goodness.

The idea of good development directly corresponds to the perhaps more familiar idea of the good society. The relationship between them is straightforward: good development is the best way toward a good society, and the good society is the ultimate destiny of good development. In other words, good development is the dynamic, and the good society the static idea of political goodness. Yet, since policy is a process of incremental betterment rather than the exercise of designing an optimal state, and since the notion of an optimal state is liable to be misunderstood as a concrete utopia, the notion of good development is preferred here.[1]

Still, even the notion of good development is liable to problematic readings. If it is read as an exercise to find and implement an existing (albeit hidden) "optimal" solution (or path), it will draw a picture of society that is problematically reductionist in one of two ways. Either it portrays a society as homogeneous and largely free of conflicts of interest, as if all members shared a common purpose without competing for privileges (Ueda 2003: 61), or it adopts the utilitarian stance that all conflicting interests of its members can be traded off against each other with deterministic precision. Either way, supposing that there is an optimal development path out there would reify "the society" and reduce ethics to a deterministic problem of puzzle-solving with all its problematic implications that have been discussed above (pp. 68, 87). Economic theory deserves particular mention for its unreserved propagation of a utilitarian concept of "social welfare". Even if the new (Paretian) welfare economics retreated from the position of cardinality and interpersonal comparability (cf. p. 10) of utility and, consequently, claimed that social welfare cannot be measured (Samuelson 1938), indeterminacy came to be recognized only with respect to measurement, not as a matter of principle. Incomplete rankings are still believed to provide ethical evaluations with deterministic certainty. At the same time, the "old welfare economics" practice of quantifying social welfare and, thereby, relying on interpersonal comparisons of utility remains in place in many parts of economic theory and often creeps in through the backdoor even where cardinality is explicitly denied (Myrdal 1953/1930: 87; van Praag and Frijters 1999: 414–15).

Ultimately, the reification of good development as "social welfare", i.e. as a concrete goal to be pursued (and maximized), subordinates the individual to a greater cause (cf. the critique by Adam Smith quoted above, p. 85). "Social welfare" or "world utility" (Thielemann) becomes a *moral subject*, and, since it is regarded as the social dominant end, it ends up being the *only* moral subject (Thielemann 1996: 52ff.). Consequently, the individual is stripped of his human dignity, having "value" (rather than rights) only because and to the degree that he contributes to "world utility". Thus, this "communistic fiction" (Myrdal 1953/1930: 54, 101) transforms the indeterminate problem of judging and balancing competing claims into a technical problem of maximizing a homogeneous good.

Rather than reifying the social good, a conception of good development should therefore be understood as a regulative idea, providing normative orientation rather than a blueprint for a "social technique for a good cause" (Ulrich 2008: 85). In analogy to the idea of a good life (cf. p. 77), the term "good development" should be understood as a terminological placeholder for the complex set of ethical principles that provide orientation for the distinction between better and worse paths of societal development.

The term "development" (without the adjective "good") holds a rather firmly established place in the political and economic literature where it basically connotes economic growth of low-income economies. The distinction between high-income and low-income countries in terms of "developed" and "underdeveloped" countries (or "least developed countries") is frequently made, and it clearly is a normative judgment. Yet, this terminology suggests that the "developed" countries are in some final stage of development where nothing remains to be improved. It also implies that a low consumption level necessarily reflects a lower quality of life and is intrinsically undesirable. Such a view is not only once again deterministic, suggesting that there is an objective point of view from which normative questions can be definitely evaluated, but also in apparent contradiction with the profound sense of social crisis experienced in many of the "developed" countries and with the sense of well-being found in some low-income societies. It remains true, of course, that low-income countries tend to suffer from more and graver socio-economic problems, but it would be wrong to take income as the only and ultimate yardstick of development.

In this context, development will therefore be understood, roughly speaking, as the never-ending endeavor to correct injustice and promote well-being. Put simply, good development is about doing the right and the good in matters of societal change.

This concept of development must be embedded into a temporally and spatially universal scope. Good development cannot be restricted to the present population of a given society, but must include future generations and other societies as well. Legitimacy is not modular: it demands justifiability before *all* potentially affected moral subjects and cannot be meaningfully established within isolated segments of humanity. Development at the expense of future generations or members of other societies would perhaps be development for the present inhabitants of that society, but not good development without qualifications.

This concept of development would mean, strictly speaking, that the expression "good development" is a pleonasm: if social change is not good, development is not taking place. However, to emphasize the ethical claim of development that usually remains implicit, and to avoid confusion with a definition of development as economic growth, the adjective "good" shall be maintained where deemed necessary.

The deeper reason for the impossibility – or inadmissibility – to collapse the problem of good development into an exercise of maximizing the good lies in the two-dimensionality of ethics. To be sure, good development aims at the promotion of people's well-being (teleological dimension), but equating good development with the maximization of the sum of people's well-being would mean to conceal the problem of legitimacy by "solving" it in an ad hoc manner. On the other hand, being concerned solely with legitimacy bears the risk of losing sight of the question of which objectives should be legitimately pursued *under the condition of* legitimacy. As we have seen above (p. 77), the idea of legitimacy is constitutively dependent on a conception of the good.

The remaining discussion of the concept of good development shall follow the lines of the two-dimensional model of ethics outlined above (Figure 4.1). It is therefore based on the conjecture that good development is not about well-being alone (teleological dimension), nor about legitimacy alone (deontological dimension), but about legitimately promoting well-being (cf. Ulrich 2008: 186f.).

The flourishing society: development toward what?

Analogous to the concept of the good life for individuals, the notion of a flourishing society should be seen as a formal concept and as an inclusive end, rather than as a dominant end (cf. p. 71). As such, we must not hope that even a sophisticated and refined concept of the flourishing society would identify concrete goals a society should strive for, or at least none that are not self-evident anyway and therefore offer little additional insight. Nevertheless, the concept is useful to describe the general idea of a society that is characterized by well-being of its citizens rather than misery, by health rather than disease, and by joy rather than suffering.

However, societies, unlike individuals, are no organisms, and the analogy between the flourishing society and the good life should not be stretched too far. Whereas an individual may experience conflicts between mutually exclusive *desires*, a society inevitably breeds conflicts between the *interests* of *moral subjects* who, in contrast to an individual's conflicting desires, are bearers of moral rights. Moreover, whereas the person can sovereignly settle internal conflicts of desires without raising any moral issues (as long as the resulting *actions* do not violate anybody's moral rights), there is no such societal institution that could settle conflicts between individuals with similar authority. In other words, a society does not have objectives or rights; only the individuals that constitute it do.

Yet, on the other hand, a society is not simply the sum of its members. As the example of the frame-of-reference effect (ch. 3) shows, individual decisions can cancel each other out even if they have the same sign. We therefore have to take social dynamics into account when generalizing from individual preferences and behavior to the societal, let alone global, level.

Such social dynamics appear to be important not only when individuals take their decisions, but already when their views and opinions meet in public debate. After all, people do not take their decisions in isolation as if they were entirely self-sufficient monads. They turn to others in their "exploration in the field of values" (Knight, cf. p. 72 above) and continually develop, and occasionally revise, their preferences.

Incumbent theories of development take little interest in this teleological (or prudential) dimension. Typically, prudential questions are bypassed by assuming that agents perfectly know what is best for them. Often, this positive stance is backed up by the normative assertion that it would be illegitimate to question a person's interests since "the game of push-pin is of equal value with the arts and sciences of music and poetry" (Bentham 1843/1775). Yet, this dictum is ambiguous and unsatisfactory. If "equal value" is understood in a deontological sense, the sentence would mean that it is as *legitimate* to like poetry as it is to like playing pushpins. Subject to some conditions of rationality (cf. ch. 4), this would indeed seem to be irrefutable. If, however, "equal value" is meant in a teleological sense ("equal value for Jeremy"), it would mean that it is as reasonable for a person to like poetry as it is to like pushpins. Such an interpretation would be problematic. Claiming that, for any given person, any taste is as reasonable as any other would either mean that, as a matter of fact, people do actually have those preferences that are the best they can have, or that it really does not matter to a specific person's good life what preferences she has. The first interpretation would draw an image of human beings of godlike rationality and sensibility from some point of adulthood onwards (unless perfect prudence is ascribed to children as well, which would be even harder to defend). The second would mock the idea of a person (Frankfurt 1971) and, consequently, that of a good life. Both interpretations would be wildly counterintuitive. After all, even superficial introspection reveals the deep tensions between unreflected desires and our conception of a good life. We are sometimes seducible, impatient, impulsive, addicted, etc., to the degree that we sometimes regret to have had certain preferences (Barkhaus and Hollstein 2003: 302). What is more, our preferences are quite frequently mutually inconsistent or outright contradictory (Ariely and Loewenstein 2006; Tversky and Kahneman 1981, 1982), raising the question of how the prudence of preferences can *not* be questioned. For the time being, the point to note is that preferences can be more or less meaningful in terms of the concerned individual's own conception of a good life, and that prudence matters to good development.

With their preferences unfinished, people constantly look for orientation to identify, order, and evaluate reasons they may have for wanting or not wanting, doing or not doing what is within their reach. In their search for orientation, people are particularly likely to be influenced by the norms that happen to prevail around them. While the prevailing trends may sometimes put individuals off, namely when they want to distinguish themselves from the masses (Vendrik 1993: 113), they more often pull people in the same direction (sometimes called "herding" or the "bandwagon effect"; cf. ibid.). Notably, when people have no clear preferences or knowledge to begin with, they may be influenced by even completely arbitrary points of reference, such as an apparent random number (Tversky and Kahneman 1982: 14). Apparently, this decision heuristic is a recipe for a self-reinforcing circle: the more prevalent a belief, the more it will move yet-undecided individuals to adopt it. Theoretically, such a circle can entrench social patterns that do not necessarily reflect original convictions of a majority but instead may reflect a minority position that at some point in time gained the upper hand by an historic accident.

At the same time, we may expect that the exchange of views and arguments may result in some conscious revision of interests by virtue of reasoned self-examination. People may be moved to change their incumbent preferences because they understand that they impose unjustifiable costs on others, rather than because they follow the crowd for lack of a better reason. They may also, however, be led to radicalize their views when they exchange their views with others who tend to confirm their own position (Sunstein 2002).

It is in this sense that we may speak of *social preferences*: not in the sense of a preference of a monolithic society, neither in the sense of the aggregation of isolated individual preferences, but as that set of preferences that results from the interplay of individual interests and social dynamics of the various kinds described.

The existence of social dynamics also implies that preferences are hardly ever truly private in the sense of being a pristine attribute of an isolated person, entirely independent of other people's views and opinions or of institutional and cultural settings. As a consequence, it would be wrong to equate any kind of outside influence as "manipulation" of, or "interference" with, a person's preferences. Where manipulation and interference begin is a normative evaluation, and a complex one at that, rather than a technical on–off question of whether a person is exposed to the views of others. Indeed, people often actively seek the views and reasons of others to make up their mind or to confirm or to challenge their held views, and in hindsight a person will often be grateful for having been exposed to arguments that made her change her convictions.

Thus, while social preferences are always *constituted* by the preferences of individuals, they cannot be *reduced* to them, since individuals are no isolated monads. Rather, individuals are interrelated and at the same time autonomous social beings who seek orientation in their society and are in principle prepared to review their preferences in the light of the moral rights of others. Social preferences are in this sense distinct from the aggregated individual preferences. Yet, they are real to the extent that they are effectively influencing the course of societal development.

Now, if social preferences are thus constituted, there is nothing that guarantees that the effective social preferences will be either meaningful or legitimate, i.e. that they will further good lives or that they would be duly respecting the rights of all individuals. Even if social preferences were the result of a homogeneous aggregation of individuals' preferences according to some neat algorithm, they would be considered legitimate only within a calculating concept of ethics (such as utilitarianism), an option that has been rejected above (cf. p. 85). On top of that objection, the potentially problematic effects of social dynamics may drive a wedge between individual and social preferences (and that implies: between individual preferences and social results), sometimes even reversing the pattern of private preferences, as in the case of positional competition (cf. p. 44).

It is, in particular, for this reason that a conception of good development must also be concerned with the teleological dimension of development. In addition to a fair and just social order that civilizes the social contest of conflicting interests (as will be discussed in the following section), a comprehensive conception of good development must not be indifferent with respect to the social preferences that will prevail. Instead, it must provide orientation for the evaluation of social preferences in terms of desirability and meaningfulness. After all, the problem of positional competition, for example, appears to be not primarily a moral, but a *prudential* problem. In other words, positional competition and the associated social waste will arise even – though perhaps to a lesser degree – in a society of perfectly responsible citizens, as long as they do not understand and address positional competition, e.g. by putting in place smart rules of the game that coordinate their competing preferences.[2]

As an example of positional competition, consider the problem of doping among athletes. In the absence of any regulation of doping, reasonable and responsible athletes would probably not take substances that have serious effects on their health, but they would most certainly engage in less detrimental practices that are "smart for one, dumb for all" (Frank 1999: 146), and it would be impossible to tell for any individual athlete, however concerned about the legitimacy of her behavior, where to draw the line. Even artificial devices as innocent as isotonic drinks and high altitude training – in fact, even any ordinary training beyond the point up to which it is undertaken for the sake of one's personal excellence – imply a relative advantage for the individual, but a real expense without a net benefit for all athletes taken together. The problem is, to slightly adapt an insightful remark by Layard (1980: 744), that "it is not clear just how an athlete observing the rules of fairness would know when to stop artificially enhancing her performance".[3] Thus, we need a teleological dimension within a concept of good development in order to distinguish more and less *desirable* outcomes where several outcomes would be *equally legitimate* in a deontological perspective.

In addition, the teleological dimension is essential where individuals cannot (or not yet) represent and defend their own interests, i.e. in the case of children, future generations, or the mentally impaired. While it is a deontological question why, how, and to which degree the future interests of yet unborn human beings need to be respected, this question can only be meaningfully addressed on the basis of some teleological notion of a good society, however preliminary and incomplete. Saying that we must respect the interests of future generations has little significance unless we have an idea what it is that we must respect, i.e. unless we have some *substantive* concept of social objectives. While this is of course also true for present generations' interests, present generations can (and do) voice and defend their interests themselves, largely eliminating the need to establish substantive (but not formal) conceptions of a good life (cf. p. 70). Future generations, presently living children, and mentally impaired persons can normally not argumentatively present their interests today so that their views have to be anticipated, in all uncertainty, by presently living people able to participate in public debate.

Even if such an account of social preferences may appear to be unorthodox to the social scientist, the underlying idea is probably intuitively familiar to most people. Wherever people feel something like a social identity as members of a nation, a community, a tribe, etc. – i.e. practically everywhere – they have an understanding of social preferences, whether they affirm or reject them. In modern societies, the most manifest reflection and catalyst of social preferences is perhaps the mass media. The criteria by which they evaluate a society's success in newspaper headlines give a pretty accurate indication of that society's teleological priorities. Apparently, the most prominent criterion for societal success in today's world is aggregate consumption, or gross national product (GNP).[4] Admittedly, additional criteria are also regularly employed, such as employment, respect for human rights, liberty in its various interpretations, or income inequality, but none of these, I would claim, comes close to GNP (and GNP *growth*) in terms of the prominence with which it is discussed and the reverence in which it is held. Moreover, these additional concerns are frequently raised merely because they are considered instrumentally important for GNP growth rather than because of their independent merit.[5] The impact of the prominence of GNP as a social preference is apparent. Not only is the GNP handwriting visible on the institutional infrastructure, it is also widely accepted – and frequently used – as a last justification of political decisions.

The point here is not to discuss whether GNP is an appropriate social preference (on this, see ch. 6 and ch. 7).[6] Rather, the upshot is that some such social preferences will always emerge in the mass media-moderated debates of a modern society and that it makes a great difference which these are. It will therefore be a formal characteristic of a good society to explicitly reflect on these preferences in a public debate, rather than blindly affirming those that it has inherited from its own past or copied from other societies.

The just society: development for whom?

While it may be expected that most citizens of any given society are in principle prepared to review their personal preferences when being confronted with counter-arguments in a public debate on social preferences, one must not expect anything close to a consensus on social objectives. A great deal of genuine discord will remain in all societies that do not effectively suppress autonomous thinking. The deontological challenge of good development, then, is to settle conflicts of interest communicatively rather than strategically, in debate rather than by bargaining, through arguments rather than by power – in a word, ethically (Ulrich 2008: 21). Thus, good development is not only a matter of moving toward collective goals, but also of settling conflicts of interest in a way that does not violate anybody's moral rights, i.e. legitimately.

The idea that justice could be taken care of by the moral integrity of a society's members alone must be discarded as a dangerous utopia, at least for any society that consists of more than just a handful of individuals. This is not only because one cannot expect perfect moral integrity all of the time from mortal human beings or because one must reckon with the presence of some outright bad-willed individuals in every society, but also because even a society of perfectly responsible individuals would not necessarily live together peacefully. They may disagree, in good faith, on their conceptions of justice or they may perceive another's behavior to be violating their own rights, thus coming to believe that they are morally entitled to retaliate against the perceived injustice with a similar assault on the interests of the other. Wars are perhaps more often the consequence of a lack of mutual trust and understanding than of bad faith. We must probably accept that the road to hell is paved with good intentions.

Since peaceful coexistence, without doubt a key characteristic of good development, cannot rely on moral integrity alone, all societies establish some rules of the game – in the form of social norms and laws – that its members are obliged to follow. The effectiveness of these rules, formal and informal, is typically backed by the threat of painful sanctions in the case of their violation, but also by means of rewards ("incentives") in the case of compliance. While sanctions and rewards address people's self-interest, this feature of social rules should be considered complementary rather than primordial. To the degree that rules are the result of deliberative democratic procedures (for more on this, cf. ch. 6 below), a considerable share of a society's members apparently *want* to be subjected to them. Rules then also have the function of assuring a responsible individual that all others will be obliged to the same sacrifices. In the absence of such an assurance, the price that a responsible person would have to pay for his compliance would become excessively painful, and the reward for free riding excessively seductive. In the absence of any enforced tax legislation, for example, an individual would not know what his fair contribution would be and, observing occasional free riding, would feel exploited by parts of society, thus probably feeling entitled to withdraw his contributions altogether. Hence, it would be no contradiction for a person to vote for a 50 percent income tax rate but then, out of a concern of justice (equal treatment), pay whatever rate comes to be adopted, even if it is less than what he advocated. In effect, then, laws (also) coordinate the choices of morally concerned individuals by establishing indispensable normative orientation rather than merely being instruments to enforce desired behavior from purely self-interested individuals (cf. Ulrich 2008: 301f.).

In both of these roles – coordination and enforcement – publicly legitimized rules of the game serve to partially disburden the individual from detailed moral case-by-case judgments. To the degree that a person is confronting a moral question for which rules have been designed, she can justify her following these rules simply by referring to the justification that was once given for these rules. Put simply, she does not need to worry about the detailed ramifications of her decision if she follows justified rules (again, as long as the question she is confronting is what the rules have been designed for). This does not mean that she is not taking an ethical perspective or that she does not need to justify her decision. It simply means that her ethical judgment now is reduced to the problem of whether or not she is right to follow the rules, i.e. whether the rules themselves are just and whether the situation she confronts is what the rules have been designed to address. In other words, rules allow the person to *economize* on moral considerations but not to *dispense* with them.

Two judgments therefore remain even in the presence of unambiguous rules: first, the question of whether the rules themselves are just, and second, whether the situation at hand is what the rules have been designed for (i.e. whether one is following the spirit of the rules and not just the letter of the law).

Following rules, even in the form of laws, is thus not automatically legitimate. After all, for a rule to be a law is a formal property and no unconditional moral qualification. Even societies under totalitarian regimes have laws, many of which will be considered outright immoral by most standards. Whether a law is to be considered just or unjust is a matter of a procedural and a consequential aspect. The procedural aspect is about the genesis of a law, i.e. about the procedures that have led to its enactment. When the procedure itself was legitimate, the law will have the presumption of legitimacy on its side. However, neither do legitimate procedures guarantee that the participants of the respective procedure act in good faith, that they understand the issue, and that the resulting law is in fact legitimate, nor do illegitimate procedures inevitably lead to illegitimate laws. Thus, in addition to the procedural aspect, laws have to be evaluated with respect to the consequences their general observation will have.

The general principle of justice for social rules is of course the same as that for the legitimacy of individual behavior (cf. p. 82): a rule is just when it is justifiable against all possible objections that might arise in a universal discourse. Again, this principle is a regulative idea whose role it is to *orient* the interminable search for justice, not to *validate* specific rules. Any specific rule must of course be defended, or criticized, in terms of concrete reasons. While this is not the place to develop a comprehensive conception of justice, it should be clear that different criteria are not mutually exclusive. It is only a metaphysical a priori belief in homogeneity and determinacy that makes some philosophical schools defend dominant-end conceptions of justice that reduce justice to the satisfaction of a single substantive criterion (cf. the critique of dominant-end conception of the good life, p. 74). Yet, there is no reason why primary goods (Rawls), fair procedure (Nozick), utility (Bentham), capabilities (Sen, Nussbaum), merit, economic citizen rights (Ulrich), and so on cannot each be relevant, partly overlapping, and often complementary aspects of justice.

Even following just rules may be illegitimate, however, namely when the normative question one is confronting is not what the rules have been designed for. In other words, laws and unwritten social norms will never be complete in the sense of providing rules for all possible normative questions. They may sometimes even explicitly encourage behavior that is thought to be illegitimate when that is considered the lesser evil in terms of the societal consequences, as, for example, in the case of tax amnesty laws that grant non-prosecution guarantees and reduced tax rates to tax dodgers who repatriate their illegal funds from abroad. More often, however, the problem of following justified laws and even social norms lies in the mismatch between a relatively stiff apparatus of rules and an infinitely complex reality. For example, insurance contracts can hardly ever be specified, let alone enforced, to such an extent that moral hazard (i.e. irresponsibly risky behavior because the insured person knows she will not have to pay for a possible damage) can be excluded. Nevertheless, the rules of insurance are intended to cover the risks of *responsible* behavior alone. When damages from *irresponsible* behavior are also covered legally that does not mean that such behavior and the resulting claims become legitimate. It merely reflects the impossibility to exclude moral hazard within the limitations of legal clauses the compliance with which must be independently verifiable. This is not to say that following rules against their spirit is automatically illegitimate. It does mean, however, that one is always still obliged to morally decide whether to follow rules, or whether to exceed or even violate them.

The deontological problem of good development can therefore not be entirely handed over to the rules of the game, and the individual cannot be absolved from all moral demands. Rather, the rules of the game must be *complemented*, but of course not replaced, by the moral integrity of the "players" – who actually stop being mere "players" to become *citizens* once they recognize moral obligations beyond the rules of the game. One does not have to rely on self-sacrificing heroes when demanding moral integrity beyond abiding by the rules of the game. For one thing, the idea of morality already ensures that the costs of moral behavior be commensurate with the reasons for such demands (cf. p. 76). More importantly, however, it would be problematic to suppose a general antagonism between moral motivation and self-interest, as if human motivation was constituted of pre-social self-interest and a social conscience as two separate systems (but it would of course be equally problematic to subsume one under the other; cf. p. 84). Rather, one may expect from people even in complex anonymous societies (who, after all, remain social beings whose identity is partly constituted by being part of a group) not to *want* to pursue their own interests unduly at the expense of the rest of society. A committed citizen will experience such a moral demand not as a constraint of her liberty, but as naturally following from her identity as part of a *res publica* (from the Latin for "public affair"), an attitude that has been termed "republican ethos" by Ulrich (2008: 283). She will consider the challenge of succeeding in her conception of a good life in the presence of conflicts of interest not as a bargaining contest against opponents, but as a never-ending endeavor to pursue her interests under the condition of respecting others' moral rights. Rather than, while strictly playing by the rules, taking reckless advantage of her superior bargaining power vis-à-vis the disadvantaged, she only desires legitimate success for herself.

If good development is really an ethical idea, then it must be justifiable not only within the society concerned. Rather, it must be justifiable also with respect to the members of other societies, as well as with respect to future generations. These are of course not additional requirements, but rather obvious consequences of taking the universalization principle seriously. When the consequences of a society's development cannot be justified beyond one's own society or beyond the present generation, this cannot be called *good* development.

From principles to procedures: "applying" development ethics

Scholars in the field of development theory might raise an objection against the reflections on development ethics made in the previous section. They would probably criticize that these considerations are not applicable since they are indeterminate and incomplete, providing no clear answers to pressing problems. Indeed, when studying the literature on development, especially that emanating from economics, one finds an impressive zeal for concreteness and conclusive problem solving. Yet, it should be clear that one cannot solve a development problem – indeed, not even identify one – if one does not already have a conception of good development, however implicit and incomplete. In the economic literature, however, such conceptions are not only mostly implicit, but also allow (ostensible) matter-of-fact constraints to determine the criteria of legitimacy, rather than to evaluate matter-of-fact constraints in the light of a conception of legitimacy that is prior to these. Even in an essay with the promising title "On the Goals of Development" by Kaushik Basu (2001), a committed development economist, one looks in vain for any fundamental reflection on the orientating principles of good development (notwithstanding the overall merit of the text in other respects). Instead, development is once more reduced to a matter of consumption, keeping alive the dead-end debate of "aggregate welfare versus inequality"[7] and culminating in a proposal for a new "goal" of development as an increase of the average income of the lowest 20 percent of the income distribution ("quintile income").

Such a handling of normative issues is symptomatic and goes far beyond development economics, including, in particular, social choice theory and welfare economics as a whole, but also much of the sustainability movement. It reflects what could be called an obsession with accounting and a priority for procedures before principles. The premise of determinacy, including, in particular, evaluational completeness (cf. p. 68), admits only those concepts of goodness that can exactly account for all possible evaluational problems. Utilitarianism offers exactly this and has therefore been gratefully embraced by economists as the default option for evaluational questions, occasionally corrected for distributional concerns in order to avoid counterintuitive outcomes (leading to a choice between the alternatives, welfare and equality). Throughout the economic literature, the specification of a conception of goodness seems to be a rather straightforward exercise and is in fact often an unconscious decision to stick with the default option of utilitarianism.[8] As a consequence, the normative challenge no longer consists in the specification of a conception of good development, but instead in the specification of practical procedures to measure or bring about outcomes that are (objectively) desirable. Symptomatically, the "goals" in Basu's essay refer to operational targets rather than substantive objectives that make reference to the idea of the good life. In other words, the question of the appropriate orientating principles is regarded as solved (or ignored altogether) and good development, i.e. ethics, reduced to a specification of operational procedures.

This is not to say that the arguments that are presented in that literature are necessarily invalid. In fact, the gap that arises from the failure to explicate the underlying orientating principles is not a black void. It is partly filled by an intuitive understanding of these principles. It is thanks to this intuitive understanding that the participants (or most of them) of such debates actually agree on the rules of the discussion game and that they are able to appraise the validity of normative arguments without having an explicit conception of ethics. More specifically, they already understand that a good (i.e. valid) argument (for development objectives or else) is one that could not be rejected in an ideal discourse, and in developing their ideas and defending their reasoning, they continually invoke this regulative idea as the ultimate criterion. After all, raising a claim to validity or legitimacy really is nothing else but a claim that an idea would survive in an ideal discourse (Sen 2004b: 320).

In this perspective, concrete proposals can be seen as demarcations on the valid scope of a discourse, in the sense that claims beyond such demarcations become pointless because their indefensibility has been theoretically established. For example, when utilitarians claim that the good consists in utility maximization, they implicitly say that a meaningful discourse should be restricted to the questions consistent with this condition, e.g. questions of counting and weighting. Claims beyond this domain, e.g. rights-based arguments, would be pointless since such arguments are taken to be unable to survive in an ideal discourse.

The principle of discourse ethics itself does not restrict the scope of discourses in the same way as other, more specific, ethical conceptions do. While it can escape the same regulative idea of validity no more than other conceptions of ethics can, it uses reflection to reveal the rules of the argumentative game within which we try to establish (tentative) validity instead of arguing *within* these rules, taking the rules themselves for granted (however unconsciously) (Apel 1973: 406; Habermas 1983: 141).

The development debate has recently made major progress in terms of ethical sophistication thanks to the *capability approach*, meanwhile understood to be practically synonymous with the "human development approach", which has been spearheaded by Amartya Sen and Martha Nussbaum and arguably prepared by Aristotle.[9] This approach is not only increasingly recognized in the academic literature, but also at the center of current debates in policy circles (especially since 1990 in the United Nations Development Programme, UNDP). A closer look at the capability approach will reveal some valuable insights into the relation between principles and procedures in development ethical debates, as well as illustrate some aspects of the role of happiness in a conception of good development.[10]

In its most recent version by Amartya Sen (1999b, 2005, 2009), the capability approach posits, roughly speaking, that the primarily relevant informational space for the evaluation of (in)equality is the space of capabilities, i.e. the substantive freedoms to choose among functionings one has reason to value (Sen 1999b: 74–5). It also argues that good development is not a matter of maximizing any single good, not even capabilities, but rather a matter of weighing competing goods and rights in a process of public reasoning. While Sen's capabilities approach has its origin in (a discontentment with) economic theory and continues a dialogue with mainstream economic development theory, it is a notable exception by its ambition to go beyond mere accounting and procedural questions and its courage to propose an explicitly and inherently incomplete theory of societal well-being. As Sen cogently argues:

> An approach that can ... compare inequalities without any room for ambiguity or incompleteness may well be at odds with the nature of these ideas ... if an underlying idea has an essential ambiguity, a *precise* formulation of that idea must try to *capture* that ambiguity rather than lose it.
>
> (Sen 1995: 48–9, emphasis orig.)

Still, even Sen does not explicate his ethical point of view. His orientating ideas remain implicit. By insisting on Rawls's (1993: 212ff.) notion of *public reasoning*[11] as the last instance to judge social priorities, he proposes what can be seen as an analogy with the discourse ethical idea of the unlimited public discourse: delegating final decisions to public reasoning means, according to Sen, that "[t] he status of these ethical claims must be dependent ultimately on their survivability in unobstructed discussion" (Sen 2004b: 349). However, Sen still presents this criterion as a procedural requirement or criterion, not as a counterfactual regulative idea against which a procedural requirement is to be evaluated. In other words, he does not reveal and substantiate the evaluative framework that makes him single out exactly this procedure (public reasoning). The regulative idea of a universal discourse as the meta-instance of legitimacy does not imply a practical discourse (or "unobstructed discussion") as a *factual* instance to settle questions of legitimacy. Moreover, the idea to settle actual judgments in a factual discourse must face the criticism that it is not at all clear (1) how the necessity of public discussion itself would be established in a particular case, given the impossibility to publicly discuss all minor issues (cf. p. 128) and (2) how "survivability" could be established. After all, one cannot expect that a factual discourse will lead to an actual consensus in more than a few exceptional (and usually uninteresting) cases. Thus, while a practical "unobstructed discussion" may after all be the least bad – and that means most justifiable – procedure to actually take decisions concerning the *res publica*, this can only be justified in the light of an ideal conception of ethics, such as the discourse ethical regulative idea of a universal discourse.

Sen's failure to reveal this orientational principle does of course not mean that his conclusions in terms of practical procedures are invalid. It does mean, however, that his reasoning remains more vulnerable than it needs to be because it lacks a foundational basis in the form of an orientational principle of ethics. His proposals are very plausible indeed, but they provide few independent arguments to convince those who do not share his intuition.

Sen's contribution can therefore be characterized as follows. It goes beyond conventional economic theories of justice by recognizing and capturing the indeterminate nature of ethics. Instead of specifying a complete set of relevant concerns and precise evaluation algorithms, he merely suggests one primary class of concerns (namely capabilities) as the major informational base and delegates the problem of evaluation to public reasoning. Sen's approach is therefore no longer an accounting technique, but it remains limited to procedural, rather than foundational, questions. It does respect basic principles of ethics (in particular, indeterminacy and the role of practical reason), but its orientating idea remains implicit.

Sen's proposal to delegate the procedural question of settling evaluational questions to an "unobstructed discussion" is as plausible as it should be self-evident. Indeed, what is remarkable about his proposal is that he finds it necessary to defend it against a number of (anticipated) objections from the economic profession, in particular against the presupposition of development and welfare theorists that evaluational questions can be solved by impersonal algorithms aggregating objective parameters, implicitly discarding the possibility that a society might raise valid objections against the resulting evaluations. While the political status of Sen's (and others') proposals is not always clear, it is apparent that they deserve some explicit consideration if major misconceptions or misunderstandings are to be avoided. As this question is also relevant in the present context, the next chapter will take up this issue in more detail.

Public debates are not always about *conflicts* of interests. They are sometimes about these interests themselves, i.e. about their meaningfulness with respect to the lives of the concerned individuals themselves. In such teleological debates, the contesting parties do not claim that the opposing view is *illegitimate* and ought to be revised, but rather that the opposing view might be *unreasonable* in light of the opposing party's own conception(s) of a good life and that it might be in that party's broader interest to revise it. If it does not revise its view, the contesting party will not feel treated unfairly, as it would in moral debates. Rather, it would feel that the opposing party fails to understand its own broader interest, holding on to an imprudent, but nevertheless legitimate, interest. Of course, teleological debates remain under the imperative of legitimacy, i.e. only those interests and decisions are admissible which are also legitimate, and in practice both dimensions may be invoked simultaneously ("your illegitimate claim is not even in your own interest").

It is admittedly difficult to specify procedures by which the meaningfulness of preferences can be ascertained. Apparently, there can be no objective criterion or procedure to settle the question of the appropriateness of certain preferences for a given person's conception of a good life. Yet, again, the question of procedures is secondary to the question of principles, and the difficulty to come up with unambiguous *procedures* in no way precludes the possibility and utility to specify ideal *principles* to orientate the evaluation of preferences in terms of their meaningfulness. By the same token, the inadmissibility of forceful outside intervention to influence legitimate preferences in no way reduces the admissibility of *questioning* even legitimate preferences (where questioning is of course not the same thing as judging).

Good development, therefore, requires that preferences meet some conditions of prudence. Kant, for example, suggested maturity and autonomy as fundamental requirements of good development (though he did of course not use that particular term) and indeed as the essence of Enlightenment (Kant 1977/1784). Later philosophers came up with similar requirements. Henry Sidgwick (1907/1874: I/IX/3), for example, argued that "[t]he notion of 'Good' ... has an ideal element: it is something that is not always actually desired and aimed at by human beings". More specifically, he held the " 'ultimate good on the whole for me' to mean what I should practically desire if my desires were in harmony with reason, assuming my own existence alone to be considered". This conception inspired Rawls's notion of *deliberative rationality* that he believes to be a requirement for a rational plan (of life or else) for a person. By deliberative rationality, Rawls means a process of:

> careful reflection in which the agent reviewed, in the light of all the relevant facts, what it would be like to carry out these plans and thereby ascertained the course of action that would best realize his more fundamental desires.
>
> (Rawls 1999/1971: 366)

Once more, the idea of prudential preferences is the flip side of a free will. We can only err in the choice of our preferences – indeed, we can *choose* preferences in the first place – only because we have a free will. As a corollary, to somebody who denies the free will, it will be self-evident that preferences cannot be imprudent. This is why, for example, Gary Becker and Kevin Murphy, methodologically ruling out freedom of will, cannot see that addiction is in any way different from any other sort of behavior.

> The claims of some heavy drinkers and smokers that they want to but cannot end their addictions seem to us no different than the claims of single persons that they want to but are unable to marry or from the claims of disorganized persons that they want to become better organized. What these claims mean is that a person will make certain changes – for example, marry or stop smoking – when he finds a way to raise long-term benefits sufficiently above the short-term costs of adjustment.
>
> (Becker and Murphy 1988: 693)

To Becker and Murphy, the costs and benefits from doing this or that simply exist for any given person. Since there is nothing to want or to choose about these preferences, it simply does not make sense to ask whether these preferences are rational. People just have the preferences they have, and there is not another standard beyond manifest preferences by which these preferences themselves could be evaluated.

On the other hand, any conception of human choice that does not go as far as to deny the free will must necessarily include a counterfactual regulative idea of prudence, or rationality. This idea requires, roughly speaking, that preferences be well-informed, reflected, and authentic, rather than unreflected, uninformed, and indoctrinated (cf. p. 95).

Whether there are legitimate procedures to further such conditions is an entirely different question, but the answer to that question need not be as negative as libertarians tend to think. At this point, we can say that, for preferences to be *well-informed*, people obviously ought to have access to relevant information and the ability to understand it; for preferences to be *reflected*, people can be encouraged to question and scrutinize their own preferences; and for preferences to be *autonomous*, people need to "emerge from their self-incurred immaturity"

(Kant 1977/1784: 53). While there is limited outside *control* over these aspects, there are a number of ways in which the *conditions* for these requirements can be enhanced, as will be discussed below (p. 138). For the time being, we shall turn to the role of happiness in a conception of good development.

A conception of good development and the role of happiness

In much of the new literature on happiness, there is an implicit, sometimes even explicit, understanding that happiness is to be maximized, which of course means that good development is the same as maximizing happiness. For example, in a well-researched book *Happiness: Lessons from a New Science*, Richard Layard (2005: 224, also ch. 8) argues that, since "we are programmed to seek happiness", it is "self-evident that the best society is the happiest". As reported above (p. 97), Ng (1978, 1980, 1996, 1997, 2003) is another economist to advocate such a view, going as far as recommending the direct stimulation of the pleasure center of the brain to increase happiness.

There are basically two kinds of objections against the happiness maximization view. The first, teleological, objection is that happiness is not a sufficient criterion for a good life. The second, deontological, objection is that happiness provides no orientation for how to deal with conflicts of interest or, in other words, that the proposed "solution" (namely, to maximize sum-total happiness where interests conflict) is indefensible.

In a teleological perspective, for happiness to serve as the unique objective of development, it would have to be the good life itself. Yet, as has been argued above (p. 88), happiness is much more a symptom of a good life and an inclusive end than a substantive good. If it were a perfect indicator of a life's goodness, it could be argued that it should be maximized nevertheless since the maximization of the indicator would ensure that the underlying concept was maximized as well. However, it would take a whole set of rigid assumptions to argue that happiness perfectly reflects the goodness of a life. Yet, this would mean to effectively exclude the possibility that a person may reasonably value other things than happiness and value these things independently of their contribution to happiness (e.g. authenticity, or the completion of a work of art). This would smack of paternalism and could certainly not claim cross-cultural validity. Some cultures clearly give higher priority to happiness than others (cf. p. 38), and there seems to be no ethical (and that means universal) basis for criticizing a culture for giving less than first priority to happiness.

In addition, one cannot derive firm normative conclusions from a person's experienced degree of happiness. A person may feel happy even in scandalously deprived living conditions because she has come to terms with a hopeless situation or because she has been indoctrinated with a fundamentalist ethic teaching her that she does not deserve better. As Sen eloquently argues:

> It is through "coming to terms" with one's hopeless predicament that life is made somewhat bearable by the traditional underdogs, such as oppressed

minorities in intolerant communities, sweated workers in exploitative industrial arrangements, precarious share-croppers living in a world of uncertainty, or subdued housewives in deeply sexist cultures. The hopelessly
deprived people may lack the courage to desire any radical change and typically tend to adjust their desires and expectations to what little they see as
feasible. They train themselves to take pleasure in small mercies. [...] To
overlook the intensity of their disadvantage merely because of their ability
to build a little joy in their lives is hardly a good way of achieving an adequate understanding of the demands of social justice.

(Sen 2009: 282–4)[12]

Conversely, a "grumbling rich man may well be less happy than the contented
peasant, but he does have a higher standard of living than that peasant" (Sen
1983: 160). In effect, using the terminology introduced above (p. 85), a person
may approve of her life where she should not, i.e. where her normative evaluation is blind against the unjust denial of rights and opportunities. Conversely,
she may not approve of it where she should, i.e. where her normative evaluation
is blind against the privileges she enjoys and perceives deprivations where there
are none. Thus, happiness is no guarantee for a dignified life, and its absence is
no sure indication of an undignified life. This is not to say that it is normatively
irrelevant whether the "grumbling rich man" is happy or not, but that happiness
is only one among several possible aspects of a good life.

In a deontological perspective, the happiness maximization rule fails because
it does not recognize the subject quality of human beings (cf. p. 79). For
example, if torturing crime suspects resulted in a however marginal increase in
sum-total happiness, the happiness maximization rule would advocate torture
(Thomä 2003: 155), effectively giving zero weight to the consideration of rights.
Or as, once more, Sen (1982: 7) hypothesized, "[t]here might have been good
utilitarian reasons for forcing men to fight wild animals in the Colosseum with
the utility gain of the thousands of spectators outweighing the utility loss of the
few forced men". Rule utilitarianism[13] is sometimes invoked to refute such
uncomfortable conclusions, but it does not, in principle, rule out that the (rule)
utilitarian calculus will lead to such outcomes in specific scenarios.

Beyond these conceptual objections against happiness maximization, it is
entirely unclear how utilitarianism should be broken down into procedures that
do not violate basic democratic principles. As a mechanical algorithm, the utilitarian principle would demand to estimate the happiness payoffs of alternative
choices and then choose the alternative with the highest payoff. The challenge of
development would thus be reduced to a technical exercise, namely to estimate
with the highest possible degree of precision the happiness payoffs involved, and
the utilitarian recommendations would remain completely insulated from the
necessity of democratic legitimization, entirely bypassing the public debate
(Thomä 2003: 155). Chapter 6 will discuss this problem in more detail.

Even though happiness is not the single ultimate objective of good development, it can, and should, still play a number of vital roles in a conception of good

development. First of all, it should be noted that rejecting utilitarianism's impersonal arithmetic is not the same as saying that its underlying motivation – to wit, taking subjective evaluations seriously – is invalid. It is not the idea of taking pleasure and happiness seriously that is problematic, but the *reduction* of ethical questions (teleological or deontological) to a calculus of pleasure and pain. It would be no embarrassment to discourse ethics if the unobstructed discourse occasionally sustained the same recommendations as the utilitarian principle. Expecting otherwise would imply that the discussion partners give zero normative significance to pleasure and pain, which would be outright implausible. One may rather expect that considerations of the sum-total of pleasure-minus-pain will be accepted by the discussion partners as the effective criterion whenever all non-utilitarian considerations are uncontentious. For example, when my neighbor has a headache, I will feel obliged to turn the volume of my music lower than usual because my neighbor's pain from exposure to loud music would be larger than my pleasure (or, deontologically speaking, my additional pleasure would not justify my inflicting additional pain on my neighbor). The fact that, in such a circumscribed situation, the moral judgment may boil down to the maximization of net pleasure is not in contradiction with discourse ethics (or, for that matter, a whole range of other conceptions of ethics). In fact, pain/pleasure considerations are naturally embedded in the principle of discourse ethics. The upshot is that they remain one consideration among others, rather than being the single organizing principle.

To the degree that people claim a legitimate interest in happiness, happiness clearly has a role in a conception of good development as one element of a good life. Yet, there is no conceptual or theoretical necessity for every single individual to give particular priority to happiness. In other words, happiness plays no privileged or constitutive role in good development. It is on the same footing with any other sincere interest to which people lay claim, even though happiness happens to be a rather natural and common interest when compared to many others. Deriving from this a normative a priori status, however, would mean committing the naturalistic fallacy, as, for example, Layard does in the quote at the beginning of this section ("we are programmed to seek happiness...").

To be precise, however, we must distinguish between the three constituents of happiness distinguished above (positive affect, approval, and rationality). In fact, it is the positive affect component of happiness that plays this role as a particularistic interest. As has been argued earlier (p. 70), people may reasonably differ with respect to the importance of positive affect in their lives, both within and across cultures, and it would be a questionable judgment, rather than a self-evident truth, to say that a good life must be happy. In this context, it is to be noted that the American Declaration of Independence proclaims the *right* to the *pursuit* of happiness, which is of course not a duty to achieve it.

As Bruckner (2001) emphatically argues, modern individualistic societies have reinterpreted the right to the pursuit to happiness into a duty against an invisible deity. "We have all rights these days, except for one: to be unhappy" (ibid.: 11). Whoever does not live up to the socially prescribed "*euphorie perpétuelle*" (the original title of his book) is condemned, his life considered a failure (ibid.: 13). Against this hedonistic imperative, he replies, "I love my life too much to desire only happiness" (ibid.: 14), and Nietzsche polemically said, "[m] an does *not* strive after happiness; only the Englishman does that" (Nietzsche 1988: VI/61, transl. J.H., cf. also Thomä 2003: 169; Ehrenreich 2009).

However, in contrast to positive affect, the second and third constituents of happiness, approval and rationality, are not particularistic tastes. Rather, saying that the life I lead is a good life *requires* that I approve of it. Whoever is able to take an evaluative stance toward his own life – i.e. any sane and mature human being – knows what it means to approve of his life and, as a matter of tautology, will find it good and desirable to lead a life he approves of. Thus, valuing a life one approves of – that is, desiring reasons for being happy – is not a preference that needs to be justified or that could be wrong in the light of one's reflected self-interest. Rather, it is a necessary, though not sufficient, condition of a good life. That this approval has to satisfy some conditions of rationality (including authenticity and being well informed) has already been demonstrated above (p. 89), and it should be clear that this condition, in its turn, is again not a matter of a taste but an absolute requirement. The specific reasons a person has for being happy are of course another matter and in principle need to be justified, but this does not change the fact that a life is only good when the respective person approves of it.

Hence, we can conclude that one half of the conditions for happiness, namely those for leading a life one approves of, is a constitutive element of good development, while the other half, namely the conditions for experiencing positive affect, is not. However, while the conditions for experiencing positive affect are no constitutive element of good development, positive affect may be expected to be advanced as a particular desire, together with many other particular desires. In short, while happiness is no constitutive element of the idea of good development, it will often be a substantive social preference of a given society and will, to that extent, be a feature of a specific development path.

Beyond featuring, in the limited sense outlined here, as a teleological element of good development, happiness plays a conceptually more central role as what could be called a heuristic device. Without pre-judging whether or to which degree happiness is desirable, assessing potential private interests and social preferences *in the light of happiness* will often help to educate judgments and choices. One may think of a number of roles happiness might play as such a heuristic device. Since the next chapter will discuss the concrete procedural implications of these roles of happiness, this discussion will be rather concise.

1   Happiness is a symptom for a good life. As has been argued above (p. 96), happiness is primarily a symptom for the presence of reasons to be happy. Thus, when a person is happy, we know that that person has *reasons* for happiness. What is perhaps more important, the observation of marked unhappiness is a sure sign of suffering, and a society should feel obliged to investigate the reasons for unhappiness whenever it affects people in a systematic manner. In this role, happiness provides one more piece of

information for the evaluation of a person's life without, however, being that evaluation itself. Good development is therefore also a matter of reducing the number and the extent of suffering of unhappy people. Moreover, criteria of distributive justice can be enriched in the light of happiness information.

2   Happiness elucidates teleological orientation. Since people and societies do not have given interests, they will look for orientation for the construction and revision of their preferences. In this process, happiness can help to elucidate alternatives by raising the question of whether something contributes to happiness and whether something is an instrumental contribution or a constitutive element of happiness. In particular, such questions can effectively reveal and scrutinize silent assumption underlying social preferences regarding the contribution to happiness of different sources. It can in particular reveal psychological fallacies and unrecognized social dynamics that come in the way of good development.

3   Happiness can recommend supererogatory acts. While deontological debates are about obligations ("what needs to be done"), happiness can introduce a supererogatory perspective, i.e. what would be desirable without being an obligation. Taking happiness as a point of reference, public debates will not remain limited to the staking of claims and the demanding of corresponding duties, but will go beyond that to ask what would improve people's well-being even in the absence of a moral obligation to do so. As an open-ended and both teleological and deontological concept, good development includes supererogation as a desirable contribution.

4   Happiness includes the role of the person. The objectification of science and political discourse has resulted in a tendency to regard human beings as passive objects of societal circumstances, rather than as subjects. In this perspective, well-being becomes a function of living conditions alone. The happiness perspectives can reintegrate the role of the person into this discourse by drawing attention to the evident fact that happiness is also a matter of the attitude a person takes vis-à-vis her living conditions. For example, rather than rashly concluding that an unhappy person must be deprived of something, this perspective suggests that an unhappy person may as well be desiring too much. As John Stuart Mill already remarked, "I regard any considerable increase of human happiness, through mere changes in outward circumstances, unaccompanied by changes in the state of desires, as hopeless (Mill 1969/1833: 15).

5   Happiness is culturally sensitive. Being an inclusive end (cf. p. 77), happiness is not committed to any substantive values (except for positive affect as one among others) nor any weighting of such values. It is therefore open to cultural variation as far as the concrete reasons for happiness are concerned. Since, moreover, happiness plays no privileged role in a universal conception of good development, it does not stipulate any particular prioritization of happiness, which might conflict with some cultures' legitimate social preferences (cf. the quote by Ahuvia on p. 20).

Apart from the contribution that can be expected from the reflection on happiness to deontological questions of good development, the recognition of the principle of morality can contribute to a conception of legitimate, universalizable happiness. Spinoza expressed the principal deontological contribution to happiness most succinctly:

> Every man's true happiness and blessedness consist solely in the enjoyment of what is good, not in the pride that he alone is enjoying it, to the exclusion of others. He who thinks himself the more blessed because he is enjoying benefits which others are not, or because he is more blessed or more fortunate than his fellows, is ignorant of true happiness and blessedness, and the joy which he feels is either childish or envious and malicious.
>
> (Spinoza 1951/1670: 43)

> Hence, men who are governed by reason ... desire for themselves nothing, which they do not also desire for the rest of mankind, and, consequently, are just, faithful, and honourable in their conduct.
>
> (Spinoza 1951/1677: 202)

Spinoza's dictum highlights a major danger when thinking of good development in terms of happiness alone: that of overlooking that happiness is not universalizable to the degree that it is based on privileges, i.e. on "oligarchic" (Harrod 1958) benefits that are desired, but cannot be enjoyed, by everybody at the same time. Or, in more technical terms, that happiness often is a matter of positional goods (cf. p. 43).

Spinoza's judgment appears to be condemning the joy derived from the misfortunes of others, i.e. *Schadenfreude*, and therefore would seem quite acceptable by most standards. Keeping in mind what has been said about positional competition (cf. p. 43), however, a closer look reveals that a person need not necessarily be moved by *Schadenfreude* to derive happiness from being "more fortunate than his fellows". A world-record sprinter, for example, will be happy that he is faster than everybody else, which is of course the same thing as saying that he is happy that nobody is as fast as he is. It would seem harsh, not to say absurd, to condemn this happiness or the underlying aspiration for not being universalizable. But if this is so, should somebody be condemned for the happiness she derives from having outperformed her fellow candidates for a contested job opening? Or from owning an original Rembrandt painting? Or from having an above-average salary and consumption? Most people who own original paintings or rare stamps, for example, may not be aware that their satisfaction depends on the social scarcity of these goods, and they may have no misgivings at all about other collectors' fortunes (and no *Schadenfreude* in particular). Yet, it remains a fact that their happiness systematically depends on most others being below them in terms of relative position, and it is apparent that a stamp collector, an athlete, or a job applicant desires for himself something that he does not also desire for the rest of mankind, to use Spinoza's words.

There are a number of reasons why Spinoza's judgment may appear too harsh, or why it needs to be differentiated. First of all, a good life does not depend on owning an original Rembrandt painting. Even though an art lover will probably feel less happy for not having one, the success of his life as a whole should not depend on it – i.e. a Rembrandt painting and many other positional goods are not constitutive of a good life. By implication, the person owning a Rembrandt does not reduce the capability of others to lead a good life. In other words, in the perspective of a good life, many positional goods are just not important enough that one should condemn their owners for that privilege.

Second, even where a positional good is constitutive of a good life, it is only one aspect of a good life, and having a low relative position with respect to such a good does not necessarily mean that one's life is going badly, just as being high on that good does not guarantee that one's life is going well. For example, an individual may reasonably consider it a constitutive element of her conception of a good life to study at a good university. When she does not get admitted to her favorite school, she may feel seriously disappointed, but as long as the other elements of her conception of a good life are not compromised, her life need not fail for that reason.

Third, it may be argued that the existence of positional competition has beneficial consequences for society because it stimulates people to develop their talents and be creative and productive. From primary school grades to the Nobel prize, positional rewards indeed appear to motivate excellence and result in benefits to society and occasionally even to the individual (namely to the degree that positional incentives compensate for the irrationality of, say, myopic students). Now, if the existence of the positional competition game is desirable, one can of course not condemn the players for winning it, at least as long as they are respecting the rules of the game and the dignity of the other players. In other words, the winner could justify his positional benefits against Spinoza's objection by arguing that he is just being a player (and a responsible one at that) of a game that is considered desirable by society.

Yet, saying that positional competition for, say, school grades is desirable still leaves open the question of degree. In particular, it does not mean that positional competition should be entirely unbound, training students to define themselves and each other by grades alone. It seems more reasonable, to stick with this specific example, to restrict the competition for grades to such a degree that it stimulates excellence and leads to an efficient selection of talent, without dominating the substantive objectives of education and without entirely subordinating students' lives to educational achievement. As Layard (1980: 734–44) argues:

> the clearest indication of a bad selection system is the extent to which its victims are obsessed by the process of selection. For the costs of education are not just direct costs and earnings foregone, but also the anxieties which students experience.

Competition, positional or otherwise, comes with a cost that needs to be balanced against its benefits.

Thus, when the positional game is desirable, the rules just, and the players playing fair, it might be argued that the losers of positional competition have no right to complain about the outcome, i.e. that their moral rights are not violated. Whether this conclusion is acceptable will of course depend critically on what one holds to be a desirable competition, just rules, and fair play. Again, the metaphor of a game should not suggest that the "players" may do anything that is within the rules, even if these are just (cf. p. 111). They should respect not only the rules, but also the other players, simply because even within the "game" of competition they are dealing with other human beings who continue to be vulnerable even within the rules of the game.

But still, even with responsible winners, there is the possibility that the cumulative outcome of a number of competitions will be ethically problematic, even if each of these games individually is not. It may be unproblematic for a person to lose out on the high school grading competition, on the university admission competition, or on the job competition, but losing repeatedly on all accounts will severely compromise a person's ability to lead a good life. If losing in a fair competition could be blamed entirely on a person's own reprehensible conduct, one might consider such an outcome justified in the same way as the loss of freedom of a convicted criminal. However, such a meritocratic justification hardly applies to positional competition because social scarcity implies that someone *must* lose, even if no players, including the losers, can be blamed for any negligence. And since losing in terms of *relative* position is an *absolute* disadvantage, a person may suffer unjustifiable disadvantages without being guilty of reprehensible conduct.

This result is of course not surprising since competition, especially, but not only, for position, cannot primarily be justified by its meritocratic justice – whatever that would exactly mean – but for its functional features. More precisely, competition and the plight of its losers are justified (if they can be justified) by the indirect efficiency gains of competition for society as a whole (in particular, for the consumer side of the production game), not by the inherent (meritocratic or distributional) justice of the individual payoffs.[14] This becomes especially clear whenever the discrepancy between these payoffs and the corresponding merit escalates and receives public criticism, as in the case of extremely polarized patterns of income distribution or exploding executive compensations. Thus, while some discrepancy between merit and individual payoff is an inherent and in principle justifiable feature of positional competition, the degree of this discrepancy must remain within limits that can actually be justified before the losers of the game by commensurate efficiency benefits.[15] This is why the recent tendency toward "winner-take-all markets" (Frank and Cook 1996) really represents a different quality of competition and involves the escalation of an ethical problem that is no unavoidable aspect of competition as such.

Returning to the point of departure for this digression, namely Spinoza's dictum that one must not be happy for the privileges one enjoys, we can therefore state that it can hardly be considered illegitimate as such to aspire, and achieve, a superior position in some respect, but that such competition can be ethically problematic if it does not meet some conditions of fairness, and even if it meets such conditions but leads to "cumulative misfortune" on the part of individual citizens. Yet, Spinoza clearly had a point that is not qualified by the demonstration of the possibility of fair and just positional competition. As has been pointed out earlier, winning or losing the positional competition for a particular benefit is not the same as having or not having a good life. Consequently, being happy for having got a job that others did not get is not the same as being happy that one has a better life than others, and saying that the one is legitimate does not imply that the other would be legitimate as well. This, I guess, is what Spinoza had in mind: one shall not derive happiness from the fact that one has a better life than others do. It may be possible to justify the desire for positional benefits on some accounts, but desiring positional superiority in the success of the life as a whole would seem impossible to defend. Put differently, one's positional desires should be consistent with the desire that all others also have a good life, and the happiness of others should not subtract from one's own happiness.

Seen from another perspective, this distinction is the same as that between envy and a justified sense of relative deprivation (cf. p. 94). Spinoza's dictum holds true both ways: not only should a person not derive happiness from the fact that others' lives are worse than her own, but also a person should not be unhappy because others lead better lives than she does. The first would be malice, the latter envy, and both appear to be sentiments that are difficult to defend.

Not all negative sentiments regarding the good fortune of others have to be an expression of envy, however. This is especially true to the extent that relative fortune is *instrumentally* important for leading a good life, most visibly perhaps in the case of secondary inflation (cf. p. 46). Since the prevalent consumption pattern provides the terms on which social inclusion and exclusion are defined, the superior consumption pattern of some hurt the relatively poor in absolute terms, and they need not be moved by envy in order to consider themselves deprived and see the superior possessions of others with bitterness. For the eighteenth century laborer without a linen shirt (p. 55) and, Smith might have added in our days, today's high school kid without a mobile phone, the linen shirts and mobile phones of others constitute the predicament of their social exclusion and not simply an object of envy.

There is, moreover, a qualitative difference between the case where a person desires to be above all others and the case where a person desires not to be below all others (cf. p. 43). Figuratively speaking, it is a difference of whether I desire a linen shirt in order to be able to appear in public without shame, or whether I desire a silk shirt in order to stand out and get the admiration of others. As long as my concern is to keep up with the Joneses, i.e. to maintain a position that most others can also occupy at the same time, my concern is universalizable. However, if I am concerned with surpassing the Joneses, i.e. with achieving an above-average position, I am playing a game that must, in the end, have a loser (cf. Lichtenberg 1996).

Happiness that may be legitimately pursued, i.e. happiness that is consistent with good development, must therefore not be based on malice or on indifference with respect to the fortune of others, but it may still functionally depend on others not having much better lives than oneself (cf. Lichtenberg 1996). Yet, to which degree this is so is not a matter of logical or historical necessity, but rather a matter of the role of position within a society. Evaluating everything from intelligence to professional achievement in terms of rankings appears to be a recipe to increase the weight of status considerations in people's assessment of human worth and, therefore, a sure recipe to obstruct the access to happiness for a portion of society. Moreover, as more and more socially scarce goods are commercialized, i.e. allocated by the price mechanism instead of being administered on another basis, the *absolute* advantage that is bought by *relative* wealth increases, and people will have more reason to run faster in the rat race for relative income (cf. Hirsch 1976: 91). In short, the privatization of socially scarce goods intensifies the desirability of relative wealth to the individual and therefore the deadweight loss from zero-sum positional competition as well as the absolute disadvantages of being relatively poor.

This is of course not the place to come up with concrete recommendations with respect to privatization. Again, positional competition may, to some extent, be desirable, and the question of whether or to which degree privatization is desirable depends on a host of other aspects as well. The point to note here is that good development will require a conscious examination and evaluation of the issue of positional competition. A blind trust in a benevolent invisible hand or the orientation at GDP figures alone will most certainly conceal the potential costs and injustices of positional competition, while an orientation at happiness may enlighten debates and choices involving positionality. In particular, the importance of relative position for happiness and, therefore, the deadweight loss from positional competition will increase with the status-mindedness of a society, which in turn depends on the absolute rewards for status and the intrinsic value a culture attaches to status.

Properly interpreted, Spinoza's dictum can indeed become a fundamental principle of good development. To be sure, it must not be interpreted with hair-splitting concreteness. To "desire for oneself nothing which one does not also desire for the rest of mankind" cannot, for the reasons given above, reasonably refer to the desire to win a medal at the Olympics or to get a particular job. Rather, this rule is valid with respect to the greater idea of a good life as such: one shall not desire for oneself a better life than for the rest of mankind. Winning a medal at the Olympics or getting a particular job is not inconsistent with the desire that others have, on the whole, a life that is as good as I wish my own life to be. There are endless areas to compete in, and when A is an excellent chess player, B may still be a famed artist, and C an exceptional carpenter. It is only when the good life itself becomes a positional good – or when it comes to depend excessively on a small set of positional goods – that it becomes difficult even for a good-willed person to heed Spinoza's rule, for then one's own good life necessarily requires others' lives to be worse.[16]

In effect, we are now back at the familiar universalization principle, just that the focus is now specifically on the reasons for happiness. What Spinoza says, ultimately, is that one's reasons for happiness should be consistent with the legitimate happiness of others – strikingly reminiscent of Kant's first formulation of the categorical imperative. This even led Ludwig Marcuse (1962: 119, transl. J.H.) to claim that the quoted passage ("desire for themselves nothing...", p. 000) "was Spinoza's formulation of the categorical imperative, one century before Kant, with the difference that Spinoza experienced the happiness of shared humanness that was denied to Kant".

Good development, therefore, is also about respecting the rights of all others to pursue their conceptions of a good life. It is, in other words, not only a matter of happiness, but also of the symmetry of human dignity and the universalization principle (cf. p. 79). Still, happiness can play an important role in the evaluational part of good development when it comes to specifying these rights in public debate. Happiness can elucidate the teleological preferences and choices at stake, filling the formal categories (rights, capabilities, legitimate claims) with a common concern that is hermeneutically accessible to everyone. Happiness will thus be a major candidate for the *content* of the open-ended public deliberation on what ought to be done, even though it cannot at the same time serve as its *criterion*. Teleological criteria and deontological principles are complementary and irreducible aspects of good development.

6 Happiness-oriented societal development under the premise of democracy

Reflections on good development, whether implicit or explicit, will ultimately be measured against their practical significance. This is not to say that they need to be "applicable" in the sense of delivering blueprints for political agendas, but that they must provide some contextually relevant understanding that can ultimately contribute to better development, rather than remaining normatively indistinctive or even tautological. This chapter will point out the specific contributions the preceding reflections may make to good development. Before doing so, however, it seems necessary to examine the precise status and the adequate form of such a contribution.

Most welfare economic studies, but also many other discussions of societal issues, conclude with "policy recommendations" that make specific proposals to solve a perceived deficit. In 99 out of 100 cases, the authors take it for granted that policy recommendations (1) address only policy makers, that (2) they must come in terms of changing the rules of the game, basically boiling down to changing incentives for selfish *homines oeconomici*, and that (3) they must be justified in terms of objective social benefits (usually in terms of maximizing social welfare). Upon closer examination, however, it becomes clear that these premises are mutually inconsistent, systematically incomplete, and at variance with basic principles of democracy.

The very term of "policy recommendations" is of course already suggestive and does much to obstruct a more adequate understanding of the potential contributions of normative research on societal issues. I shall therefore not adopt this term here but rather use the expression "practical implications". At this point, it shall also be re-emphasized that the term "development" refers not only to the low-income countries but to the challenge to correct injustice and promote well-being with which all societies are permanently and eternally confronted (cf. p. 102).

Democracy and policy recommendations

In present days, practically all normative research and the "policy recommendations" therein contained accept the premise of democracy. While there is no consensus with respect to the exact conception of democracy, there appears to be an overwhelming consensus that the recommended policies should not be implemented against universal public resistance and that policies must ultimately be justifiable in terms of, and respond to, the will of the people. Even if one wants to doubt the factual accuracy of this analysis, the above discussion of ethics (p. 68) should provide sufficient justification to accept its normative validity: a policy that ignores the will of the people cannot be a good policy since it violates a basic principle of procedural justice.

Under this premise of democracy, the practice of formulating specific policy recommendations may, at first sight, look problematic. Specifically, it may appear ethically illegitimate and factually ineffective for social scientists to propose specific policies. After all, it is the people as a whole, not only experts, who should decide upon policies (ethical argument) and who do, as a matter of fact, elect policy makers (factual argument). A classical libertarian argument would then complete this reasoning by declaring people to be rational: since every individual knows best what is good for herself, democracy simply demands that elected policy makers reflect people's preferences. Happiness-based policies in particular would look suspicious in this perspective because they take an interest in people's private lives and subjective experiences, a sphere that libertarians believe is sacrosanct and needs to be categorically protected from outside interference. Besides being illegitimate, this interest in people's private lives would also be superfluous because people's rationality would ensure that the preferences they voice in the democratic process take care of their personal happiness so that no outside interest would be required.

Such a conception of liberal democracy (which is of course more refined than can be sketched here) raises some valid points against the practice of formulating policy recommendations in general and against happiness maximization policies in particular, but it would replace an overspecification of societal design by an underspecification of democracy. Saying that policy recommendations, and normative research in general, are neither necessary nor legitimate because the superior rationality of people combined with the benevolence of an invisible hand guarantees the best of all possible worlds would be a metaphysical confession rather than a rational argument. Thus, a more refined and ethically reflected concept of democracy is needed, one that is rigidly argued without excluding the moral dimension of human beings. The most convincing concept along this line, I will argue, is that of deliberative democracy, as developed within political philosophy.[1]

The idea of deliberative democracy can be roughly characterized as "a system that combines accountability with a measure of reflection and reason-giving" (Sunstein 2002). In contrast to most other conceptions of democracy – in particular to contractarian and libertarian conceptions such as social choice theory and the public choice school – it does not blindly accept the tastes and preferences people bring to bear on the democratic process, and it does not assume that people are necessarily and always selfish, i.e. driven by strategic considerations alone. Rather, deliberative democracy demands that choices be made through a process of deliberation in which people demand and give justification for the preferences they are defending. This process does of course not usually lead to a consensus, nor does it guarantee a legitimate outcome, but demanding such properties of a conception of democracy would again make sense only within a deterministic conception of ethics that has been repeatedly rejected throughout this text. In this context, it is noteworthy that the preference aggregation "paradox" first demonstrated by Arrow (1951) in what came to be known as "Arrow's impossibility theorem" is a paradox only within a deterministic paradigm (cf. Ulrich 1993/1986: 212f.). It should not surprise that the *ethical* conditions it stipulates cannot be jointly satisfied by a *deterministic* framework of preference accounting and that the hundreds – or probably thousands – of articles provoked by Arrow's findings could not solve the "paradox".[2]

Thus, consensus or determinacy should be considered neither requirements nor virtues of democratic decision procedures. Instead, what may be expected from deliberative democracy is that people's preferences that will ultimately find public expression (sometimes, but not necessarily, in elections) will be somewhat better reflected and more sensitive to other people's moral rights and interests. Moreover, the very process of publicly reflecting and justifying competing interests should be considered an *intrinsic* procedural benefit of deliberative democracy, as well as a *functional* precondition for trust and accountability.

One criticism at the idea of deliberative democracy would go that it is impractical to have extensive public deliberation on each and every single decision. Apart from decisions restricted to tiny communities, the large majority of decisions must be decided without much or any public deliberation. Not only would it be impossible to discuss every minor decision publicly, but it would be an undue demand on citizens' time and energy to oblige them to form and express an opinion on every public matter. Therefore, deliberative democracy would be an undesirable and unfeasible model of democracy. Instead, decisions would have to be taken by elected decision-makers who dispose of sufficient formal authority.

Fortunately, we do not have to choose between these two radical alternatives (universal and permanent deliberation vs. authoritarian decision-making). The critique just presented is in fact a critique at a caricature of deliberative democracy, not at its spirit. Well-understood, deliberative democracy demands that decisions *can* be challenged and submitted to a public debate whenever they meet substantial opposition, not that each and every decision is actually preceded by such a debate. The "constraint of deliberative economy" (Dryzek 2001: 652), i.e. the need to limit the deliberative demands on citizens, must of course be taken into account in a conception of democracy that also respects the right of each citizen to not have her life consumed by politics (cf. Warren 1996: 46).

Even if public deliberation does not actually precede each and every individual decision, the real possibility to publicly challenge decisions will have the effect of pressuring decision-makers into taking decisions *as if* public deliberation had taken place because they know that public contestation is just around the corner. In other words, the mere possibility of contestation obliges decision-makers to anticipate and be responsive to contestation. At the same time, this same possibility of contestation (and its occasional exercise) will inspire a degree of trust in office holders on the side of citizens because both sides know that repeated failure to respect the anticipated outcome of public deliberation will not be tolerated (ibid.: 47).

While a relatively small number of rather contentious decisions will be the subject of actual public deliberation, the large majority of decisions that are rather uncontentious (either because they have been settled earlier or because they are evidently not contentious) will have to fall under the authority of office holders in order to economize on deliberation. This authority is neither absolute nor arbitrary, however. The power it lends to office holders is again dependent on the silent approval and the resulting trust of the public, i.e. on the absence of public challenge where it would be possible. Authority that is in this way deserved and based on trust is therefore not antagonistic to democracy, but rather makes democracy possible by allocating limited deliberative resources to those issues that are most contentious.

From the perspective of the citizens, in turn, trust-based authority means that the institutionalized possibility of challenge allows individuals to partially suspend judgment on specific issues (Warren 1996: 57). It does not mean that citizens surrender their judgment to officeholders between elections. Rather, their judgment moves to a higher order, concerning the question of whether their trust in the person taking a specific decision is justified, rather than whether a specific decision is correct. It is this higher-order judgment that allows citizens to partially suspend their lower-order judgments. "Democratic authority" (ibid.: 47) must therefore be a constitutive element of deliberative democracy and not just a necessary evil for which an advocate of deliberative democracy would have to apologize.

Public deliberation must be open to all citizens, but it would be misplaced egalitarianism to demand, or expect, that the extent of participation and influence would be exactly the same for every individual. Evidently, legitimately elected office holders would play a distinguished role. They are granted privileges that are justified by the very fact that they have been explicitly entrusted with decision-making powers on behalf of the electorate. But it is not only democratic representation that confers privileged decision-making powers. Judges, for example, are often indirectly elected (i.e. appointed or elected by representatives of the people), but whether they are trusted also depends on their expertise as judges. After all, we do not respect Supreme Court decisions only because its members are appointed through a process that we consider legitimate, but also because we consider its members competent and believe they use their authority in good faith (i.e. impartially). While the democratic authority of judges still derives largely from the procedural legitimacy of their public office, other individuals command democratic authority almost independent from democratic procedures. Physicians, jet pilots, genetic engineers, etc. dispose of such a degree of expert knowledge that we gladly surrender our judgment to theirs if we have reason to trust them. As a consequence, these experts hold considerable direct decision-making powers (whether to do a surgery, whether to do an emergency landing, whether to convict a criminal suspect) but also indirect power by virtue of the weight of their voice in public debates. Yet, while ordinary citizens may reasonably challenge the normative conclusions that experts derive from their instrumental knowledge (e.g. whether a newly invented weapon should be produced), they will often be unable to challenge the factual knowledge as such (e.g. how lethal that weapon is). As far as factual knowledge is concerned, they have no alternative but to infer each expert's trustworthiness from the discourse among the experts and from established screening devices such as university degrees and career steps.

As far as the normative discourse is concerned, people may expect that expert opinions inform and enlighten their judgment by revealing overlooked aspects or contributing new arguments simply because often the experts have also reflected more than others on the normative implications of their subject matter. However, experts have no systematically better faculty to make moral judgments than ordinary citizens. There is no reason to assume that, for example, a person with expert knowledge of the detailed functioning of a weapon will come to a better judgment concerning the question of whether that weapon should be produced than a lay person who merely knows about the morally relevant aspects of that weapon. You clearly do not have to be a nuclear physicist to have a well-argued opinion on nuclear armament policy.

Since political decisions are never ethically neutral (or "objective"), there cannot be a single political decision that can legitimately be excluded from the realm of public deliberation and instead be decided by decision algorithms or experts alone. For development policies in general, this means that they must indeed be subjected to (the possibility of) public deliberation, rather than be decided by experts in development economics or other social scientists. This is not to say that social scientists are not allowed to formulate policy recommendations. It only means that these recommendations must not have the last word. In other words, policy recommendations must not bypass the deliberative democratic process; they must become an *input* to public deliberation. It would not be for the better of a democratic society if social scientists kept silent about their normative considerations. These can enrich the public debate with new arguments that are overlooked by those who do not dedicate most of their time to the issue in question. However, heeding the advice of an expert is not the same as blindly adopting it.

This conception of deliberative democracy already indicates the limits within which policy recommendations must remain. First, they must not aim at seriously undermining the foundations of deliberative democracy itself. This demand is analogous to the prohibition of self-abolishment contained in most states' constitutions or to the prohibition of parties deemed unconstitutional. Saying that such policy recommendations are not admissible is of course meant in the sense of not being morally admissible, rather than in the sense of being illegal. Not being morally admissible, in turn, means that they should stand no chance of being seriously considered in a functioning deliberative democracy.

Second, policy recommendations have to be presented in terms of the justifiability of the proposed recommendation, rather than in terms of purely mechanical arguments based on alleged natural social laws. It would be a category mistake to claim that a particular policy recommendation is "objectively" the right thing to do because it enhances "social welfare", "efficiency", or "aggregate happiness". For example, the fact that having more leisure time tends to have a positive effect on SWB does not justify the policy recommendation to extend the number of holidays workers should be entitled to. Such a recommendation would be awkwardly removed from the contextual legitimizing considerations that must bear on such a decision (cf. Thomä 2003: 155). Such a justification reflects a view of citizens as happiness vectors and of politicians as social engineers, whose task it is to optimize a mechanical social happiness function. There may be many good reasons to extend holiday entitlements, but an argument based on statistical evidence alone fails to provide reasons that might politically legitimize such a decision in the face of potential conflicts between opposing rights and interest. Statistical evidence may be one valuable piece of information, but it cannot decide the deontological question of whether a particular policy is legitimate.

In addition to these rather formal conditions for policy recommendations, the preceding argument rests on a conception of democracy where the citizens bring with themselves some minimum ethical predisposition or, in simpler words, some good will. While any conception of democracy must be robust against undemocratic and immoral attitudes of a minority, it cannot meaningfully be built upon the assumption of the complete absence of a sense of morality. The implications of such a conception shall be elaborated in the following section.

The imputation of morality

The idea of deliberative democracy rests on the premise that citizens have a sense of morality. More specifically, this premise consists of two interrelated but nevertheless distinct claims. First, it includes the factual claim that people generally are not only and always selfish but are in principle prepared to act upon moral imperatives they recognize. Second, it includes the normative claim that people ought to pursue their self-interest only under the condition of legitimacy. Correspondingly, opponents have raised two objections against this premise of morality. First, they believe that it is *unrealistic* to expect that people are moved by moral considerations. Second, they argue that it would be *illegitimate* to appeal to people's morality.

While both issues (factual and normative, realism and legitimacy) are inextricably linked with each other (one's position on one systematically implies that on the other), they still remain distinct and will therefore have to be discussed separately.

To begin with, the issue is not, once more, whether people are angels or devils, i.e. whether they always act from the moral point of view or whether they never do so, but whether most people are generally prepared to respect the rights of others out of non-strategic, i.e. moral, considerations. The criterion is not whether I pursue my own interests or those of others ("egoism" vs. "altruism") and neither whether I respect another's interest at any cost to myself, but whether

I sincerely care also about another person's moral rights and allow it to become, in principle, a reason to act against my immediate self-interest. The pursuit of one's self-interest is not evidence of a lack of morality. It is the lack of respect for others' moral rights *in* the pursuit of one's self-interest that is immoral, and the continuous and universal lack of such respect is what defines immorality.

The claim that the (factual) premise of morality is *illusory* is problematic for at least three reasons, apart from the theoretical problems of this view that have already been discussed above (p. 79). First, empirical evidence strongly suggests that people are responsive to the claims and opinions of others with which they are confronted. Empirical evidence on voting behavior, for example, suggests that people's voting decisions are much better explained by the "responsibility hypothesis" than by self-interest. For example, rather than reelecting the present government whenever their own economic situation is secure, their decision shows a concern for the overall situation of the economy (Frey and Stutzer 2002: 123; cf. also the literature cited there). It has also been convincingly demonstrated that people indeed change their stated preferences upon reflection and after being exposed to opposing (but also to supporting) arguments (cf. Sunstein 2002).

Second, starting from the premise of immorality would carry with it the danger of becoming a self-fulfilling prophecy. When democratic decision procedures are designed to merely aggregate unquestioned preferences rather than to help people make up their minds about which preferences they consider justifiable, one can indeed not expect citizens to be sensitive to the moral claims of others. It is like putting two persons in a boxing ring. Knowing that the rules of the game are designed under the assumption that the two opponents fight each other without compassion, they will conform to that expectation. Yet, put the same two persons in a golf competition and they will, in all likelihood, respect the unenforceable moral code of the game.

Third, it is impossible to argue that human beings in general are immoral without contradicting oneself. This is because, as Habermas (1983: 140–1) has shown, the very idea of communication imputes to the participants a commitment to the universalization principle (cf. p. 81), and somebody who engages in communication is implicitly claiming to respect that commitment. Thus, a person who argues that human beings have no sense of morality would be invoking what she is claiming to reject and therefore commit a performative contradiction (cf. p. 83), similar to Epimenides the Cretan's famous claim that "all Cretans are liars".

A skeptic might still object that, even though people are not in general immoral, it is *illegitimate* to demand that people change their preferences. Usually, this objection is motivated by the deontological interpretation of Bentham's "push-pin and poetry" dictum (cf. p. 104) and basically says that preferences cannot be judged because they are subjective ("*de gustibus non est desputandum*"). The point is not that Bentham's statement as such would be problematic, but rather that it is not problematic only because he took an "innocent" (Bentham) example. As long as no rights of human beings (or, what would be more difficult to defend, animate beings or even non-animate nature) are involved, there indeed seems to be no basis to judge preferences. As soon as preferences have a social dimension, however, they may be contested. This is not only a problem of internalizing negative externalities. Compensating people for the damages inflicted on them does not in itself legitimize an act. As Brian Barry argues in an analogous context:

> We will all agree that doing harm is in general not cancelled out by doing good, and conversely that doing some good does not license one to do harm provided it does not exceed the amount of good. For example, if you paid for the realignments of a dangerous highway intersection and saved an average of two lives a year, that would not mean that you could shoot one motorist per year and simply reckon on coming out ahead.[3]
>
> (Barry 1991: 264, quoted in Neumayer 1999: 40)

The same case can be made of most negative externalities. A rich person may have no difficulties to pay the victims of his feudal lifestyle into accepting his negative externalities, but it would still be much better had he different, more universalizable preferences. For example, a very rich person may be able and willing to pay a community of indigenous fishermen just enough money for them to accept the pollution of their lake by the unfiltered waste oil from his fleet of pleasure yachts. Such a deal would clearly be to the (subjective) advantage of both, as all free deals are by their very nature – otherwise the contracting parties would not consent to the deal in the first place. Yet, one might wonder whether the rich man should not *want* to use his money in a more responsible way, e.g. in a way that generates meaningful work or in a way that improves the situation of people desperate enough to trade their fishing grounds for a small amount of money. Or, to give a more trivial example, a person might decide to spend her leisure time riding her bicycle instead of driving her SUV around and would thus reduce social costs even if she had paid some "optimal" amount of eco-taxes for the truck's gasoline. Rather than compensating those who suffer from one's choices, it would clearly be better to have such preferences that do not make others suffer and require compensation in the first place. This is not to say that all preferences that have a negative impact on others are necessarily illegitimate (if that was so, few legitimate ones would remain). The point is that the question of whether or not a specific preference with a negative impact on others is justified or not is an ethical problem. Simply declaring all personal preferences as beyond questioning "solves" this ethical problem in an unacceptable way, burying the issue under a dogma rather than facing up to it. Of course, purely private preferences do exist (e.g. which color I paint the walls of my living room), and whether or not somebody is unhappy about them is ethically irrelevant, even if utilitarianism (and the Pareto criterion) suggest otherwise (Sen 1970). But which preferences are private and which are not is again an ethical question (Ulrich 2008: 299).

As a corollary, the idea that the person responsible for a negative externality must compensate her "victims" must rest on a concept of legitimate preferences.

If I happen to dislike the sight of people wearing striped socks, that would probably not be a sufficient reason to oblige people wearing striped socks to compensate me for the discomfort they cause me. Similarly, one may have good reason to consider the noise of a factory an illegitimate nuisance for which the victims have a right to be compensated, but at the same time regard the noise of playing children a legitimate externality for which the "victims" cannot claim compensation.

Perhaps more importantly, the strong objection against questioning preferences on the side of libertarians is often in fact an objection against prescribing or forbidding preferences. Yet, it is a long way from questioning preferences to prescribing or forbidding preferences, and saying that the one is legitimate does not at all imply that the other is so as well. Questioning means demanding justification rather than judging something to be unjustifiable, let alone preventing someone from doing something. In the above example, saying that it would be legitimate to question the desire of the millionaire to drive a fleet of pleasure yachts and dispose of the waste oil in the cheapest possible way is not the same thing as saying that his desire is necessarily unjustifiable. Moreover, even if one concludes that it would be unjustifiable, it would be another step to argue that he should be actively prevented from doing so.

Apart from these ethical considerations, it would be inconsistent and arbitrary to formulate policy recommendations and at the same time dispense citizens from any moral responsibility. This is because policy recommendations will inevitably make moral demands on the decision-makers that are being addressed as long as they are justified by reference to some social benefit. The only way to avoid this would be to motivate one's policy recommendations by showing why the addressed decision-makers should have purely strategic reasons to adopt the proposed measures, i.e. by showing that the proposed measure would pay off for decision-makers privately ("we recommend reducing taxes in order to secure victory in the next elections"). Fortunately, we may safely assume that sincere academic policy recommendations are usually inspired under the premise that they must be legitimate (at least in a national perspective, even if not necessarily from a global point of view) rather than only advantageous for the addressed audience.

Yet, if decision-makers are called upon to do what is right rather than what pays off for them privately, it would be inconsistent to exempt all others (i.e. those who are not public decision-makers) from this demand. Moreover, people may actually want to know what their role ought to be to make a proposed policy successful. As has been illustrated above (p. 108), public and explicit formulation of citizen duties may sometimes even be necessary in order to reassure people that their commitment will be matched by those of many others. Demanding a commitment to the *res publica* from people is therefore not ideological or manipulative, but rather the logical next step when formulating policy recommendations that address policy makers.

While it would certainly be inappropriate for academic writings to come up with specific citizen commandments, what can be said is that citizens may be expected and called upon to respect the rights of others in their pursuit of their respective interests, i.e. we may expect them to develop a republican ethos (cf. p. 111). Whether we may realistically expect that a large majority does so to a considerable degree is an entirely different issue, and the answer to this question makes no difference to the normative conclusion that individuals with a free will have the moral obligation to respect the rights of others. In contrast to most libertarian and contractarian models of democracy, a conception of *republican liberalism* (Ulrich 2008: 278ff.) leaves some of the burden of morality with the individual instead of shifting it entirely to the rules of the game. In other words, it envisions the possibility of communicative interaction between citizens, rather than merely strategic interaction of purely self-oriented *homines oeconomici*.

In the context of happiness, republican liberalism would not only demand morality, i.e. respect of others' rights, but also recommend prudence, i.e. the thoughtful transformation of living conditions into a life worth living. The freedom that republican liberalism demands for the individual carries with it the responsibility to make good use of this freedom. Free citizens cannot expect everything from the living conditions that others do or do not create for them; they still have to *lead* their lives. Under given living conditions, a person can be happy or unhappy, depending largely on what she makes out of her living conditions and how she interprets them. The unhappiness of a person cannot be necessarily blamed on her living conditions. A person's unhappiness that results from dissatisfaction with her living standard, for example, might be due to envy with respect to others who are deservedly better off. Drawing the line between envy and a justified sense of being disadvantaged is one aspect of the individual's responsibility.

Saying that a person has responsibility for her own happiness does not mean that the individual is obliged to make herself feel happy whenever possible. Such a deontological "duty of happiness" (Bruckner) would indeed be an untenable demand that would not only be an undue moral imposition on people's private lives but also an overspecification of the good life. Rather, responsibility here means that, given a person's living conditions, each person has the freedom to be more or less happy. Whether a person wants to feel rather happy or not is her own business, but if she does feel unhappy despite favorable living conditions (because of envy, for example) then she cannot blame that on others.

Sometimes people may have reason to be unhappy. It would be odd to demand cheerfulness from a funeral congregation. It is even argued sometimes that it is healthy for a society to feel unhappy with poor living conditions because unhappiness can motivate people to bring about change and to pressure decision-makers into improving living conditions. However, being happy or unhappy and being critical and constructive as a citizen should be seen as independent characteristics. If, thanks to a positive general attitude, a person is happy despite terrible living conditions, there seems to be no reason why that person should not also demand an improvement of living conditions. After all, it would be quite a limited view of the person to expect that citizens are concerned only with their personal happiness (cf. ch. 4).

This connects well with the republican co-responsibility for appropriate rules of the game. If fierce competition within the rules of the game punishes individual actors for moral behavior, they cannot simply justify illegitimate behavior by pointing to the "constraints" on their choices as long as they do not, within the extent that may reasonably be demanded, actively lobby for rules that reward, rather than punish, responsible behavior (Ulrich 2008: 409ff.). As an example, consider the case of a country without environmental legislation. The forces of competition would punish those firms that try to limit their emissions voluntarily as they suffer economic disadvantages with respect to their competitors. At the limit, their sense of responsibility will be punished by a takeover or by bankruptcy. However, a company cannot justify its failure to limit emissions by pointing to this threat only; it would also have to demonstrate that it undertakes a reasonable effort to lobby for environmental regulation and to change the incentives its industry faces.

An analogous principle holds for "positional" happiness. In many situations marked by precarious living conditions, a given individual may be able to escape discomfort and hardship thanks to a high relative position (e.g. the owners of real estate). Yet, to the degree that this escape is based on positional benefits, her strategy cannot be emulated by an arbitrary number of people. In positional competition, while everybody has the chance to win, not everybody can be a winner. Thus, the winners would be wrong to suppose that everybody could emulate their success and that they are only reaping a benefit that everybody could get if only everybody followed their path. While it does not follow from this that it is necessarily illegitimate to enjoy positional privileges, it does follow that positional success is no generalizable answer to the problem of precarious living conditions, and this in turn suggests that those enjoying or going after positional benefits are under an obligation to work toward conditions that allow all people to pursue more universalizable paths of success.

While republican liberalism does demand *that* people let themselves be guided by considerations of morality, it does not demand which specific norms they should follow and not even that all members of a community must share the same set of norms and values. In other words, it does not require a substantive agreement on (teleological) values and (deontological) norms, as communitarianism does, but "only" the unconditional acceptance of the universalization principle, the recognition of which does not depend on pre-rational beliefs or axioms. Thus, citizens with a republican ethos will not stop living in conflict with each other, but they will deal with these conflicts in a civilized manner, always trying to settle them by arguments rather than by power.

How the happiness perspective could influence development paths

From the preceding considerations, it follows that the difference the happiness perspective could make for development is not adequately captured by classical policy recommendations that address decision-makers only. Instead, taking happiness seriously can make a difference to the very discourse that underlies and legitimizes policies, as well as to the way people lead and evaluate their lives under given living conditions.

This section will outline some of the ways in which the idea of happiness can make a difference to development. If, occasionally, these sound much like policy recommendations, then what has been said above holds: that policy recommendations are legitimate as inputs to public deliberation, i.e. as unpretentious suggestions that are submitted to the public for critical scrutiny. Yet, since good development is not only about policies but also about what people make out of their lives under given policies, some of the proposed influences will not work through policies at all but rather directly through the interpretations and decisions of individuals.

The distinctions between the four possible effects that will be discussed in the following are not very sharp. Nevertheless, they can be classified along two dimensions with two categories each, giving rise to a two-by-two matrix as in Table 6.1. The horizontal dimension denotes the systematic status of the effect, distinguishing between a constructive and a consequential effect.[4] The constructive effect refers to the way individuals think about their lives and the world and how societies debate their concepts of development, rather than to the results of such thinking and debating. The decisions that might result from such a changed construction will be referred to as consequential effects. These can therefore be considered as the anticipated consequences of a discourse that takes happiness seriously.

The vertical dimension denotes the level of aggregation of the effect, making a distinction between the individual and the societal level. Of course, a society ultimately consists of individuals, but since a society is more – or sometimes less – than simply the sum of its individual members (cf. p. 105), a separate consideration of both levels of aggregation is warranted.

Typical policy recommendations jump directly to the fourth quadrant, i.e. to the political measures that should be taken. However, as has been argued in this chapter, policy changes should be sought only through a process of public deliberation, not directly and behind the back of the public. It is therefore more illuminating to also lay out *in which ways* the happiness perspective may affect public deliberation, which in turn depends on how the mental constructions of individuals will be changed when happiness is taken seriously. The four

Table 6.1 Classification of potential effects of the happiness perspective

| | | Systematic status | |
		Constructive	Consequential
Level of aggregation	Individual	I – The individual's construction of the world	II – Educative effects
	Society	III – The practice of public deliberation	IV – Public policy

different effects should therefore not be understood as four separate policy recommendations but rather as the anticipation of the reflections and the deliberative process that would precede any political changes and that might set in once
the happiness perspective occupies a prominent place in the public debate. Much
of the following will already have been touched upon above; a major purpose of
this section, then, is to systematize the preceding considerations in terms of this
two-by-two matrix.

The individual's construction of the world (I)

If Frank Knight (1999/1924: 1) is correct that "life is at bottom an exploration in
the field of values, an attempt to discover values, rather than on the basis of
knowledge of them to produce and enjoy them to the greatest possible extent"
(cf. p. 72), then the reflection on happiness can offer one point of reference that
orientates this "exploration in the field of values". In particular, the examination
of one's values in terms of happiness can challenge common precepts that a
person may have blindly adopted under the subtle pressure of widespread
endorsement. Lane (2000b: 70), for example, argues that "the market culture
teaches us that money is the source of well-being [and people,] lacking privileged knowledge of the causes of their feelings, ... accept conventional answers".
People may even know the causes of their feelings but still base their decisions
on criteria that are publicly endorsed rather than on what will make them more
satisfied, as has been corroborated by experiments eliciting different orderings in
the space of liking than in the space of wanting (i.e. choosing) as reported above
(cf. p. 62). This discrepancy must not necessarily be "wrong" or irrational, but it
strikes us as surprising and possibly imprudent. Evaluating values and choices
also in terms of happiness may then lead to better-reflected and more consistent
preferences.

Exposure to discourses that address only policy measures and the rules of
the game, while ignoring the role of the individuals that will have to live under
the thus-created living conditions, may also make a person blind toward her
own role within a good life. At the limit, she may believe that her well-being
and her happiness depend entirely on her living conditions. Yet, consciously
thinking about what makes one's life happy – rather than successful by objective criteria or enviable – may remind a person of the simple fact that a good
life depends also on how one relates to one's living conditions: that a good life
is not only about satisfying desires, but also about reflecting and controlling
these desires. More profoundly, this recognition may make a person (more)
aware that desires are not heteronomously given, but also – to a degree – autonomously chosen, and that it is in a person's interest to question and cultivate her
desires (cf. p. 70).

This is not to say that a mature person will or should become immune to
external living conditions. The stoic and Buddhist ideal of absolute control over
one's emotional experiences may be one legitimate ideal, but it certainly is not
the only legitimate one. A person may legitimately prefer a succession of

euphoric and depressed episodes to a continuous stream of controlled content-ment.[5] Conscious reflection on happiness may also have the effect of a person realizing that she has been manipulated into taking a defeatist attitude and toler-ating humiliation, with the result that the person will eventually be less happy. In other words, which conclusion a person draws from a conscious evaluation of her life in terms of happiness can neither be anticipated nor prescribed in general terms. What matters and should be rather uncontroversial, however, is that a person will take a more mature perspective on her life and make better-informed choices after having considered happiness explicitly.

Paradoxically, the serious contemplation of one's life in terms of happiness may lead a person to realize that happiness is not everything that matters to a good life. Even though initially, everything we want will appear as being instru-mental to happiness, closer examination quickly reveals that we value many things independently of their contributions toward happiness, even though they do, incidentally, tend to contribute to happiness (cf. p. 96). Moreover, a person may realize that happiness is not a substantive end that can itself be pursued, but rather an inclusive end that still needs to be filled with content.

Educative effects (II)

A person who has made up her mind with respect to the role she wants happiness to take in her life will likely draw a couple of concrete conclusions from psycho-logical evidence regarding typical cognitive fallacies. As reported above (p. 59), people make a number of systematical errors in predicting how satisfied they will be as a result of a particular event or decision. Once she gains knowledge of the relevant cognitive fallacies, she will probably anticipate her unconscious adaptation to new comforts and therefore spend less on goods that bring only temporary happiness and more on those whose happiness payoff lasts longer. When contemplating to move to a place she considers more attractive, she will be able to correct her spontaneous prediction of her satisfaction in the new envir-onment by consciously taking into account less salient aspects of everyday life and by trying to anticipate how she will feel over a longer period rather than only focusing on a small set of salient aspects and the initial sensation of novelty.

This is not to say that a person who takes happiness seriously will – let alone should – optimize all her decisions in terms of their happiness payoff. The point is merely that people sometimes take decisions also in order to be happy – and very often under the condition that the decision will at least not make them unhappy – and to the degree that this is the case, knowing about cognitive falla-cies will improve decisions that would otherwise be based on popular wisdom that has been blindly accepted for lack of a better theory.

This will be especially relevant for situations in which people or entire socie-ties face far-reaching decisions, as do (quasi) subsistence societies that contem-plate the possibility of pursuing economic progress. In a vivid account of the society of Ladakh (in NW India) facing, and going through, such a process,

Helena Norberg-Hodge describes a potential fallacy waiting for those who are offered an option that is so distant from their experiences that they have a hard time imagining the consequences.

> For millions of youths in rural areas of the world, modern Western culture appears far superior to their own. It is not surprising since, looking as they do from the outside, all they can see is the material side of the modern world – the side in which Western culture excels. They cannot so readily see the social or psychological dimensions – the stress, the loneliness, the fear of growing old. Nor can they see environmental decay, inflation, or unemployment. On the other hand, they know their own culture inside out, including all its limitations and imperfections.
>
> (Norberg-Hodge 1991: 97–8)

To be sure, Norberg-Hodge's report is an anecdotal account and can probably not be generalized. But one need not agree with her overall evaluation of modernization (which is rather negative) to see that decisions will better serve the decision-makers' authentic interests when people know about cognitive fallacies and get a chance to correct them to some degree, whether or not that ultimately makes a difference to the decision itself.

Much of what happiness research has to say about the happiness paradox cannot be applied by the individual. The insight that positional competition and secondary inflation erode the happiness of each individual only teaches the individual *why* he desires a higher income and why the fulfillment of that desire will not result in more happiness, but it does not show him how he, individually, can break that circle. In other words, self-help, prudence, or wisdom do not hold the answer to the happiness paradox, even though they may help a given person avoid some cognitive fallacies.

The practice of public deliberation (III)

When people defend their views in public deliberation, they must anticipate which arguments will be accepted as sensible and valid by the public, rather than directly stating their arguments as they see them privately. This is particularly apparent in the case of representatives of special interest groups who feel obliged to put their arguments in terms of reasons that will conform to the public's criteria of acceptability. Even where a government has dictatorial power, it feels compelled to wrap its decisions into moral terms that lay a claim to universal validity (Tugendhat 1995: 12).

The public's criteria of acceptability are not arbitrary, but they are contingent on the particular cultural and historical setting. In particular, they depend on the unwritten moral code that happens to prevail in a particular society and at a given point in time. Yet, the criteria of acceptability go beyond questions of morality in a narrow sense. They also regulate, for example, which teleological values are considered valid interests that deserve (deontological) consideration or which form an argument has to take. For example, homosexual love is not always and everywhere considered a sensible value to be respected and protected, and even though this is often labeled a "moral" issue, it is, from a modern ethical perspective, primarily a matter of a purely teleological preference and therefore not a moral issue in the sense of being about deontological duties. Thus, every public has its implicit or explicit success criteria for a person's life, and these determine which reasons are admitted into the debate and which are rejected or ignored as unreasonable or insensible.

It is these success criteria that Ahuvia and Lane have in mind when they say that "[d]efenders of collectivism give away the store when they allow Western psychologists to set the success criteria for a culture" (cf. p. 20), or that "the market culture teaches us that money is the source of well-being" (cf. p. 140). Indeed, success criteria that Western psychologists consider "natural" and which they do not find necessary to justify may not seem natural at all to psychologists from other cultures. In a study by two eminent US American psychologists, for example, "psychological well-being" is equated with "psychological adjustment", a technical concept comprising "self-actualization" and "vitality" (Kasser and Ryan 1993: 411–12), two concepts that are clearly not equally valued in all cultures. It also seems plausible that it is the internalization of these public success criteria, especially those that Lane ascribes to the "market culture", that leads respondents in the above-mentioned experiment (p. 62) to chose the higher-paying job over that in which they declared they would be more satisfied. As the authors of the study themselves hypothesize:

> When people are asked to assess the hedonic value of some future states (e.g. job offers) they try to imagine what it would feel like to experience those states. But when asked to choose among these states, they tend to search for reasons or arguments to justify their choice.
>
> (Tversky and Griffin 1991: 114)

It appears that people feel compelled to justify their choices by the accepted public success criteria – rather than by their personal well-being – which in turn are strongly influenced, and reflected, by the way a society measures and communicates its success. As it happens, societies today measure their success in terms of purely objective and "hard" indicators – such as GDP, life expectancy, years of schooling, physicians per 1,000 inhabitants, etc. Subjective measures are practically absent, with the consequence that we do not know if a society is happy with its wealth, whether modern medicine prolongs fulfilled or miserable lives, or whether schools train their students to be competitive production factors or whether they also educate them to be emotionally stable individuals and mature citizens. This ban on the subjective aspects of life probably makes people exaggerate objective criteria and overlook subjective aspects in their decisions. Why else would a billionaire go to great lengths to get yet another percentage point of return on his assets, or would a sports star with a multi-million-dollar salary humiliate himself by appearing in silly TV ads to earn yet another million?[6] The pure form of this subordination of subjective aspects to objective success criteria can be imagined as a father questioning his son's wishes by saying "Happiness! – How much of that do you own?" (Spaemann 2000/1989: 22).

If this interpretation is correct, then a conscious consideration of happiness by many individuals (as described on p. 72) may have the effect of altering the set of accepted public success criteria and vice versa: a change in the public success criteria might change the outlook of many individuals on their lives. On the societal level, taking happiness seriously would strengthen the recognition of subjective reasons that correspond to an intersubjective reality. In such an environment, citizens would feel entitled to demand justification for particular policy proposals in terms of subjective well-being, rather than in terms of objective criteria alone. They would not find it ridiculous if newspapers asked to what degree the government's economic growth target will enhance people's happiness.

Indeed, it can be argued that the greatest effect of officially declaring "Gross National Happiness" (GNH) a primary policy objective would be such a subtle change in the practice of public deliberation, rather than a radical change of public policy. In Bhutan, the small Himalaya Kingdom of 800,000 inhabitants and the only country to have adopted GNH as an official concept, happiness is a standard subject of most public speeches by government officials and it is a salient concept in many public debates. Gross National Happiness also features prominently in the country's young constitution, stipulating, for example, that it is the task of the government to "provide good governance, and ensure peace, security, well-being and happiness of the people" (Kingdom of Bhutan 2008: art. 20,1).

On a smaller scale and in a less conspicuous move, the "Local Government Act 2000" enacted by the Parliament of the United Kingdom gives local authorities the power "to do anything which they consider is likely to achieve ... the promotion or improvement" of the economic, social, or environmental well-being of their area (Printer of Acts of Parliament 2000: I/2/1). Thus, for the first time, municipalities can undertake policies that contribute directly to people's well-being without having to refer to specific pieces of legislation that usually stipulate objective requirements (Marks 2004: 328).

Giving public recognition to happiness may also play an important role in provoking teleological debates in which a society's priorities and its social preferences (cf. p. 106) can be clarified. Instead of debating only either technical questions – i.e. the efficiency of different ways to achieve a given objective – or deontological problems – i.e. the legitimacy of different ways to achieve an agreed goal – teleological debates are about objectives as such and may in particular question a presumed agreement on what a society regards as worth being pursued. Keeping in mind that happiness should be understood as an inclusive end (cf. p. 77), such debates should not simply posit happiness as the ultimate (dominant) end and merely discuss the ways in which it shall be pursued, which would mean repeating the same errors, but rather about the contents of happiness and of a flourishing society.

Public policy (IV)

A changed practice of public deliberation may have significant but unforeseeable consequences on public policy. Even though it is not the major focus of this study to anticipate the precise policy changes that may result when happiness is taken seriously as a policy objective, a few conjectures shall be made. In the spirit of what has been said above (p. 128) about the legitimacy of academic policy recommendations, the following is to be understood as reasoned conjectures about what a society that has thoroughly debated happiness might decide to do differently, rather than as recommendations that have been "objectively" established as being in the interest of a society.

The most profound consequence would probably be institutional and legal provisions to reduce the harm done by positional competition. A society that has understood that positional competition can be a zero-sum or even a negative-sum game (cf. p. 44), and that particular sources of happiness are not universalizable (cf. p. 116), will recognize that it stands to gain something for nothing by limiting positional competition.

Some excesses of positional competition could be addressed by legislation. Robert Frank (1999), for example, proposes to replace current income taxation by a progressive consumption tax (i.e. technically speaking, by a progressive income tax plus total tax deductibility for net savings). Instead of discouraging work and encouraging consumption, as conventional income taxation does, a consumption tax would not discourage work but consumption. Its progressivity would ensure that people who already have a high spending profile would pay more taxes on a given product than someone who buys the same product but has a low spending record for that year. This way, consumption at the top would be relatively more heavily discouraged than at the bottom, thus addressing the effect of expenditure cascades (cf. p. 47).

Richard Layard, too, believes that taxation is an efficient way to deal with positional competition with respect to consumption. Positional externalities, he argues, should be treated like all other externalities (i.e. like those that have been denominated "direct externalities" in Chapter 3), namely by internalizing the damage they do to others by taxing the "pollutant". He estimates that the appropriate tax rate that would correct for positional external effects and for cognitive fallacies (i.e. unanticipated effects on the same individual in the future) would be around 60 percent (Layard 2003: 11). As this value is close to the actual overall tax rate (direct plus indirect taxes) in many rich countries, his estimate does not suggest any additional taxation. It does, however, change the evaluational perspective of taxation. Instead of being a necessary evil or a redistributive mechanism justified by a concern for justice alone, taxation becomes efficient even in the logic of economic theory itself. As Layard observes further, "We should be clear that such taxation is almost certainly reducing our measured GDP, by reducing work effort. But we should be equally clear that this does not matter, because GDP is a faulty measure of well-being" (Layard 2003: 11).

A similar case can be made for forced saving schemes in which a certain percentage of all employees' incomes is directly subtracted from the paycheck and later paid out as retirement benefits. If people could choose whether to sign up to such a scheme, they might not want to do so for reasons of positional advantages (e.g. paying for a better school for their children, buying a house in a better neighborhood, etc.). Obliging people to save a fixed portion of their salary may be an effective way to curb such positional competition and its adverse effect on retirement savings (Frank 1999: 169). In addition, it may correct for shortsightedness and other types of irrationality. Ample empirical evidence suggests that saving behavior is particularly prone to receiving too little reflection and that decisions – and even more the absence of any conscious decisions – about how much to save for retirement are often regretted later in life.[7]

Another major candidate for regulative measures to reduce positional competition would be working-time regulations. In fact, the regulation stipulating maximum working hours and limits on overtime that is already in place in many societies – in fact, the very existence of labor unions – can be considered a response to the problem of positional competition among (potential) employees. For all those employees who have less bargaining power than their (potential) employers, competition among employees would drive working hours up to the number of hours that is optimal from the point of view of the employers. In such a situation, only binding rules can limit this (from the employees' perspective) detrimental rat race. Only when the individual employee is denied the choice to work more hours than others can all employees together be protected from the pressure to compete with each other in terms of working hours.

Whether or not the limits on working hours currently in place in different societies are appropriate shall not be judged here. The point is that the social function of collective agreements and laws limiting working times is only fully understood when their effect on positional competition is also appreciated.

Moreover, it should be noted that the differences in actual working hours per year – taking into account overtime and effective holidays – are enormous, even among countries with similar levels of income and productivity, with Italians and Americans working 30 percent more hours than the Dutch (Figure 6.1). It would be difficult to believe that these differences exclusively reflect the different societies' authentic preferences for the tradeoff between leisure time and consumption (in which case there would of course be no case for changing these countries' working time regimes). If tastes alone do not explain these differences, however, it would appear natural to conclude that all societies do not draw the same conclusions from the phenomenon of positional competition and that, therefore, at least some are working more than they would if they understood positional competition.

A similar case can be made with respect to working conditions in general. For the individual worker it may be impossible to negotiate, for example, particular improvements in work safety, and even if he could pay for the improvement

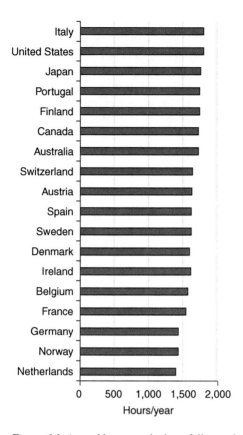

Figure 6.1 Annual hours worked per fully employed person, 2008 (source: ILO Key
Indicators of the Labour Market, Table 6b (http://kilm.ilo.org)).

Note
Hours are annual hours actually worked per person.

(say, safety equipment) himself, the private benefit might not justify the private
costs. By contrast, when collective rules oblige all companies to adhere to particular safety measures, no company suffers a competitive disadvantage because
its competitors are equally affected. Even if it has to lower salaries because of
the absolute costs of these measures, the loss to each worker will be less than
what each individual worker would have paid for the same measures privately
(Frank 1999: 169–70).

Another type of positional competition that could be reduced by legislative
measures is the attendance of cram courses that students attend in the hope of
improving their chances for admission to top universities. Obviously, the number
of students who take such courses does not affect the number of applicants that
will be admitted to top universities. Therefore, while attending a preparatory
course improves the chances of any individual student, for all applicants as a

whole, the existence of such courses does not improve anybody's chances to get admitted to the school of his choice (or if it does, then only because some students cannot afford to attend such courses, thereby reducing competition for the wealthier kids and distorting the intended talent screening effect) (Frank 1999: 155). If such courses have a social benefit in terms of educating people, then this benefit must be weighed against the time and effort students spend studying (and teachers teaching). But if it was concluded that the educational benefit is worth the price, then one would have to conclude that the knowledge imparted by cram courses was actually the job of the high school or of the university. Either way, the existence of preparatory courses reflects either a wasteful allocation of resources or the failure of regular educational institutions.

Apart from legislative measures, a society mindful of happiness and aware of positional competition, secondary inflation, and adaptive aspirations might take different decisions in a number of ways. For example, it could decide to design school curricula and examination methods in such a way that students are not excessively encouraged to define their success in relative terms with respect to others ("Am I the best in class?") but in absolute terms, i.e. with respect to their potential ("Did I do as well as I can?"). If students compare themselves with their classmates, one's relative success will be the others' failure, but if they compare themselves with their respective potential, one's success does not subtract from that of any other (Layard 1980).

Another area where positional competition could be reduced without resorting to legislation would be within-firm competition. A company might discourage positional competition for job promotions, e.g. by basing the selection process on non-positional criteria. It might also measure and reward the success of individuals or departments with respect to an absolute benchmark, rather than with respect to its relative position in a ranking, thus encouraging cooperation and information-sharing within the firm.

As any other political decision, any measure to limit positional competition would have to be checked for its legitimacy in the light of possible infringements on individuals' legitimate interests, and the benefit of limiting positional competition will always have to be balanced against the infringement on personal liberties. Laws to limit working hours, for example, may be in the interest of most people, but there will always be some who would sincerely prefer to work more than the maximum time established by society. There may even be some athletes who are prepared to pay a high price in terms of health damages for the use of steroids, not because they want to be better than others but because they want to excel absolutely.

Yet, concluding from this that limits on positional competition must always be illegitimate because they infringe on some individuals' personal freedoms would reflect an incomplete grasp of the idea of freedom. Of course, a ban on doping takes away an athlete's freedom to improve her performance by all means. Yet, on the other hand, this same ban is the basis for another freedom, namely her freedom to stand a real chance to win a competition without putting her health at risk. It would be plainly absurd to be concerned only with the freedom to choose between all options that happen to be available in the absence of any restricting rules – negative freedom – and not at all with the set of options itself which defines the scope of possible choices – positive freedom.[8] Without a ban on doping, the option to win a sports competition without health damage would simply not be effectively available. Whether or not a ban on doping is ultimately justified is a particular judgment that must be made by some process of public deliberation. If a ban is decided, however, this means that athletes have decided that, to them, the (positive) freedom they gain justifies the loss of the (negative) freedom they sacrifice.

Policies to control positional competition are faced with a particular difficulty to the extent that positional competition extends beyond a jurisdiction's boundaries. If one society agrees on restrictive measures but other societies do not, it may end up paying a high price. It would be like banning doping for only one half of the runners. They would remain healthy, but they would have no chance of winning against the doped competitors. In such a case, it would be in the interest – and arguably also a moral obligation – of the party attempting to reduce positional competition to try to convince all (potential) competitors of the benefits of a collective agreement. In how far that is possible in a given case is of course another matter.

Finally, measuring happiness could be contemplated as a policy measure. This would of course not have a direct impact on people's happiness, but it would certainly raise awareness of happiness. Considering the weight of prominent public indicators, especially GDP growth, in the public debate, it would seem no exaggeration to expect a significant impact from an official happiness index.

However, just having an official indicator does not guarantee that it receives the attention of the media and, ultimately, of citizens. Many countries generate thousands of indicators each year but only a handful find their way into the mass media. Moreover, some more or less public indicators of happiness are already raised in many countries (e.g. in the European Union by the Eurobarometer survey conducted twice a year by the European Commission, in the US annually by the General Social Survey), but they hardly get any public attention. Still, an official engagement by a country's government might be enough to propel happiness indicators into public awareness, as the example of Bhutan shows.

Bhutan is an interesting case because, despite its adoption of the concept of Gross National Happiness as an official policy objective, it has not actually measured SWB until very recently (in 2007). This was not due to a lack of resources, but because its leadership – political and intellectual – was for a long time not convinced that it would be a good idea to measure SWB. The topic was intensely debated during a conference on GNH that took place in Bhutan's capital, Thimphu, in 2003 (cf. Ura and Galay 2004). On the one hand, it was argued, having a single index number of happiness would help to communicate the issue and attract interest from the media. As political activists are fond of saying, "what doesn't get measured doesn't get managed". This was also the reason that moved Amartya Sen (1999a) to support the Human Development

Index (HDI) – "a measure of the same level of vulgarity as GNP", as he quotes Mahbub ul Haq, the then-director of the United Nations Development Program (UNDP) – in spite of his skepticism at "attempting to catch in one simple number a complex reality about human development and deprivation".

On the other hand, a single number alone can never adequately guide policy and only provides information about one aspect of a complex reality. Trying to express "social welfare" in a single number will always be a grossly reductionist exercise (cf. p. 85). In the context of happiness, a particular danger would consist in the possibility that such an indicator might be hijacked by a hedonistic and utilitarian interpretation, suggesting that it measures pleasure and demanding that the resulting number ought to be maximized at any cost.

In other words, a single happiness index might take the same path as GDP growth measures. In itself, such an index is innocent, providing a valid piece of information on the state and development of a society. Yet, once its underlying rationale is forgotten and its meaning exaggerated, it can seriously disorient public debates. The problem starts when an indicator is no longer seen as an input into a public debate, but as its substitute; not as one reason among others for or against a specific political program, but as its end.

Limitations of the happiness perspective

Its potential for positive changes notwithstanding, the happiness perspective faces some significant limitations, and also some dangers, when it is employed as an orientating concept for good development. Above all, it holds no neat solutions to solve the problem of good development because it is a teleological concept, whereas good development is both a teleological and a deontological problem. Even a society whose members are mature, autonomous citizens and have made up their minds about what they really want in their lives will face conflicts of interest that will have to be settled by moral principles. Good development is not about harmonizing or equalizing people's interests, but about dealing with conflicts of interests in a way that does justice to each individual's rights. Good development, moreover, requires dealing morally not only with conflicts of interests between the members of the society concerned, but also with conflicts of interests extending to other societies and even to future generations.

Representing deontological problems (conflicts of interest) as teleological ones (pursuing the right objectives) would mean sacrificing the dignity of the individual and reifying "social welfare" as a moral subject with a right to be respected (and maximized). Moreover, it would only be consistent with a deterministic conception of the human mind, a highly problematic and implausible conception, as has been argued above.

As long as a deterministic paradigm prevails, even the most humane objective turns inhumane when it is proclaimed as the ultimate goal to be maximized. There can be no single goal that is worth being pursued at any cost simply because, in a society composed of autonomous (i.e. not determined) subjects, good development is not simply about achieving a goal, but about achieving a number of goals in a particular, i.e. moral, way.

It will be more appropriate, therefore, to consider the happiness perspective as complementary to deontological perspectives and, indeed, to other teleological aspects. After all, it does not capture a number of (teleological) objectives people might reasonably have, including such apparent ones as a long life – it does not make much sense to say that one will be more happy alive than dead.

The happiness perspective alone cannot give conclusive answers to the problem of good development. It depends on additional perspectives and principles in order to make a positive contribution to good development. Once it is embedded into a comprehensive conception of good development, however, it can make a real difference.

7 Orientation for a knowledgeable world

If the preceding reflections had to be expressed in a single message, it would be that the idea of happiness can provide orientation for societies which *know how* to do almost everything, but have lost the sense of direction that helps them understand *what* they should want to do. Apparently, economic growth and technological progress do not automatically mean good development.

The preceding chapters have established the empirical evidence on the relationship between living conditions and subjective well-being (ch. 2), suggested explanations for the observed paradoxes (ch. 3), developed a normative conception of happiness (ch. 4), embedded this conception into a conception of good development (ch. 5), and spelled out the implications of these findings for development (ch. 6). It is now time to wrap up the discussion and take stock of what has been achieved and of what remains to be understood.

What the happiness perspective can contribute to good development

Happiness does not hold a magical formula, a grand societal project, or a policy blueprint that holds the answer to the problem of development. Happiness maximization in particular must be discarded as a guide to development policy. It would also be a misconception if happiness was elevated to being the ultimate objective of human striving and the epitome of a good life. This is not because there is something wrong about being happy, but because people care about more than being happy. In particular, they care about the self-transcendent reasons they have for being happy.

It is precisely for this reason that happiness may play a substantial indicative role in conceptions of good development. As an inclusive end (cf. p. 000), it acts as an umbrella concept that unites a variety of things that make a life a good life, both those that bring pleasure and those that are valued for self-transcendent reasons. In other words, happiness matters because a happy person has reason for being happy, and the teleological accomplishment of development is a matter of realizing what people have reason to value. Happiness should not be promoted as a substantive good, i.e. without regard to the contents of happiness. Such a view would ultimately favor a scenario in which a happiness drug made people enjoy a pointless experience of "perpetual euphoria" (Bruckner 2001). In this view, it would be entirely irrelevant whether people have reason for being happy as long as they *feel* happy. Even the scenario of a "Matrix"[1] in which machines control the sensory experiences of people and "farm" their bodies in a gigantic factory would not be objectionable. In fact, it would even be welcome, as long as the Matrix makes people feel happier than they would feel in real life. Making happiness the only and ultimate *objective* of development would therefore turn upside down the humanistic project of protecting and promoting the dignity of human life. It would reduce the question of the good life to a matter of a particular psychic condition. Instead, happiness should be considered one *symptom* of a succeeding life, a psychic condition that *signals* that a life is going well without itself being the content of a good life.

In this role, the happiness perspective can correct a decade-long misconception of development as "economic growth whatever the cost". For some reason, it has come to be taken for granted that the objective of development is the maximization of consumption, implying that economic growth is the best yardstick for development. Perhaps this enthusiasm for economic growth was not even based on the conviction that other things do not matter, but rather that economic growth automatically reconciles all those aspects that contribute to good development. The problem, in other words, is the reduction of good development to economic growth.

This is where the happiness perspective can make a difference, by challenging entrenched beliefs and stimulating and orientating the reflection of preferences. Because happiness is an inclusive goal, asking "What makes me happy?" puts all the (potential) contents of a good life on the table. By contrast, the question "What brings economic growth?" already imposes the premise that development is about consumption alone and thereby limits the field of vision.

The way in which the happiness perspective challenges conventional beliefs should be different for the case of individual choices than for the case of collective decisions. The individual should test her conventional wisdom against the question "What makes me happy?" She may want to know if the importance she attaches – without much reflection – to a high salary, a new car, or an evening with her friends stands up to critical scrutiny. As far as societal issues are concerned, however, the question should be "What contents of happiness can be generalized for society as a whole?" The members of a society may then realize that there are a number of things that can be achieved by each citizen individually, but not by all, or most, citizens at the same time, and that there is therefore no point in improving the conditions under which individuals compete for these benefits. They may then conclude that they should focus their efforts on managing such absolutely scarce benefits in a fair way and on increasing the availability of those benefits that can be spread out to a large number of people.

A society that looks toward happiness for orientation will probably not do everything differently. It will, however, strive to create conditions for a society in which production and consumption are subordinated to a good life rather than the other way round. It will not reduce citizens to consumers, and workers to production factors. Where it has to choose, it will opt for quality of life at the expense of economic growth and not for the contrary.

Development is not only a matter of furthering the good life. As has been emphasized throughout this study, it is also a matter of justice, and justice in turn cannot be reduced to happiness or any other teleological concept. Still, the happiness perspective can inform deontological questions by substantiating the content of what deontological debates are about. Deontological questions are not necessarily about happiness. They may also be about, say, freedom independently from its effect on happiness. Mostly, however, happiness will be one important consideration among others in deontological issues. Taking it explicitly into consideration may then contribute to clarifying the rights and duties at stake. When, for example, the proposal to build a hydropower dam is discussed, the happiness effects on the losers and winners, which partly reflect economic consequences as well, may be considered more relevant to the evaluation of the project's legitimacy than the economic effects in monetary terms alone.

More generally speaking, the salience of happiness in public debates might promote the recognition of the subjective perspective, i.e. of the relevance of subjective perceptions and evaluations. Restricting the public debate to objective aspects alone would severely deprive it. It would become entirely irrelevant how people transform living conditions into fulfilled lives and whether they are the masters or the slaves of their preferences and desires. In such a society, a person would feel compelled to justify her interest in, say, protecting natural scenery in terms of objective benefits ("revenues from tourism", "long-term profitability", or "value of biodiversity for medical research"), instead of simply saying that it is a source of mental and spiritual well-being.

To sum up, the contribution the happiness perspective can make to development lies in a reconsideration of the teleological dimension of development without reducing it to a single objective. It can shake up conventional answers that suggest that the evident goal of development is economic growth and that technological progress will automatically bring well-being. It can awaken us to the fact that development is not primarily limited by a lack of technological possibilities, but by a lack of orientation concerning the question to which uses we should want to put the possibilities we have.

Economic growth and good development

The point of departure for this study was the observation that economic growth has apparently not delivered the degree of happiness that may have been expected. Throughout the text, the relationship between consumption and subjective well-being has been touched upon and it has been argued that economic growth does not automatically contribute to more happiness.

It would be inappropriate, however, to portray the relationship between economic growth and happiness as antagonistic, i.e. as if economic growth systematically came at the expense of happiness. As far as the evidence on happiness is concerned, there is nothing that suggests that economic growth has on balance a negative effect on well-being, merely that historically it has on average not had a clear positive effect, as economists and the public at large have been assuming all along. Apparently, the positive and negative effects of economic growth are basically canceling each other out.

This historical record does not imply a systematic relationship, though. The fact that we observe that happiness has not risen during a period of economic progress does not permit the conclusion that this is a systematic necessity. It may well be that we have simply done a poor job in transforming possibilities into happiness and that we could have done better. After all, there are actually some cases in which SWB has risen over time.

The question is not, therefore, whether economic growth is a good thing or a bad thing, but rather what the systematic status of economic growth should be in our thinking about development. The answer to this question follows in a pretty straight-forward way from the preceding reflections: economic growth should be pursued as a means, i.e. only if and to the degree that it contributes to good development. It should not be pursued as an end in itself or as a strategy that guarantees good development. One will probably find that many policies that are recommended by a narrow economic growth perspective will also appear desirable in the happiness perspective. This is no embarrassment. To the contrary, one should become suspicious if the measures that appear reasonable in the happiness perspective do not occasionally make sense from other perspectives as well. The difference between the economic growth perspective and the happiness perspective is not one of diametric opposition, but one of the perspective in which one orders the priorities.

Pitting economic growth against happiness would also be inappropriate for a more fundamental reason. Treating economic growth as a political variable of the same nature as, for example, education or infrastructure, i.e. as a substantive output that has defined costs and consequences, obscures the distinct role of economic growth. It simply does not make sense to ask whether economic growth as such is desirable or not because economic growth can manifest itself in many different and even directly opposing ways. For example, it can be associated with additional environmental pollution (as in the case of air travel becoming cheaper) or with a reduction of pollution (as in the case of more efficient renewable energy generation). It can be a result of people working more hours or of the invention of time-saving technologies, etc. The only substantive outcome that will always, by definition, go together with economic growth is an increase in a society's production and, therefore, consumption in terms of the aggregated exchange value of these goods and services (but if the additional production goes into efforts to repair damages caused by economic growth, actual consumption will not increase and may actually decrease). In other words, economic growth means that people can have more of the things they are willing to pay for, but it can also come with substantial costs. Whether the overall effect is to be assessed positively or negatively, or which rate of growth is deemed appropriate, depends on the concrete manifestation of economic growth.

In the long run, economic growth is a matter of technological progress. Additional working hours, capital investments (through corresponding savings), a reduction of unemployment, etc. increase the level of output (and the growth rate of one or two years) but do not bring a sustained increase in growth rates. Technological progress, however, is an unlimited source of economic growth and it is practically a one-way street. The technology available to a society can only increase, not decrease, except in the case of catastrophic events or some peculiar circumstances (e.g. patenting of formerly public knowledge). Moreover, its increase is almost unavoidable because one cannot effectively prevent people from finding more efficient ways to do certain tasks or from inventing and offering goods and services that satisfy people's desires in a more efficient, i.e. less resource-intensive, way. This in turn means that a society will quite naturally have a tendency to grow as long as its members prefer to do their work in less, rather than in more, time and to the degree that a culture encourages inventiveness. Of course, a society may manage to accelerate technological progress by certain policies, but even if it does not actively stimulate it, technological growth will take place, not least because knowledge tends to spread across frontiers. Thus, a society that manages to keep unemployment from rising (and prevents other macroeconomic imbalances) will see economic growth in the long run simply because people implement ideas that allow them to satisfy effective demand with fewer resources.

It therefore does not make much sense to ponder the desirability of development without economic growth. Economic growth as such is not a possible problem; the elevation of economic growth to a substantive end is. A society that succeeds in terms of good development – improving conditions for people to have reasons for happiness and doing so under the condition of justice – will naturally have just the perfect rate of economic growth.

A more meaningful question than "How much (if any) economic growth is desirable?" is therefore "Which use should we make of our (rising) productive potential?" This question entails, once more, a teleological ("Which objectives are worth being pursued?") and a deontological dimension ("In which way can we pursue these objectives without violating anybody's moral rights?"). In other words, we should be concerned with good development rather than with derivative indicators, and since economic growth is not a meaningful substantive end, it should have no privileged place in a conception of good development. As long as policies are right, one need not worry about economic growth.

Concluding remarks

Good development is not all about happiness. Reducing it to happiness alone would belie the two-dimensionality and the indeterminacy of good development. Still, happiness holds important clues for the way we think about and construct development because it is a particular characteristic of good development: it is an inclusive indicator that reflects globally whether a person has reason for being happy. It therefore permits inferences with respect to good development. It is an indicator that reflects with reasonable precision whether essential *desiderata* have been realized. At the same time, it is also one legitimate *desideratum* among others, though it should not be portrayed as a privileged, let alone as the only, one. As Bruckner (2001: 14) remarks, one may love one's life too much to desire nothing but happiness (cf. p. 120).

Happiness research is a particularly promising way to address the question of good development because it provides a natural bridge between empirical and conceptual questions. Empirical happiness research has produced, and will continue to produce, valuable insights into the way people and societies evaluate their living conditions. Conceptually, happiness as a non-technical concept is naturally understood by practically everybody (which, by the way, is one of the reasons why empirical research leads to valid and reliable data). The deeper reflection on happiness as practiced mainly by philosophers can therefore connect to prior knowledge and thus avoid the danger of "ivory tower research".

Someone who expected a clear solution or policy recipe for the challenge of good development may be disappointed by the insights gained by this study. Yet, as has been argued here, the bottleneck to good development is not so much the knowledge of how to achieve given objectives, but the lack of orientation regarding which objectives are worthwhile to be pursued, i.e. what we should want, both individually and collectively. This is not to say that there are no other bottlenecks as well or that there are no differences between high-income and low-income countries, but any given society stands to benefit from a more comprehensive reflection on preferences through the lens of happiness.

Notes

2 The evidence on happiness

1 As long as the term "subjective well-being" has not been introduced, I will use the term "happiness" instead. While this is obviously inaccurate, the patient reader will be alerted to the non-trivial difference between the two concepts on the pages to follow.

2 An entire interdisciplinary congress in 2003 was even devoted to "The paradoxes of happiness in economics" (Bruni and Porta 2005, 2007).

3 The reference to the body does not mean that a bodily *stimulus* must be involved, but that any emotional *response* will also find expression physiologically (e.g. in changed pulse frequency or in facial expressions).

4 Two correlations of 0.50 (Campbell *et al.* 1976: 34) and 0.63 (Andrews and Withey 1976: 85) have been reported, which compare with a test-retest correlation of 0.70 (test-retest correlations are discussed again on p. 16). The corresponding correlation between national averages of a sample of 45 countries produced a correlation of 0.90 (own calculation based on data in Veenhoven 1997: 36–7).

5 That happiness also involves some limited objective aspects and should not be understood as an entirely subjective notion is shown later (p. 95), but it shall not distract us at this stage.

6 The same point has been made by Sen with respect to the particular concepts of "equality" (Sen 1983/1979) and "poverty" (Sen 1983): "There is ... an irreducible absolutist core in the idea of poverty. ... [P]overty is an absolute notion in the space of capabilities but very often it will take a relative form in the space of commodities or characteristics" (ibid.: 159, 161).

7 The following discussion will draw extensively on evidence that I have compiled earlier in the unpublished Master's thesis "Happiness and Economics" (Hirata 2001a).

8 Wierzbicka (1999: 25) testifies that she, "as a native speaker of Polish, would never interpret Ekman's smiling faces in terms of 'enjoyment', because there is no such category in the Polish lexicon", and Stanislaw Baranczak (1990: 13), professor of Polish literature at Harvard University, asserts that "Slavic languages don't have an exact equivalent for the verb 'to enjoy'" (quoted in Wierzbicka 1999: 248).

9 The term "effect" will be used in the context of statistical analysis in the sense of being associated with a change of another variable, i.e. without implying any causality.

10 I will use the term *significant* for the statistical significance corresponding to $p \leq 0.05$, and *highly significant* for $p \leq 0.025$.

11 The authors report a larger coefficient (0.34), but since it relates to the natural logarithm of income rather than the logarithm to the basis 2 of income it needs to be corrected by the factor 0.693 ($=\log\hat{e}x/\log\hat{2}x$) to reflect the effect of doubling the underlying variable.

12 The coefficient reported by Deaton is larger (0.838) for the same reason as stated in the previous note.

13 The authors use a compound measure of SWB composed of two separate measures of happiness and life satisfaction. Looking at both measures separately, the trend was much more positive in happiness (positive trend in 45 out of 52 countries) than in life satisfaction (positive in 33 out of 52 countries; ibid.).

14 "Districts" are Federal Electoral Districts, of which there are (or were in 1971) 264, with an average population of 82,000 (Tomes 1986: 434).

15 Higher skew, in spite of implying a less "balanced" distribution, had a positive effect on an individual's happiness as predicted by range-frequency theory (Parducci 1995). This is because the dependent variable here is *individual* SWB, and *given a person's income and the lower and upper bound of the income distribution*, a thinner right-hand tail (=fewer very rich people) means a more favorable comparison of that income (fewer people above and more people below one's income).

16 Studies that corroborate these findings are Clark and Oswald (1994), Clark *et al.* (2001) and Di Tella *et al.* (2003). I am not aware of any study that finds no significant negative correlation between SWB and unemployment (even though the latter study finds that the very long-term unemployed get habituated to their situation so that their SWB approaches that of the reemployed long-term unemployed).

17 In a longitudinal study of 180 nuns, those in the highest SWB quartile lived 9.4 years longer on average than those in the lowest quartile (where SWB was assessed between age 18 and 32 by means of an independent assessment of autobiographies for positive and negative affect words) (Danner *et al.* 2001: 809; cf. also Diener 2003: 113).

18 Self-efficacy was measured in one survey by the question "How do you feel about yourself?", and in another, "How do you feel about yourself – what you are accomplishing and how you handle problems?"

19 A respondent's number of friends was estimated by asking "How about your friendships: would you say that you have a good many friends that you could count on if you had any sort of trouble, an average number, or not too many very good friends?" (Campbell *et al.* 1976: 358).

20 These comparisons refer to an ordinal rather than cardinal scaling of SWB. Differences do therefore not refer to numerical SWB values, but to the *probability* of being "completely happy" (score 10 out of 10). Interpreting SWB as a cardinal measure does not alter the general pattern. The Geneva/Basel-Land difference (0.45) would then be larger than the highest/lowest income group difference (0.33) but smaller than the effect of divorce (0.63) (Frey and Stutzer 2002: 188–9).

21 Hofstede describes this dimension as follows:

> *Individualism* pertains to *societies in which the ties between individuals are loose: everyone is expected to look after himself or herself and his or her immediate family. Collectivism* as its opposite pertains to *societies in which people from birth onwards are integrated into strong, cohesive in-groups, which throughout people's lifetime continue to protect them in exchange for unquestioning loyalty.*
>
> (Hofstede 1991: 51, emphasis orig.)

3 Relative income and happiness

1 Ronald Inglehart has published extensively on the World Values Surveys (Inglehart and Rabier 1986; Inglehart 1990, 1997, 2000; Inglehart *et al.* 2008). See also the institutional website: www.worldvaluessurvey.org.

2 This fallacy is committed, for example, by Frey and Stutzer (2002: 90–1) and Diener *et al.* (1995: 862). Apparently erroneous, or otherwise misleading, figures of huge positive time trends in a number of countries have been brought into circulation by Diener and Oishi (2000: 203) and uncritically been cited as evidence by Hagerty and

Veenhoven (2003: 3–5) and Layard (2005: 33, fn. 9). For a critical view of these results, cf. Easterlin (2005) and Hirata (2003: 12).

3 I am here talking of the possibility that *some* such societies exist or existed, without implying that subsistence societies generally tend to be more or less contented than modern societies (cf. Ueda 2003: 12).

4 I am using the term "prudent" here to avoid being pinned down to the technical meaning *rational* has assumed in the economic "rational choice" literature, even though I of course mean *rational* in its philosophical (and colloquial) sense of *governed by reason*.

5 For another relevant quote from the *Wealth of Nations*, cf. p. 000.

6 At first sight, one may be led to believe that the additional business of the watch industry also needs to be counted as a benefit, but this is again merely a shift within a zero-sum game since business is only diverted from other (non-positional) industries toward the watch industry. Only if people started working more in order to buy better watches would the watch industry's revenues really constitute additional business, but then this could again not be counted as a net welfare gain because the additional work effort (a social cost) would not be matched by a social benefit.

7 The term "secondary inflation" has been first introduced in Hirata (2001a: 36), and first published in Vendrik and Hirata (2003: 7).

8 Sen himself shows that the idea of functionings goes back to Aristotle (e.g. Aristotle 1934: 1094a 1). It also featured prominently, though not under that name, in a study by James Duesenberry (1949: 20) in which he wrote that "people do not, for the most part, desire specific goods but desire goods which will serve certain purposes".

9 The frequently encountered claim that such defensive expenditures "raise GDP" is of course wrong because they do not raise productivity nor working hours. They merely divert resources from wanted to needed goods, i.e. from constructive to defensive consumption. They "raise GDP" only with respect to a hypothetical scenario in which people would work correspondingly fewer hours. What remains true, of course, is that the national accounts count defensive expenditures with a positive sign (as any other expenditure) and thereby conceal reductions of well-being that derive from a diversion of resources from productive to defensive expenditures.

10 Indeed, Sen explicitly suggests that "being happy" is one of several "[complex] functionings relevant for well-being" (Sen 1993: 36), even though on another occasion he states that "[a functioning] has to be distinguished ... from the happiness generated by the functioning" (Sen 1985a: 10).

11 The effect to assess reality against expectations has even been observed in monkeys that refused to eat lettuce (which they would otherwise accept) that they discovered under a cup where they were made to expect an even more preferred banana (Tinklepaugh 1928, reported in Parducci 1995).

12 Other terms used interchangeably with "negative externalities" are "negative external effects", "negative spillover effects" and "external diseconomies". Importantly, externalities can also be positive, as will be discussed presently.

13 The term "direct externalities" or a corresponding concept is not used in the literature since no need is seen to distinguish "ordinary" direct externalities from frame of reference externalities.

14 The externalities discussed in the following are indeed attributed to various phenomena, from competition to modernization, to consumerism, to economic growth as such. Each of these concepts is complex in itself and cannot possibly be satisfactorily discussed here. I will therefore use the term "economic progress" as a general notion to capture the historical phenomenon of "economic advance and modernization" (Landes 1998: x).

15 The prisoner's dilemma describes a situation in which the sum of individually rational decisions is an overall outcome that is undesirable from the perspective of each decision-maker. For an elaborate discussion of the prisoner's dilemma and its implications for the concept of rationality, cf. Sen (1983/1973).

16 The revealed preference approach has been dominating the economic science since Paul Samuelson's pioneering 1938 article. It has been aptly criticized by Sen (1983/1977, 1987).

17 I am avoiding the term "rational" since it has come to be associated with entirely different meanings in philosophy and economics (cf. Zafirovski 1999). Cf. also note 4.

18 One study comparing nations (Rehdanz and Maddison 2003) found a significant correlation between climate and SWB, but a visual inspection of their graph (ibid.: 8) strongly suggests that their result is largely due to the formerly Communist countries that happen to have cold climates but had suffered a considerable fall in SWB levels (Inglehart 1997: 63) in the wake of the dissolution of their social(ist) infrastructure, rather than because of climate.

19 Just to avoid misunderstandings, I should state that this ambition does not imply a norm of SWB maximization. Understanding whether SWB can be enhanced does not need to rest on a desire to maximize it at any cost. Cf. p. 000 for more on this.

20 Due to the problem of multicollinearity and small sample sizes, the evaluation of predictors of SWB across countries is highly problematic. High-income countries share a lot of common characteristics that may all be causes or consequences of SWB, such as respect for human rights, basic need fulfillment, civic liberties, low incidence of corruption, long life expectancy, etc., and it is practically impossible to appraise their respective contributions.

4 Happiness and ethics

1 This question has been dealt with by a large number of philosophers, beginning with Plato and Aristotle and having found new popularity very recently. Cf. Annas (1993), Fenner (2004), Himmelmann (2003), McMahon (2004, 2005b), Seel (1999/1995), Spaemann (2000/1989), Wolf (1996), and the contributions in Schummer (1998), in Steinfath (1998), and in Studia Philosophica (1997).

2 The conception of ethics defended here is in large part inspired by the conception of Integrative Economic Ethics as developed by Peter Ulrich (2008) and the sources there referred to (in particular, Apel 1973, Habermas 1981, and Tugendhat 1995).

3 The term "area ethics" is suggested by Ulrich (2008: 81) in opposition to the established term "applied ethics" that problematically suggests that ethics can reveal factual or instrumental knowledge that can be applied to situations with pre-defined objectives. Instead, the job of area ethics should be seen in the generation of orientating knowledge that provides guidance where the objectives themselves are at issue. Cf., for the distinction between instrumental knowledge and orientating knowledge, Mittelstrass (1982: 19ff.).

4 Cf. Ulrich (2008: 101f.). I am generalizing somewhat by grouping Ulrich's third task ("the determination of the major 'site' of morality to put the regulative idea of socio-economic rationality into practice", ibid.) together with his second ("the clarification of a (discourse-) ethically grounded regulative idea of comprehensive economic reason or socio-economic rationality", ibid.).

5 "Ethics", *Encyclopædia Britannica*. Retrieved July 24, 2005, from Encyclopædia Britannica Online: http://search.eb.com/eb/article?tocId=60020.

6 A more formal account of this conception of behavior as utility maximization can be found in almost any introductory microeconomics textbook.

7 For carefully argued criticism at the utility maximization conception of human behavior, cf. Etzioni (1988), Rawls (1999/1971), Sen (1983/1977), Thomä (2003), Tversky *et al.* (1988), and Ulrich (2008).

8 For a "pure" example of reason-motivated behavior, one might think of the case of honoring a promise given to a deceased friend. However, reason-motivated behavior is not limited, I would argue, to moral considerations, as the example of wanting to congratulate a friend should make clear.

9 The relevant passage from Aristotle (1934: 1156b8–10) reads "…but it is those who wish the good of their friends for their friends' sake who are friends in the fullest sense, since they love each other for themselves and not accidentally". For a more thorough and more benevolent interpretation of Aristotle and the role of relational goods, cf. Bruni (2009/2006: 21ff.).

10 For a related argument, cf. Thomä (2003: 143, 151).

11 As the source for this conception of a formal account of well-being, Seel credits Ernst Tugendhat (1984: 33, 54).

12 For an illuminating interpretation of Sen's capability approach as a hermeneutic variant of a neo-Kantian ethic, cf. Jesús Conill (2004).

13 This paragraph is a brief adaptation of Ulrich (2008: 31ff.).

14 For competent critiques of utilitarianism, cf., for example, Rawls (1999/1971: 480ff.), Sen (1999b: 77ff.), Smith (1976/1759: 89f., 188), and Ulrich (1993/1986, 2008).

15 This quote is commonly attributed to John Maynard Keynes, but wrongly so, according to Wikiquote. Cf. http://en.wikiquote.org/wiki/John_Maynard_Keynes.

16 John Rawls, too, considers rationality a precondition of happiness:

> Indeed, with certain qualifications (§83) we can think of a person as being happy when he is in the way of a successful execution (more or less) of a rational plan of life drawn up under (more or less) favorable conditions, and he is reasonably confident that his plan can be carried through.
>
> (Rawls 1999/1971: 359)

17 Thomas Common, *Thus Spake Zarathustra* by F. Nietzsche, 6th edn. 1967, p. 364, quoted in Perricone (1999).

18 Felipe De Brigard's study also shows that around 50 percent of respondents would choose to remain connected to Nozick's happiness machine, even if the alternative was an unspecified life or a life of a "millionaire artist living in Monaco". While these results are intriguing and cast some doubt on the general acceptance of Nozick's conclusions in the literature, De Brigard's experiment is about choice rather than happiness.

19 Buddhists might not agree with this conclusion but argue that one can, and should, not lose one's happiness even at the loss of a loved one. However, they would probably have a different concept of happiness in mind than the one I have tried to explicate in this chapter, which is based on the meaning of happiness as it is used in the English language in an occidental cultural context.

5 Happiness and good development

1 This choice corresponds closely to Amartya Sen's reasons for giving preference to "realization-focused approaches" over "transcendental institutionalism" (Sen 2009: 5ff.).

2 To be more precise, one should say that *excessive* positional competition should be addressed by smart rules of the game because even the smartest rules should probably still allow, or even encourage, some degree of positional competition.

3 The problem described here is of course a case of a prisoners' dilemma. Yet, since the problem at hand is not a problem of purely strategic behavior, discussing it in terms of the prisoners' dilemma might lead to some confusion.

4 I shall make no distinction between gross *national* product and gross *domestic* product since the difference between the two is of no relevance here. What matters here is the underlying normative claim that a society's success is exclusively a matter of consumption rather than of leisure time, enjoyable work, capabilities, interpersonal relationships, and so on.

5 Symptomatic is a remark by Princeton economist José A. Scheinkman (2005, transl. J.H.) in which he applauds the fact that "the team of the [Brazilian] finance ministry

understood that there will be no sustainable [economic] growth in the country without an improvement of the issues of poverty and inequality".

6 For critical views of GNP as a policy objective, cf., for example, Sen (1999b).

7 For example: "If some aggregate welfare has to be sacrificed for greater equality, that is worthwhile, but if poverty has to be increased in order to have greater equality, the greater equality is not worth it" (Basu 2001: 68).

8 Utilitarianism is often complemented with libertarian arguments in economics, but it is not clear how these two perspectives can be reconciled, as Amartya Sen (1970) brilliantly showed.

9 It seems more plausible, however – both in a genetical and systematic perspective – to consider the capability approach's reference to Aristotle as a somewhat artificial *ex post* construction, at least in the case of Sen's version (Conill 2005).

10 Most of the following arguments in this section have first been presented by the author at the Second Workshop on Capabilities and Happiness in Milan in June 2005 (Hirata 2008).

11 While Sen ascribes to Rawls (1993) the term "public reasoning", Rawls himself uses the formulation "public reason" and defines it as "citizens' reasoning in the public forum about constitutional essentials and basic questions of justice" (Rawls 1993: 12). I assume Sen chose to use the expression "public reasoning" to avoid the possible metaphysical connotations of "public reason" and to better express the procedural nature of Rawls' own definition. I will stick with Sen's version for these very reasons.

12 Sen restates the same argument on several occasions, e.g., in Sen (1984a: 512, 1984b: 309, 1985b: 24, 1987: 46, 1999b: 63, 2009: 282ff.). Even though Sen uses this argument to defend the capability approach and, by implication, appears to criticize the reliance on happiness information as such, a closer reading reveals that his argument is directed against the *exclusive* reliance on happiness information and against happiness maximization, but not against *also* taking happiness information into account, as he makes clear on another occasion (Sen 1985a: 31). Cf. also Hirata (2008).

13 Cf. Harsanyi (1982: 41), who attributes the concept to Harrod (1936) and the terminology to Brandt (1959: 369, 380).

14 Cf. Rawls (1999/1971: 87–8) for an analogous argument in a contractarian perspective.

15 This was apparently also John Rawls's intuition behind his difference principle (Rawls 1999/1971: 65ff.), even though he articulated it in a problematic manner (cf. Ulrich 2008: 233f.).

16 This problem is nicely illustrated by the famous joke about the two men who are camping in the savannah when they discover a hungry lion running toward them. As one of them puts on his running shoes, his friend comments that he will never outrun the lion, not even with running shoes. "I don't need to outrun the lion," the first replies, "I only need to outrun *you*."

6 Happiness-oriented societal development under the premise of democracy

1 The following argument is adapted from an essay prepared by the author for the 2nd International Conference on Gross National Happiness (Hirata 2005).

2 This is not to imply that the "paradox" could be solved by an indeterministic framework, but that the very ambition to determine a set of preference aggregation rules that unambiguously satisfies a however modest set of cemented ethical conditions reflects a fundamental ethical misconception.

3 The example by Barry can also be read to criticize the utilitarian rule to add outcomes across individuals, but this is not the interpretation that Barry had in mind, nor the one that is of interest in this context.

4 On this distinction, cf. also Sen's (2005: 152–3) distinction between a process and an opportunity aspect of freedom.
5 Consider the following lines from the essay "Cloudy Sky" ("Bewölkter Himmel", 1919; transl. J.H.) by Hermann Hesse:

> What I never want, not even in my darkest hours, is a balanced middle between good and bad, such an uneventful, comfortable average. I would rather prefer an even stronger exaggeration of the curve – an agony even more vexing and, in exchange, even more blissful moments of exaltation.

6 Some of those who find it important to earn yet another million dollars apparently do not even notice whether or not they actually get that money, as in the case of two Goldman Sachs executives who, during more than a year, did not realize that their secretary had been diverting £4.5 million from their bank accounts (*The Economist* 2004). This might suggest that they bargained astronomical salaries for reasons other than the well-being these confer.
7 Cf. Madrian and Shea (2001), who found that shifting employees from enrolment-on-request to automatic enrolment in tax-sheltered saving schemes raised participation from just over 10 percent to 80 percent. In other words, whether people committed themselves to tax-sheltered savings schemes or not depended on whether they had to do a phone call to enroll or to sign out of the scheme, an apparently negligible cost compared to the sums at stake.
8 For the distinction between positive and negative freedom – though with a slightly different emphasis – cf. Berlin (1958) and Ulrich (2008: 245).

7 Orientation for a knowledgeable world

1 Cf. the series of three movies ("The Matrix", 1999, 2003, 2003) written and directed by Andy and Larry Wachowski.

Bibliography

Ahuvia, A.C. (1999) *Honor Versus Hedonism: A Cross-Cultural Analysis of the 'Missing Link' Between Income and Subjective Well-Being*, paper presented at the 7th Cross Cultural Research Conference, Michigan.

Ahuvia, A.C. (2002) "Individualism/Collectivism and Cultures of Happiness: A Theoretical Conjecture on the Relationship between Consumption, Culture and Subjective Well-Being at the National Level", *Journal of Happiness Studies*, 3: 23–36.

Alesina, A., Di Tella, R., and MacCulloch, R. (2004) "Inequality and Happiness: Are Europeans and Americans Different?", *Journal of Public Economics*, 88(9–10): 2009–42.

Andrews, F.M. and Withey, S.B. (1976) *Social Indicators of Well-Being*, New York: Plenum.

Angner, E. (2010) *Subjective Well-Being: When, and Why, It Matters*, paper presented at the Annual Conference of the European Society for the History of Economic Thought 2010, Amsterdam.

Annas, J. (1993) *The Morality of Happiness*, New York: Oxford University Press.

Annas, J. (2004) "Happiness as Achievement", *Dædalus*, 133(2): 44–51.

Apel, K.-O. (1973) "Das Apriori der Kommunikationsgemeinschaft und die Grundlagen der Ethik: Zum Problem einer rationalen Begründung der Ethik im Zeitalter der Wissenschaft", in Apel, K.-O. (ed.), *Transformation der Philosophie, Vol. 2: Das Apriori der Kommunikationsgemeinschaft* (engl.: *Towards a Transformation of Philosophy*, London: Routledge, 1980) (2nd ed.), Frankfurt a.M.: Suhrkamp, pp. 358–435.

Argyle, M. (1999) "Causes and Correlates of Happiness", in Kahneman, D., Diener, E., and Schwarz, N. (eds.), *Well-Being: The Foundations of Hedonic Psychology*, New York: Russell Sage Foundation, pp. 353–73.

Ariely, D. and Loewenstein, G. (2006) "The Heat of the Moment: The Effect of Sexual Arousal on Sexual Decision Making", *Journal of Behavioral Decision Making*, 19(2): 87–98.

Aristotle (1934) *Nicomachean Ethics*, translated by Rackham, H., Cambridge, MA: Harvard University Press.

Arrow, K.J. (1951) *Social Choice and Individual Values*, New York: John Wiley & Sons.

Avenel, V.G.d. (1913) *Le nivellement des jouissances*, Paris: Flammarion.

Baranczak, S. (1990) *Breathing under Water and other East European Essays*, Cambridge, MA: Harvard University Press.

Barkhaus, A. and Hollstein, B. (2003) "Ein Sozialstaat, der 'Sinn macht''? Begründung der Leitidee eines nachhaltigen aktivierenden Sozialstaates", *Zeitschrift für Wirtschafts- und Unternehmensethik*, 4(3): 287–306.

Barry, B. (1991) *Liberty and Justice: Essays in Political Theory 2*, Oxford: Clarendon Press.

Basu, K. (2001) "On the Goals of Development", in Meier, G.M. and Stiglitz, J.E. (eds.), *Frontiers of Development Economics: The Future in Perspective*, Oxford: Oxford University Press, pp. 61–86.

Beals, J. (1985) *Generational Differences in Well Being for Two European Groups*, Doctoral thesis, University of Michigan, Ann Arbor.

Becker, G.S. (1976) *The Economic Approach to Human Behavior*, Chicago: University of Chicago Press.

Becker, G.S. and Murphy, K.M. (1988) "A Theory of Rational Addiction", *Journal of Political Economy*, 96: 675–700.

Beckerman, W. (1975) *Two Cheers for the Affluent Society: A Spirited Defence of Economic Growth*, New York: St. Martin's Press.

Bentham, J. (1843/1775) "The Rationale of Reward", in *The Works of Jeremy Bentham* (ed. by J. Bowring), London: Tait, pp. 189–266.

Bentham, J. (1907/1789) *An Introduction to the Principles of Morals and Legislation*, Oxford: Clarendon Press.

Berlin, I. (1958) *Two Concepts of Liberty*, Oxford: Clarendon Press.

Berridge, K.C. (1999) "Pleasure, Pain, Desire, and Dread: Hidden Core Processes of Emotion", in Kahneman, D., Diener, E., and Schwarz, N. (eds.), *Well-Being: The Foundations of Hedonic Psychology*, New York: Russell Sage Foundation, pp. 525–57.

Blanchflower, D.G. and Oswald, A.J. (2003) *Does Inequality Reduce Happiness? Evidence from the States of the USA from the 1970s to the 1990s*, paper presented at the conference "The Paradoxes of Happiness in Economics", March 2003, Milan.

Blanchflower, D.G. and Oswald, A.J. (2004) "Well-Being Over Time in Britain and the USA", *Journal of Public Economics*, 88: 1359–86.

Blishen, B. and Atkinson, T. (1980) "Anglophone and Francophone Differences in Perceptions of the Quality of Life in Canada", in Szalai, A. and Andrews, F.M. (eds.), *The Quality of Life*, Beverly Hills: Sage, pp. 25–39.

Boulding, K.E. (1972) "Human Betterment and the Quality of Life", in Strumpel, B., Morgan, J.N., and Zahn, E. (eds.), *Human Behavior in Economic Affairs: Essays in Honor of George Katona*, Amsterdam: Elsevier, pp. 455–70.

Brandt, R.B. (1959) *Ethical Theory: The Problems of Normative and Critical Ethics*, Englewood Cliffs: Prentice-Hall.

Brickman, P., Coates, D., and Janoff-Bulman, R. (1978) "Lottery Winners and Accident Victims: Is Happiness Relative?", *Journal of Personality and Social Psychology*, 36: 917–27.

Bruckner, P. (2001) *Verdammt zum Glück: Der Fluch der Moderne*, translated by Stein, C., Berlin: Aufbau-Verlag.

Bruni, L. (2001) "Note sul consumo e sulla felicità", *Umanità Nuova*, 138.

Bruni, L. (2009/2006) *Civil Happiness: Economics and Human Flourishing in Historical Perspective*, London: Routledge.

Bruni, L. and Porta, P.L. (eds.) (2005) *Economics and Happiness: Framing the Analysis*, Oxford: Oxford University Press.

Bruni, L. and Porta, P.L. (eds.) (2007) *Handbook on the Economics of Happiness*, Cheltenham: Edward Elgar.

Campbell, A., Converse, P.E., and Rodgers, W.L. (1976) *The Quality of American Life*, New York: Russell Sage Foundation.

Cheng, H. and Furnham, A. (2001) "Attributional Style and Personality as Predictors of Happiness and Mental Health", *Journal of Happiness Studies*, 2(3): 307–27.

Clark, A.E. (2003) *Inequality-Aversion and Income Mobility: A Direct Test*, CNRS/DELTA Working Paper, Paris.

Clark, A.E. and Oswald, A.J. (1994) "Unhappiness and Unemployment", *The Economic Journal*, 104(424): 648–59.

Clark, A.E. and Oswald, A.J. (1996) "Satisfaction and Comparison Income", *Journal of Public Economics*, 61: 359–81.

Clark, A.E., Diener, E., Georgellis, Y., and Lucas, R.E. (2008) "Lags And Leads in Life Satisfaction: a Test of the Baseline Hypothesis", *The Economic Journal*, 118(529): F222–43.

Clark, A.E., Georgellis, Y., and Sanfey, P. (2001) "Scarring: The Psychological Impact of Past Unemployment", *Economica*, 68(270): 221–41.

Conill, J. (2004) *Horizontes de economía ética: Aristóteles, Adam Smith, Amartya Sen*, Madrid: Tecnos.

Conill, J. (2005) "Ethische Grundlagen des Ansatzes der Fähigkeiten von Amartya Sen", in Homann, K., Koslowski, P., and Lütge, C. (eds.), *Wirtschaftsethik der Globalisierung*, Tübingen: Mohr Siebeck, pp. 319–34.

Cornelissen, C. (1908) *Théorie du salaire et du travail salarié*, Paris: Giard et Brière.

Danner, D.D., Snowdon, D.A., and Friesen, W.V. (2001) "Positive Emotions in Early Life and Longevity: Findings from the Nun Study", *Journal of Personality and Social Psychology*, 80(5): 804–13.

Davidson, R.J. (1992) "Anterior Cerebral Asymmetry and the Nature of Emotion", *Brain and Cognition*, 20(1): 125–51.

Deaton, A. (2008) "Income, Health, and Well-Being around the World: Evidence from the Gallup World Poll", *Journal of Economic Perspectives*, 22(2): 53–72.

De Botton, A. (2004) *Status Anxiety*, London: Hamish Hamilton/Penguin.

De Brigard, F. (2010) "If You Like It, Does It Matter if It's Real?", *Philosophical Psychology*, 23(1): 43–57.

Deci, E.L. and Ryan, R.M. (1985) *Intrinsic Motivation and Self-determination in Human Behavior*, New York: Plenum.

Demir, M. and Weitekamp, L.A. (2007) "I am so Happy 'Cause Today I Found My Friend: Friendship and Personality as Predictors of Happiness", *Journal of Happiness Studies*, 8(2): 181–211.

Diener, E. (1984) "Subjective Well-Being", *Psychological Bulletin*, 95(3): 542–75.

Diener, E. (1994) "Assessing Subjective Well-Being: Progress and Opportunities", *Social Indicators Research*, 31: 103–57.

Diener, E. (2003) *The Psychology of why Inequality Might Matter, or not*, presentation at "Why Inequality Matters: Lessons for Policy from the Economics of Happiness", The Brookings Institution, 4/5 June 2003 (in: "Transcript of the second day").

Diener, E. and Diener, M. (1995) "Cross-Cultural Correlates of Life Satisfaction and Self-Esteem", *Journal of Personality and Social Psychology*, 68(4): 653–63.

Diener, E. and Fujita, F. (1995) "Resources, Personal Strivings, and Subjective Well-Being: A Nomothetic and Idiographic Approach", *Journal of Personality and Social Psychology*, 68: 926–35.

Diener, E. and Lucas, R.E. (1999) "Personality and Subjective Well-Being", in Kahneman, D., Diener, E., and Schwarz, N. (eds.), *Well-Being: The Foundations of Hedonic Psychology*, New York: Russell Sage Foundation, pp. 213–29.

Diener, E. and Oishi, S. (2000) "Money and Happiness: Income and Subjective

Well-Being across Nations", in Diener, E. and Suh, E.M. (eds.), *Culture and Subjective Well-Being*, Cambridge: MIT Press, pp. 185–218.

Diener, E. and Seligman, M.E.P. (2004) "Beyond Money: Toward an Economy of Well-Being", *Psychological Science in the Public Interest*, 5(1): 1–31.

Diener, E. and Suh, E.M. (1999) "National Differences in Subjective Well-Being", in Kahneman, D., Diener, E., and Schwarz, N. (eds.), *Well-Being: The Foundations of Hedonic Psychology*, New York: Russell Sage Foundation, pp. 434–50.

Diener, E., Diener, M., and Diener, C. (1995) "Factors Predicting the Subjective Well-Being of Nations", *Journal of Personality and Social Psychology*, 69: 851–64.

Diener, E., Larsen, R.J., Levine, S., and Emmons, R.A. (1985) "Intensity and Frequency: Dimensions Underlying Positive and Negative Affect", *Journal of Personality and Social Psychology*, 48: 1253–65.

Diener, E., Sandvik, E., Pavot, W., and Gallagher, D. (1991) "Response Artifacts in the Measurement of Subjective Well-Being", *Social Indicators Research*, 24: 35–56.

Diener, E., Sandvik, E., Seidlitz, L., and Diener, M. (1993) "The Relationship between Income and Subjective Well-Being: Relative or Absolute?", *Social Indicators Research*, 28(3): 195–223.

Di Tella, R., MacCulloch, R.J., and Oswald, A.J. (2003) "The Macroeconomics of Happiness", *Review of Economics & Statistics*, 85(4): 809–27.

Dryzek, J.S. (2001) "Legitimacy and Economy in Deliberative Democracy", *Political Theory*, 29(5): 651–69.

Duesenberry, J.S. (1949) *Income, Saving and the Theory of Consumer Behavior*, Cambridge, MA: Harvard University Press.

Easterlin, R.A. (1974) "Does Economic Growth Improve the Human Lot? Some Empirical Evidence", in David, P.A. and Reder, M.W. (eds.), *Nations and Households in Economic Growth: Essays in Honor of Moses Abramowitz*, New York and London: Academic Press, pp. 89–125.

Easterlin, R.A. (1995) "Will Raising the Incomes of All Increase the Happiness of All?", *Journal of Economic Behavior and Organization*, 27: 35–48.

Easterlin, R.A. (2001) "Income and Happiness: Towards a Unified Theory", *The Economic Journal*, 111(473): 465–84.

Easterlin, R.A. (2003) *Building a Better Theory of Well-Being*, IZA Discussion Paper No. 742, Bonn: IZA.

Easterlin, R.A. (2005) "Feeding the Illusion of Growth and Happiness: A Reply to Hagerty and Veenhoven", *Social Indicators Research*, 74(3): 429–43.

Easterlin, R.A. and Angelescu, L. (2009) *Happiness and Growth the World Over: Time Series Evidence on the Happiness-Income Paradox*, IZA Discussion Paper No. 4060, Bonn.

Easterlin, R.A. and Schaeffer, C.M. (1999) "Income and Subjective Well-Being over the Life Cycle", in Ryff, C.D. and Marshall, V.W. (eds.), *The Self and Society in Aging Processes*, New York: Springer, pp. 279–301.

Edgeworth, F.Y. (1881) *Mathematical Psychics: An Essay on the Application of Mathematics to the Moral Sciences*, London: Kegan Paul.

Ehrenreich, B. (2009) *Bright-Sided: How the Relentless Promotion of Positive Thinking Has Undermined America*, New York: Metropolitan Books.

Eich, E., Brodkin, I.A., Reeves, J.L., and Chawla, A.F. (1999) "Questions Concerning Pain", in Kahneman, D., Diener, E., and Schwarz, N. (eds.), *Well-Being: The Foundations of Hedonic Psychology*, New York: Russell Sage Foundation, pp. 155–68.

Ekman, P. (1975) "The Universal Smile: Face Muscles Talk Every Language", *Psychology Today*, 9: 35–9.

Elster, J. (2000) *Ulysses Unbound: Studies in Rationality, Precommitment, and Constraints*, Cambridge, UK: Cambridge University Press.

Etzioni, A. (1988) *The Moral Dimension*, New York: Free Press.

Fenner, D. (2004) "Glück oder Moral? Zur Verhältnisbestimmung von Individual- und Sozialethik", *Zeitschrift für philosophische Forschung*, 58(3): 428–46.

Ferrer-i-Carbonell, A. (2005) "Income and Well-Being: an Empirical Analysis of the Comparison Income Effect", *Journal of Public Economics*, 89(5–6): 997–1019.

Ferrer-i-Carbonell, A. and Frijters, P. (2004) "How Important is Methodology for the Estimates of the Determinants of Happiness?", *The Economic Journal*, 114: 641–59.

Festinger, L. (1954) "A Theory of Social Comparison", *Human Relations*, 7: 117–40.

Forschner, M. (1998) "Über das Vergnügen naturgemäßen Tuns: John Stuart Mills Konzept eines Lebens in Lust und Würde", in Schummer, J. (ed.), *Glück und Ethik*, Würzburg: Königshausen und Neumann, pp. 147–67.

Frank, R.H. (1989) "Frames of Reference and the Quality of Life", *American Economic Review*, 79(2): 80–5.

Frank, R.H. (1997) "The Frame of Reference as a Public Good", *The Economic Journal*, 107(November): 1832–47.

Frank, R.H. (1999) *Luxury Fever: Why Money Fails to Satisfy in an Era of Excess*, Princeton: Princeton University Press.

Frank, R.H. (2003) *Are Positional Externalities Different from Other Externalities?*, draft for presentation at "Why Inequality Matters: Lessons for Policy from the Economics of Happiness", The Brookings Institution, 4/5 June 2003.

Frank, R.H. and Cook, P.J. (1996) *The Winner-Take-All Society: Why the Few at the Top Get so much More than the Rest of us*, New York: Penguin Books.

Frank, R.H., Gilovich, T., and Regan, D.T. (1993) "Does Studying Economics Inhibit Cooperation?", *Journal of Economic Perspectives*, 7(2): 159–71.

Frankfurt, H.G. (1971) "Freedom of the Will and the Concept of a Person", *Journal of Philosophy*, 68(1): 5–20.

Frankfurt, H.G. (1999) *Necessity, Volition, and Love*, Cambridge, UK: Cambridge University Press.

Frankl, V.E. (2003) "Determinismus und Humanismus", in Frankl, V.E. (ed.), *Der Mensch vor der Frage nach dem Sinn* (16th ed.), München: Piper, pp. 50–64.

Frederick, S. and Loewenstein, G. (1999) "Hedonic Adaptation", in Kahneman, D., Diener, E., and Schwarz, N. (eds.), *Well-Being: The Foundations of Hedonic Psychology*, New York: Russell Sage Foundation, pp. 302–29.

Frey, B.S. and Stutzer, A. (2000) "Happiness, Economy, and Institutions", *The Economic Journal*, 110: 918–38.

Frey, B.S. and Stutzer, A. (2002) *Happiness and Economics: How the Economy and Institutions Affect Human Well-being*, Princeton: Princeton University Press.

Friedman, B. (2006) "The Moral Consequences of Economic Growth", *Society*, 43(2): 15–22.

Galbraith, J.K. (1958) *The Affluent Society*, Boston: Houghton Mifflin.

Gardner, J. and Oswald, A. (2007) "Money and Mental Wellbeing: A Longitudinal Study of Medium-sized Lottery Wins", *Journal of Health Economics*, 26(1): 49–60.

Gasper, D. (2004) *The Ethics of Development: From Economism to Human Development*, Edinburgh: Edinburgh University Press.

Giannetti, E. (2002) *Vícios privados, benefícios públicos? A ética na riqueza das nações*, São Paulo: Companhia Das Letras.

Graham, C. and Felton, A. (2005) *Does Inequality Matter to Individual Welfare? An Initial Exploration Based on Happiness Surveys from Latin America*, CSED Working Paper No. 38, Washington, DC: The Brookings Institution.

Graham, C. and Pettinato, S. (2001) *Happiness and Hardship: Opportunity and Insecurity in New Market Economies*, Washington, D.C.: Brookings Institution Press.

Gross, P. (1994) *Die Multioptionsgesellschaft*, Frankfurt a.M.: Suhrkamp.

Gurin, G., Veroff, J. and Feld, S. (1960) *Americans View their Mental Health*, New York: Basic Books.

Habermas, J. (1981) *Theorie des kommunikativen Handelns*, Frankfurt a.M.: Suhrkamp. (engl.: *Theory of Communicative Action*, Boston: Beacon, 1984.)

Habermas, J., (1983) *Moralbewusstsein und kommunikatives Handeln*, Frankfurt a.M.: Suhrkamp. (engl.: *Moral Consciousness and Communicative Action*, Cambridge: MIT Press, 1992).

Hagerty, M.R. (2000) "Social Comparisons of Income in One's Community: Evidence from National Surveys of Income and Happiness", *Journal of Personality and Social Psychology*, 78(4): 764–71.

Hagerty, M.R. and Veenhoven, R. (2003) "Wealth and Happiness Revisited: Growing National Income Does Go with Greater Happiness", *Social Indicators Research*, 64(1): 1–27.

Hardie, W.F.R. (1965) "The Final Good in Aristotle's Ethics", *Philosophy*, 40(154): 277–95.

Harrod, R.F. (1936) "Utilitarianism Revised", *Mind*, 45(178): 137–56.

Harrod, R.F. (1958) "The Possibility of Economic Satiety", in *Problems of United States Economic Development*, New York: Committee for Economic Development, pp. 207–13.

Harsanyi, J.C. (1982) "Morality and the Theory of Rational Behavior", in Sen, A.K. and Williams, B. (eds.), *Utilitarianism and Beyond*, Cambridge: Cambridge University Press, pp. 39–62.

Haybron, D.M. (2000) "Two Philosophical Problems in the Study of Happiness", *Journal of Happiness Studies*, 1: 207–25.

Headey, B. and Wearing, A. (1992) *Understanding Happiness: A Theory of Subjective Well-Being*, Melbourne: Longman Cheshire.

Headey, B., Veenhoven, R., and Wearing, A. (1991) "Top-Down versus Bottom-Up Theories of Subjective Well-Being", *Social Indicators Research*, 24: 81–100.

Helson, H. (1964) *Adaptation-level Theory: An Experimental and Systematic Approach to Behavior*, New York: Harper & Row.

Himmelmann, B. (2003) *Kants Begriff des Glücks*, Berlin: de Gruyter.

Hirata, J. (2001a) *Happiness and Economics: Enriching Economic Theory with Empirical Psychology*, Master's thesis, Maastricht University.

Hirata, J. (2001b) "Was Mother Teresa an Egoist?", *Eloquent*, 8(1): 37–8.

Hirata, J. (2003) *Happiness and Economics: Some Ethical Considerations*, discussion paper of the Institute for Business Ethics No. 99, St. Gallen: Institute for Business Ethics.

Hirata, J. (2004) "Happiness Research: Contributions to Economic Ethics", *Zeitschrift für Wirtschafts- und Unternehmensethik (zfwu)*, 5(2): 141–59.

Hirata, J. (2005) "How Should Happiness Guide Policy? Why Gross National Happiness Is not Opposed to Democracy", *Journal of Bhutan Studies*, 12: 1–22.

Hirata, J. (2008) "The Division of Labor between the Capability and the Happiness Perspective", in Bruni, L., Comim, F., and Pugno, M. (eds.), *Capabilities and Happiness*, New York: Oxford University Press, pp. 160–86.

Hirsch, F. (1976) *Social Limits to Growth*, Cambridge, MA: Harvard University Press.

Hoffman, E. (1989) *Lost in Translation: A Life in a New Language*, New York: E.P. Dutton.

Hofstede, G. (1991) *Cultures and Organizations: Software of the Mind*, Boston: McGraw-Hill.

Hooper, J. and Teresi, D. (1992) *The Three-pound Universe*, Los Angeles: St. Martin's Press.

Iijima, K. (1982) *The Feelings of Satisfaction and Happiness of the Japanese and other Peoples*, Bulletin of the Nippon Research Center (excerpts from the original paper in Japanese).

Inglehart, R. (1977) *The Silent Revolution: Changing Values and Political Styles Among Western Publics*, Princeton: Princeton University Press.

Inglehart, R. (1990) *Culture Shift in Advanced Industrial Society*, Princeton: Princeton University Press.

Inglehart, R. (1997) *Modernization and Postmodernization: Cultural, Economic, and Political Change in 43 Societies*, Princeton: Princeton University Press.

Inglehart, R. (2000) "Globalization and Postmodern Values", *The Washington Quarterly*, 23(1): 215–28.

Inglehart, R. and Rabier, J.-R. (1986) "Aspirations Adapt to Situations – But Why are the Belgians so much Happier than the French?", in Andrews, F.M. (ed.), *Research on the Quality of Life*, Ann Arbor: Institute for Social Research, University of Michigan.

Inglehart, R., Foa, R., Peterson, C., and Welzel, C. (2008) "Development, Freedom, and Rising Happiness: A Global Perspective (1981–2007)", *Perspectives on Psychological Science*, 3(4): 264–85.

James, J. (1993) *Consumption and Development*, New York: St. Martin's Press.

Kahneman, D. (1999) "Objective Happiness", in Kahneman, D., Diener, E. and Schwarz, N. (eds.), *Well-Being: The Foundations of Hedonic Psychology*, New York: Russell Sage Foundation, pp. 3–25.

Kahneman, D. (2003) "A Psychological Perspective on Economics", *American Economic Review*, 93(2): 162–8.

Kahneman, D., Wakker, P.P., and Sarin, R. (1997) "Back to Bentham? Explorations of Experienced Utility", *Quarterly Journal of Economics*, 112(2): 375–405.

Kant, I. (1977/1784) *Beantwortung der Frage: Was ist Aufklärung?*, Collected Writings Vol. XI (pp. 53–61), ed. by W. Weischedel, Frankfurt a.M.: Suhrkamp.

Kant, I. (1977/1785) *Grundlegung zur Metaphysik der Sitten*, Collected Writings Vol. VII, ed. by W. Weischedel, Frankfurt a.M.: Suhrkamp.

Kasser, T. and Ahuvia, A. (2002) "Materialistic Values and Well-being in Business Students", *European Journal of Social Psychology*, 32(1): 137–46.

Kasser, T. and Ryan, R.M. (1993) "A Dark Side of the American Dream: Correlates of Financial Success as a Central Life Aspiration", *Journal of Personality and Social Psychology*, 65(2): 410–22.

Kasser, T. and Ryan, R.M. (1996) "Further Examining the American Dream: Differential Correlates of Intrinsic and Extrinsic Goals", *Personality and Social Psychology Bulletin*, 22: 280–7.

Kingdom of Bhutan (2008) *Constitution of the Kingdom of Bhutan*. Online. www.constitution.bt/html/constitution/articles.htm (accessed 12 July 2010).

Kirchgässner, G. (2000/1991) *Homo Oeconomicus: Das ökonomische Modell individuellen Verhaltens und seine Anwendung in den Wirtschafts- und Sozialwissenschaften*, 2nd ed., Tübingen: Mohr Siebeck.

Knight, F.H. (1964) *Risk, Uncertainty, and Profit*, New York: A.M. Kelley.

Knight, F.H. (1999/1924) *The Limitations of Scientific Method in Economics*, Selected Essays, ed. by R.B. Emmett (Vol. I), Chicago: University of Chicago Press.

Landes, D.S. (1998) *The Wealth and Poverty of Nations: Why Some are so Rich and Some so Poor*, London: Little Brown.

Lane, R.E. (2000a) "Diminishing Returns to Income, Companionship – and Happiness", *Journal of Happiness Studies*, 1: 103–19.

Lane, R.E. (2000b) *The Loss of Happiness in Market Democracies*, New Haven: Yale University Press.

Lange, J. (1929) *Verbrechen als Schicksal: Studien an kriminellen Zwillingen*, Leipzig: Georg Thieme.

Larsen, R.J. and Fredrickson, B.L. (1999) "Measurement Issues in Emotion Research", in Kahneman, D., Diener, E., and Schwarz, N. (eds.), *Well-Being: The Foundations of Hedonic Psychology*, New York: Russell Sage, pp. 40–60.

Lauterbach, A. (1972) "The Social Setting of Consumer Behavior in Latin America", in Strumpel, B., Morgan, J.N. and Zahn, E., (eds.), *Human Behavior in Economic Affairs: Essays in Honor of George Katona*, Amsterdam: Elsevier, pp. 261–85.

Layard, R. (1980) "Human Satisfaction and Public Policy", *The Economic Journal*, 90(360): 737–50.

Layard, R. (2003) *Income and Happiness: Rethinking Economic Policy*, Lionel Robbins Memorial Lecture for 2003: Happiness: Has Social Science a Clue? (2 of 3), London. Online. http://cep.lse.ac.uk/events/lectures/layard/RL040303.pdf (accessed 12 September 2006).

Layard, R. (2005) *Happiness: Lessons from a New Science*, New York: Penguin.

Lazarus, R.S. (1991) *Emotion and Adaptation*, New York: Oxford University Press.

Lelord, F. (2002) *Le Voyage d'Hector ou la recherche du bonheur*, Paris: Odile Jacob.

Lichtenberg, J. (1996) "Consuming Because Others Consume", *Social Theory & Practice*, 22(3): 273–97.

Loewenstein, G. and Schkade, D. (1999) "Wouldn't it Be Nice? Predicting Future Feelings", in Kahneman, D., Diener, E., and Schwarz, N. (eds.), *Well-Being: The Foundations of Hedonic Psychology*, New York: Russell Sage Foundation, pp. 85–105.

Lucas, R.E., Clark, A.E., Georgellis, Y., and Diener, E. (2003) "Reexamining Adaptation and the Set Point Model of Happiness: Reactions to Changes in Marital Status", *Journal of Personality and Social Psychology*, 84(3): 527-39.

Lucas, R.E., Clark, A.E., Georgellis, Y., and Diener, E. (2004) "Unemployment Alters the Set Point for Life Satisfaction", *Psychological Science*, 15(1): 8–13.

Lykken, D. and Tellegen, A. (1996) "Happiness Is a Stochastic Phenomenon", *Psychological Science*, 7: 186–9.

Madrian, B.C. and Shea, D.F. (2001) "The Power of Suggestion: Inertia in 401(k) Participation and Savings Behavior", *Quarterly Journal of Economics*, 116(4): 1149–87.

Marcuse, L. (1962) *Philosophie des Glücks: Zwischen Hiob und Freud*, Munich: Paul List.

Marks, N. (2004) "Towards Evidence Based Public Policy: The Power and Potential of Using Well-being Indicators in a Political Context", in Ura, K. and Galay, K. (eds.), *Gross National Happiness and Development: Proceedings of the First International*

Seminar on Operationalization of Gross National Happiness, Thimphu: The Centre for Bhutan Studies, pp. 319–46.

Marx, K. (1887) *Capital: A Critical Analysis of Capitalist Production*, ed. by F. Engels, translated by Moore, S. and Aveling, E.B., London: Sonnenschein.

Marx, K. (1933/1849) "Wage Labor and Capital", in *Selected Works*, New York: International Publishers.

McMahon, D.M. (2004) "From the Happiness of Virtue to the Virtue of Happiness: 400 B.C.–A.D. 1780", *Dædalus*, 133(2): 5–17.

McMahon, D.M. (2005a) "Be of Good Cheer—Or Else", *The Wall Street Journal*, 26 January, p. D11.

McMahon, D.M. (2005b) *Happiness: A History*, New York: Atlantic Monthly Press.

Meadows, D.H., Meadows, D.L., Randers, J. and Behrens, W.W. (1972) *The Limits to Growth*, New York: Universe Books.

Michels, R. (1918) *Economia e felicità*, Milano: Vallardi.

Mill, J.S. (1969/1833) "Remarks on Bentham's Philosophy", in Robson, J.M. (ed.), *Collected Works of John Stuart Mill*, Toronto: Toronto University Press, pp. 4–18.

Mishan, E.J. (1979/1967) *The Costs of Economic Growth*, Harmondsworth: Penguin.

Mittelstrass, J. (1982) *Wissenschaft als Lebensform: Reden über philosophische Orientierungen in Wissenschaft und Universität*, Frankfurt a.M.: Suhrkamp.

Moan, C.E. and Heath, R.G. (1972) "Septal Stimulation for the Initiation of Heterosexual Activity in a Homosexual Male", *Journal of Behavior Therapy and Experimental Psychiatry*, 3: 23–30.

Mokdad, A.H., Serdula, M.K., Dietz, W.H., Bowman, B.A, Marks, J.S., and Koplan, J.P. (1999) "The Spread of the Obesity Epidemic in the United States, 1991–1998", *Journal of the American Medical Association (JAMA)*, 282(16): 1519–22.

Myers, D.G. (1992) *The Pursuit of Happiness: Discovering the Pathway to Fulfillment, Well-being, and Enduring Personal Joy*, New York: Avon.

Myers, D.G. (2000) "The Funds, Friends, and Faith of Happy People", *American Psychologist*, 55(1): 56–67.

Myrdal, G. (1953/1930) *The Political Element in the Development of Economic Theory*, translated from the German edition by Streeten, P., Abingdon: Routledge.

Neumayer, E. (1999) "Global Warming: Discounting Is not the Issue, but Substitutability Is", *Energy Policy*, 27: 33–43.

Ng, Y.-K. (1978) "Economic Growth and Social Welfare: The Need for a Complete Study of Happiness", *Kyklos*, 31(4): 575–87.

Ng, Y.-K. (1980) "Money and Happiness: First Lesson in Eudaimonology", *Kyklos*, 33(1): 161–3.

Ng, Y.-K. (1996) "Happiness Surveys: Some Comparability Issues and an Exploratory Survey Based on Just Perceivable Increments", *Social Indicators Research*, 38: 1–27.

Ng, Y.-K. (1997) "A Case for Happiness, Cardinalism, and Interpersonal Comparability", *The Economic Journal*, 107(445): 1848–58.

Ng, Y.-K. (2003) "From Preference to Happiness: Towards a More Complete Welfare Economics.", *Social Choice & Welfare*, 20(2): 307.

Nietzsche, F. (1988) *Sämtliche Werke. Kritische Studienausgabe*, ed. by Colli, G. and Montinari, M., Berlin: Walter de Gruyter.

Norberg-Hodge, H. (1991) *Ancient Futures: Learning from Ladakh*, London: Rider.

Nozick, R. (1989) "Happiness", in Nozick, R. (ed.), *The Examined Life: Philosophical Meditations*, New York: Simon and Schuster, pp. 99–117.

Nurkse, R. (1953) *Problems of Capital Formation in Underdeveloped Countries*, New York: Oxford University Press.

Nussbaum, M.C. (1992) "Human Functioning and Social Justice: In Defense of Aristotelian Essentialism", *Political Theory*, 20(2): 202–46.

Nussbaum, M.C. (2000) *Women and Human Development: The Capabilities Approach*, Cambridge: Cambridge University Press.

Nussbaum, M.C. (2004) "Mill between Aristotle & Bentham", *Dædalus*, 133(2): 60–8.

Nussbaum, M.C. (2006) *Frontiers of Justice: Disability, Nationality, Species Membership*, Cambridge, MA: Harvard University Press.

Olds, J. and Milner, P. (1954) "Positive Reinforcement Produced by Electrical Stimulation of the Septal Area and Other Regions of the Rat Brain", *Journal of Comparative and Physiological Psychology*, 47: 419–28.

Olson, J.M., Herman, C.P., and Zanna, M.P. (eds.) (1986) *Relative Deprivation and Social Comparison: The Ontario Symposium, Vol. 4*, Hillsdale, NJ, and London: Lawrence Erlbaum.

Oswald, A.J. (1997) "Happiness and Economic Performance", *The Economic Journal*, 107(November): 1815–31.

Pankaj, P. and Dorji, T. (2004) "Measuring Individual Happiness in Relation to Gross National Happiness in Bhutan: Some preliminary results from survey data", in Ura, K. and Galay, K. (eds.), *Gross National Happiness and Development*, Thimphu: The Centre for Bhutan Studies, pp. 375–88.

Parducci, A. (1968) "The Relativism of Absolute Judgments", *Scientific American*, 219: 84–90.

Parducci, A. (1995) *Happiness, Pleasure, and Judgement: The Contextual Theory and its Applications*, Mahwah, NJ: Erlbaum.

Perricone, J.A. (1999) "Catholic Theology of Work and Worship", *St. John's Law Review* (Summer).

Pigou, A.C. (1952/1920) *The Economics of Welfare*, 4th ed., London: Macmillan.

Plato (1998) *Gorgias*, translated by Waterfield, R., Oxford: Oxford University Press.

Plug, E.J.S. and van Praag, B.M.S. (1995) "Family Equivalence Scales within a Narrow and Broad Welfare Context: Some Comments", *Journal of Income Distribution*, 4(2): 17–32.

Popper, K.R. (1959/1934) *The Logic of Scientific Discovery*, New York: Basic Books.

Porter, M.E. (2000) "Attitudes, Values, Beliefs, and the Microeconomics of Prosperity", in Huntington, S.P. and Harrison, L.E. (eds.), *Culture Matters: How Values Shape Human Progress*, New York: Basic Books, pp. 14–28.

Printer of Acts of Parliament. (2000) *Local Government Act 2000*, London: Parliament of the United Kingdom. Online. www.opsi.gov.uk/acts/acts2000/20000022.htm (accessed 20 August 2003).

Putnam, R.D. (2000) *Bowling Alone: The Collapse and Revival of American Community*, New York: Simon & Schuster.

Rainwater, L. (1990) *Poverty and Equivalence as Social Constructions*, Luxembourg: Luxembourg Income Study Working Paper No. 55.

Rawls, J. (1982) "Social Unity and Primary Goods", in Sen, A.K. and Williams, B. (eds.), *Utilitarianism and Beyond*, Cambridge: Cambridge University Press, pp. 159–85.

Rawls, J. (1993) *Political Liberalism*, New York: Columbia University Press.

Rawls, J. (1999/1971) *A Theory of Justice*, revised ed., Oxford: Oxford University Press.

Read, C. (2005/1901) *Logic, Deductive and Inductive*, 2nd edn., Boston: Adamant.

Rehdanz, K. and Maddison, D. (2003) *Climate and Happiness*, Research Unit Sustainability and Global Change Working Paper FNU-20, Centre for Marine and Climate Research, Hamburg University.

Rhodes, N. (2000) "The Monetisation of Bhutan", *Journal of Bhutan Studies*, 2(2): 79–95.

Rice, T.W. and Steele, B.J. (2004) "Subjective Well-being and Culture across Time and Space", *Journal of Cross-Cultural Psychology*, 35(6): 633–47.

Ridge, C., Rice, T., and Cherry, M. (2009) "The Causal Link between Happiness and Democratic Welfare Regimes", in Dutt, A.K. and Radcliff, B. (eds.), *Happiness, Economics and Politics: Towards a Multi-Disciplinary Approach*, Cheltenham: Edward Elgar, pp. 271–84.

Rignano, E. (1901) *Di un Socialismo in accordo colla dottrina economica liberale*, Turin: Fratelli Bocca.

Rousseau, J.-J. (1762/1922) *Emil oder Über die Erziehung*, translated by Denhardt, H., Leipzig: Reclam.

Russell, B. (1996/1930) *The Conquest of Happiness*, New York: Liveright.

Samuelson, P.A. (1938) "A Note on the Pure Theory of Consumer's Behaviour", *Economica*, 5: 61–71.

Scheinkman, J.A. (2005) "BC ignora impacto fiscal dos juros", *O Globo*, 30 May, p. 23.

Schkade, D.A. and Kahneman, D. (1998) "Does Living in California Make People Happy? A Focusing Illusion in Judgments of Life Satisfaction", *Psychological Science*, 9: 340–6.

Schmid, H.B. (2005) "Beyond Self-goal Choice: Amartya Sen's Analysis of the Structure of Commitment and the Role of Shared Desires", *Economics and Philosophy*, 21(1): 51–63.

Schummer, J. (ed.) (1998) *Glück und Ethik*, Würzburg: Königshausen und Neumann.

Schwartz, B. (2000) "Self-Determination: The Tyranny of Freedom", *American Psychologist*, 55(1): 79–88.

Schwartz, B. (2004) *The Paradox of Choice: Why More Is Less*, New York: Ecco.

Schwarz, N. and Strack, F. (1999) "Reports of Subjective Well-Being: Judgmental Processes and their Methodological Implications", in Kahneman, D., Diener, E., and Schwarz, N. (eds.), *Well-Being: The Foundations of Hedonic Psychology*, New York: Russell Sage Foundation, pp. 61–83.

Schyns, P. (1998) "Crossnational Differences in Happiness: Economic and Cultural Factors Explored", *Social Indicators Research*, 43: 3–26.

Seel, M. (1999/1995) *Versuch über die Form des Glücks*, Frankfurt a.M.: Suhrkamp.

Sen, A.K. (1970) "The Impossibility of a Paretian Liberal", *Journal of Political Economy*, 78: 152–7.

Sen, A.K. (1982) "Rights and Agency", *Philosophy and Public Affairs*, 11(1): 3–39.

Sen, A.K. (1983) "Poor, Relatively Speaking", *Oxford Economic Papers*, 35(July): 153–69.

Sen, A.K. (1983/1973) "Behavior and the Concept of Preference", in *Choice, Welfare and Measurement*, Oxford: Basil Blackwell Publisher, pp. 54–73.

Sen, A.K. (1983/1977) "Rational Fools: A Critique of the Behavioural Foundations of Economic Theory", in *Choice, Welfare and Measurement*, Oxford: Basil Blackwell Publisher, pp. 84–106.

Sen, A.K. (1983/1979) "Equality of What?", in *Choice, Welfare and Measurement*, Oxford: Basil Blackwell Publisher, pp. 353–69.

Sen, A.K. (1984a) "Goods and People", in *Resources, Values and Development*, Cambridge, MA: Harvard University Press, pp. 509–32.

Sen, A.K. (1984b) "Rights and Capabilities", in *Resources, Values and Development*, Cambridge, MA: Harvard University Press, pp. 307–24.

Sen, A.K. (1985a) *Commodities and Capabilities*, Professor Dr. P. Hennipman Lectures in Economics, Amsterdam: North-Holland.

Sen, A.K. (1985b) "Rights as Goals", in Guest, S. and Milne, A. (eds.), *Equality and Discrimination: Essays in Freedom and Justice*, Stuttgart: Franz Steiner, pp. 11–25.

Sen, A.K. (1987) *On Ethics and Economics*, The Royer Lectures, ed. by Letiche, J.M. Oxford: Basil Blackwell.

Sen, A.K. (1993) "Capability and Well-Being", in Nussbaum, M.C. and Sen, A.K. (eds.), *The Quality of Life*, Oxford: Oxford University Press, pp. 30–53.

Sen, A.K. (1995) *Inequality Reexamined*, Cambridge, MA: Harvard University Press.

Sen, A.K. (1999a) "Assessing Human Development", in UNDP (ed.), *Human Development Report 1999*, Oxford: Oxford University Press, p. 23.

Sen, A.K. (1999b) *Development as Freedom*, Oxford: Oxford University Press.

Sen, A.K. (2004a) "Capabilities, Lists, and Public Reason: Continuing the Conversation", *Feminist Economics*, 10(3): 77–80.

Sen, A.K. (2004b) "Elements of a Theory of Human Rights", *Philosophy and Public Affairs*, 32(4): 315–56.

Sen, A.K. (2005) "Human Rights and Capabilities", *Journal of Human Development*, 6(2): 151–66.

Sen, A.K. (2009) *The Idea of Justice*, London: Penguin.

Shweder, R.A. (2000) "Moral Maps, 'First World' Conceits, and the New Evangelists", in Huntington, S.P. and Harrison, L.E. (eds.), *Culture Matters: How Values Shape Human Progress*, New York: Basic Books, pp. 158–72.

Sidgwick, H. (1907/1874) *The Methods of Ethics*, 7th ed., London: Macmillan.

Smith, A. (1976/1759) *The Theory of Moral Sentiments*, ed. by Raphael, D.D. and Macfie, A.L., Oxford: Oxford University Press.

Smith, A. (1979/1776) *An Inquiry into the Nature and Causes of the Wealth of Nations*, ed. by Campbell, R.H. and Skinner, A.S., Oxford: Oxford University Press.

Smith, A. (1980/1795) "The Principles which Lead and Direct Philosophical Enquiries; Illustrated by the History of Astronomy", in *Essays on Philosophical Subjects*, Oxford: Oxford University Press, pp. 31–105.

Solow, R.M. (1956) "A Contribution to the Theory of Economic Growth", *Quarterly Journal of Economics*, 70(1): 65–94.

Spaemann, R. (2000/1989) *Happiness and Benevolence*, translated by Alberg, J.L, Notre Dame: University of Notre Dame Press.

Spinoza, B.d. (1951/1670) "Tractatus theologico-politicus", translated by Elwes, R.H.M., in *The Chief Works of Benedict de Spinoza (vol. II)*, New York: Dover.

Spinoza, B.d. (1951/1677) "The Ethics (Ethica ordine geometrico demonstrata)", translated by Elwes, R.H.M., in *The Chief Works of Benedict de Spinoza (vol. I)*, New York: Dover.

Steinfath, H. (ed.) (1998) *Was ist ein gutes Leben? Philosophische Reflexionen*, Frankfurt a.M.: Suhrkamp.

Stevens, S.S. (1958) "Adaptation Level vs. the Relativity of Judgment", *American Journal of Psychology*, 71(4): 633–46.

Stevenson, B. and Wolfers, J. (2008) *Economic Growth and Subjective Well-Being: Reassessing the Easterlin Paradox*, IZA Discussion Paper No. 3654, Bonn.

Stouffer, S.A., Suchman, E.A., DeVinney, L.C., Star, S.A., and Williams, R.M. (1949)

The American Soldier: Adjustment during Army Life (Vol. 1), Princeton: Princeton University Press.

Studia Philosophica (1997) *Jahrbuch der Schweizerischen Philosophischen Gesellschaft: Glück und Philosophie.*

Stutzer, A. (2004) "The Role of Income Aspirations in Individual Happiness", *Journal of Economic Behavior & Organization*, 54(1): 89–109.

Suh, E.M. (2000) "Self, the Hyphen between Culture and Subjective Well-being", in Diener, E. and Suh, E.M. (eds.), *Culture and Subjective Well-Being*, Cambridge: MIT Press, pp. 63–86.

Sunstein, C.R. (2002) "On a Danger of Deliberative Democracy", *Dædalus*, 131(4): 120–4.

Taylor, C. (1977) "Why Measure Morale?", in Nydegger, C. (ed.), *Measuring Morale: A Guide to Effective Assessment*, Washington, DC: Gerontological Society, pp. 30–3.

Tellegen, A., Lykken, D.T., Bouchard, T.J. Jr, Wilcox, K.J., Segal, N.L. and Rich, S. (1988) "Personality Similarity in Twins Reared Apart and Together", *Journal of Personality and Social Psychology*, 54: 1031–9.

The Economist (2004) "Shed Pounds with a PA", 24 April, p. 30.

The Economist (2005) "The Economics of Happiness: Can't Buy it?", 13 January.

The Victorian Literary Studies Archive (2010) *Hyper-Concordance*, Nagoya University. Online. http://victorian.lang.nagoya-u.ac.jp/concordance/ (accessed 16 July 2010).

Thielemann, U. (1996) *Das Prinzip Markt: Kritik der Theorie externer Effekte*, doctoral thesis, University of St. Gallen, St. Gallen.

Thomä, D. (2003) *Vom Glück in der Moderne*, Frankfurt a.M.: Suhrkamp.

Tinklepaugh, O.L. (1928) "An Experimental Study of Representation Factors in Monkeys", *Journal of Comparative Psychology*, 8: 197–236.

Tomes, N. (1986) "Income Distribution, Happiness and Satisfaction: A Direct Test of the Interdependent Preferences Model", *Journal of Economic Psychology*, 7(4): 425–46.

Triandis, H.C. (1995) *Individualism and Collectivism: New Directions in Social Psychology*, Boulder: Westview Press.

Tugendhat, E. (1984) *Probleme der Ethik*, Stuttgart: Reclam.

Tugendhat, E. (1995) *Vorlesungen über Ethik*, 3rd ed., Frankfurt a. M.: Suhrkamp.

Tversky, A. and Griffin, D. (1991) "Endowment and Contrast in Judgments of Well-being", in Strack, F., Argyle, M., and Schwarz, N. (eds.), *Subjective Well-Being: An Interdisciplinary Perspective*, Oxford: Pergamon, pp. 101–18.

Tversky, A. and Kahneman, D. (1981) "The Framing of Decisions and the Psychology of Choice", *Science*, 211: 453–8.

Tversky, A. and Kahneman, D. (1982) "Judgment under Uncertainty: Heuristics and Biases (Introductory chapter)", in Kahneman, D., Slovic, P., and Tversky, A. (eds.), *Judgment under Uncertainty: Heuristics and Biases*, New York: Oxford University Press, pp. 3–21.

Tversky, A., Sattath, S., and Slovic, P. (1988) "Contingent Weighting in Judgment and Choice", *Psychological Review*, 95: 371–84.

Ueda, A. (2003) *Culture and Modernisation: From the Perspectives of Young People in Bhutan*, Thimphu: Centre for Bhutan Studies.

Ulrich, P. (1993/1986) *Transformationen der ökonomischen Vernunft: Fortschrittsperspektiven der modernen Industriegesellschaft*, 3rd edn., Bern: Haupt.

Ulrich, P. (2008) *Integrative Economic Ethics: Foundations of a Civilized Market Economy*, Cambridge: Cambridge University Press.

Unger, P. (1999) "The Mystery of the Physical and the Matter of Qualities: A Paper for Professor Shaffer", *Midwest Studies in Philosophy*, 23(1): 75–99.

Unger, P. (2002) "Free Will and Scientiphicalism", *Philosophy and Phenomenological Research*, 65(1): 1–25.

Ura, K. and Galay, K. (eds.) (2004) *Gross National Happiness and Development: Proceedings of the First International Seminar on Operationalization of Gross National Happiness*, Thimphu: Centre for Bhutan Studies.

van Praag, B.M.S. (1991) "Ordinal and Cardinal Utility: An Integration of the Two Dimensions of the Welfare Concept", *Journal of Econometrics*, 50(1–2): 69–89.

van Praag, B.M.S. and Frijters, P. (1999) "The Measurement of Welfare and Well-Being: The Leyden Approach", in Kahneman, D., Diener, E., and Schwarz, N. (eds.), *Well-Being: The Foundations of Hedonic Psychology*, New York: Russell Sage Foundation, pp. 413–33.

Veblen, T. (1994/1899) *The Theory of the Leisure Class*, New York: Penguin.

Veenhoven, R. (1987) "Cultural Bias in Ratings of Perceived Life Quality: A Comment on Ostroot & Snyder", *Social Indicators Research*, 18: 329–34.

Veenhoven, R. (1991) "Questions on Happiness: Classical Topics, Modern Answers, Blind Spots", in Strack, F., Argyle, M., and Schwarz, N. (eds.), *Subjective Well-Being: An Interdisciplinary Perspective*, Oxford: Pergamon, pp. 7–26.

Veenhoven, R. (1993) *Happiness in Nations: Subjective Appreciation of Life in 56 Nations 1946–1992*, Studies in Socio-Cultural Transformation. Rotterdam: RISBO.

Veenhoven, R. (1996) "Developments in Satisfaction-Research", *Social Indicators Research*, 37: 1–46.

Veenhoven, R. (1997) "Advances in Understanding Happiness", *Revue Québécoise de Psychologie*, 18: 29–79.

Veenhoven, R. (1999) "Quality-of-life in Individualistic Society: A Comparison of 43 Nations in the Early 1990s", *Social Indicators Research*, 48: 157–86.

Veenhoven, R. (2007) *Trend Average Happiness in Nations 1946–2006: How Much People Like the Life They Live*, Trend Report 2007–1, World Database of Happiness. Online. http://worlddatabaseofhappiness.eur.nl/hap_nat/findingreports/TrendReport-007-1.pdf (accessed 12 July 2010).

Vendrik, M. (1993) *Collective Habits and Social Norms in Labour Supply: From Micromotives to Macrobehavior*, Doctoral thesis, University of Maastricht, Maastricht.

Vendrik, M. and Hirata, J. (2003) "Experienced versus Decision Utility of Income: Relative or Absolute Happiness", in Bruni, L. and Porta, P.L. (eds.), *Handbook of the Economics of Happiness*, Cheltenham: Edward Elgar, pp. 185–208.

Warren, M.E. (1996) "Deliberative Democracy and Authority", *American Political Science Review*, 90(1): 46–60.

Weber, M. (1975/1920) "Die protestantische Ethik und der Geist des Kapitalismus", in Winckelmann, J. (ed.), *Die protestantische Ethik I: Eine Aufsatzsammlung*, 4th edn., Tübingen: Siebenstern, pp. 27–277.

Wierzbicka, A. (1999) *Emotions Across Languages and Cultures: Diversity and Universals*, Cambridge: Cambridge University Press.

Winkelmann, L. and Winkelmann, R. (1998) "Why Are the Unemployed so Unhappy? Evidence from Panel Data", *Economica*, 65: 1–15.

Wolf, U. (1996) *Die Philosophie und die Frage nach dem guten Leben*, Reinbek bei Hamburg: Rowohlt.

Zafirovski, M. (1999) "What is Really Rational Choice? Beyond the Utilitarian Concept of Rationality", *Current Sociology*, 47(1): 47–113.

Name index

Subject index

Page numbers in *italic* denote tables, those in **bold** denote figures.